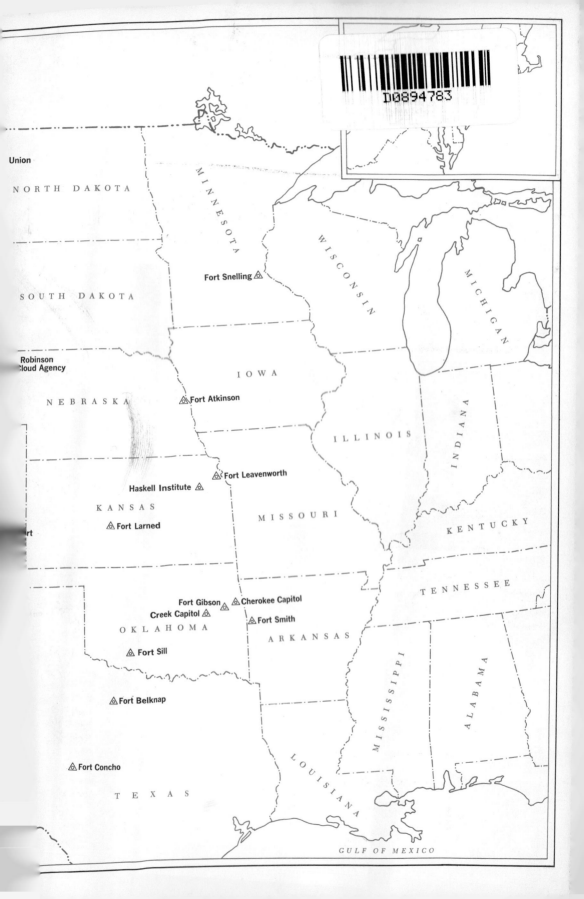

Union

NORTH DAKOTA

MINNESOTA

WISCONSIN

MICHIGAN

SOUTH DAKOTA

Fort Snelling ⚠

Robinson
Cloud Agency

IOWA

NEBRASKA

⚠ Fort Atkinson

ILLINOIS

INDIANA

⚠ Fort Leavenworth

Haskell Institute ⚠

KANSAS

MISSOURI

KENTUCKY

⚠ Fort Larned

rt

Fort Gibson ⚠ ⚠ Cherokee Capitol
Creek Capitol ⚠

TENNESSEE

OKLAHOMA

⚠ Fort Smith

ARKANSAS

⚠ Fort Sill

MISSISSIPPI

ALABAMA

⚠ Fort Belknap

⚠ Fort Concho

LOUISIANA

TEXAS

GULF OF MEXICO

D0894783

THIS informative and profusely illustrated book meets two important needs. It provides a compact, authoritative narrative of the turbulent relations between Indian and white man in the trans-Mississippi West during the nineteenth century, and it is an invaluable guide to the historic sites on which this history was made.

This was the period when the trapper, the explorer, and finally the settler were pushing westward into lands where the Indian had always roamed at will. The inevitable clash between the two cultures was violent and tragic. Attempts to make a farmer out of the nomadic Indian, to teach him the white man's ways, were tried and failed.

about their relationship, present condition, how to get to them and what to look for. The result, combined with the narrative history of Part I, is a fascinating and important contribution to the knowledge and appreciation of our Western heritage.

SOLDIER AND BRAVE has been prepared and written by historians and archaeologists of the National Park Service after comprehensive field work and in consultation with many experts. This is the first volume to be published in the National Park Service project, The National Survey of Historic Sites and Buildings, whose purposes are to evaluate places important in United States history and prehistory, to present a record of them, and to encourage their preservation.

SOLDIER AND BRAVE

F
591
U5

The Cavalier. This young trooper, posing proudly at Camp Cheyenne (apparently Fort Bennett, South Dakota) about 1890, represents a major agency for the transmitting of culture in the West. Photographed in 1890 by Grabill of Deadwood, South Dakota. Collections of the Library of Congress.

SOLDIER
AND BRAVE

INDIAN AND MILITARY AFFAIRS
IN THE TRANS-MISSISSIPPI WEST, IN-
CLUDING A GUIDE TO HISTORIC SITES
AND LANDMARKS

Introduction by Ray Allen Billington

Volume XII
THE NATIONAL SURVEY OF HISTORIC SITES AND BUILDINGS

NATIONAL PARK SERVICE
U.S. DEPARTMENT OF THE INTERIOR

Harper & Row, Publishers
NEW YORK, EVANSTON, AND LONDON
1963

CONTRA COSTA COLLEGE
DISCARD
SAN PABLO, CALIFORNIA

APR 3 1967

F
591
U5

SOLDIER AND BRAVE. Introduction Copyright © 1963 by Harper & Row, Publishers, Incorporated; all rights reserved. Printed in the United States of America. For information address Harper & Row, Publishers, Incorporated, 49 East 33rd Street, New York 16, N.Y.

FIRST EDITION

LIBRARY OF CONGRESS CATALOG CARD NUMBER: 63-10600

Contents

MAPS *by Harry Scott*

Introduction

Three centuries of bitter Indian warfare reached a tragic climax on the plains and mountains of America's Far West. Since the early seventeenth century, when Chief Opechancanough rallied his Powhatan tribesmen against the Virginia intruders on their lands, each advance of the frontier had been met with stubborn resistance. At times this conflict flamed into open warfare: in King Phillip's rebellion against the Massachusetts Puritans, during the French and Indian Wars of the eighteenth century, in Chief Pontiac's assault on his new British overlords in 1763, in Chief Tecumseh's vain efforts to hold back the advancing pioneers of 1812, and in the Black Hawk War. At other times the skirmishing was little known beyond the frontier settlements where raids and counterraids took their regular toll. Step by step the Indians were forced back, first beyond the Appalachians, then across the Mississippi to "permanent" reservations on the "Great American Desert," as the encroaching whites ravaged their fields and engulfed their hunting grounds.

Thus was the stage set for the last act in this drama of brutality and bravery. In the Far West the Indians could no longer strike and retreat as they had in the past. Behind them were inhospitable deserts, and behind the deserts more white men who were pressing eastward from California and Oregon with the advancing mining frontier. Their backs were to the wall, and they must fight to survive. Fight they did, with a desperation that cost the nation heavily in men, money and honor. Of the ultimate outcome there could be no doubt, for no amount of bravery could match the superior weapons and mass numbers of the encroaching whites. In three tragic decades, between 1860 and 1890, the Indians suffered the humiliating defeats that forced them to walk the white man's road toward civilization. Few conquered people in the history of mankind have paid so dearly for their defense of a way of life that the march of progress had outmoded.

This epic struggle left its landmarks behind, as monuments to the brave men, Indian and white, who fought and died that their manner of living might endure. Some have been erased by nature but others remain: eroded ruins of adobe forts; scarred battle-fields that have resisted time's ravages; crumbling remains of schools and mission stations where humanitarian men of God sought to prepare their Indian brethren for the white man's heaven; and overgrown mounds of earth marking the sites of trading posts where some less noble Americans dispensed whiskey and diseases. The relics of a dead past have resisted the corrosive influences of civilization partly because the dry air of the West serves as a natural preservative, but more because the sparse settlement of that semiarid land protected them from the ravages of humans.

Today many of these relics are in grave danger of extinction. The march of the American people westward continues at an ever-accelerating rate, to overflow areas that defied conquest before the advent of better transportation, irrigation farming and air conditioning. Already sprawling cities, located at strategic points as were the forts and trading posts and missions, are engulfing the ruins of these precious reminders of an age of conflict. Others are threatened by waterpower projects that create lakes where Indian and white once battled. If these landmarks of the American herit-age are to be preserved, positive action is necessary by both the people and their governments.

This is the problem faced by the National Park Service, and to aid in its solution this worthwhile volume has been prepared by the National Survey of Historic Sites and Buildings. Field workers have located and inspected every historic site of significance in the interplay between whites and Indians in the nineteenth century: forts, battlefields, trading posts, mission stations, schools and all the rest. Eight of these which are in the system of National Parks are described and pictured on the following pages; twenty-one more are listed as of "exceptional value" and hence eligible for designation as Registered National Historic Landmarks; and 117 more are rated as "valuable," and more briefly described. The brief historical and descriptive sketch of each landmark, the meticulous care that has been taken to locate each, and the superb contemporary and modern photographs provide Americans with a record of Indian-connected sites without parallel in our historical literature.

This is made even more understandable by a condensed history of Indian-white relations in the Far West that introduces the book. Here is told, in colorful but accurate prose, the tragic tale of the warfare that robbed the Indian of lands and game—his two essentials of life—and forced upon him a new life on a reservation as a ward of the Government. Here is told, too, the story of a gradually emerging Indian policy that sought to transform the "lords of the plains" into God-fearing tillers of the soil, complete with their own fields, citizenship, education and Christianity. And, most tragic of all, here are described the social convulsions that occurred as the Indians sought to adjust to an alien civilization that overwhelmed them with its differences and confused them with its values. Their last rebellion, in the brief Ghost Dance Wars, is understandable to all who read this moving account.

The National Park Service and Harper & Row have performed an invaluable service in offering this volume to the public. This is a book that will stimulate students of archaeology and history, and serve as a useful guide to the traveling public. Here is information on sites that await archaeological investigation and others where preliminary digs have promised rich finds. Historians can learn the exact location of many forts and trading posts that have been little known in the past, and can learn much from the careful research embodied in the capsule-like descriptions of each. They can also be reminded that the Government played an often-forgotten role in the westward advance, and—perhaps most important of all—be made to realize that only familiarity with physical remains will allow them to experience that sense of intimacy with the past that lends reality to their narratives.

But the traveling public should benefit most from the devoted labors of those who produced this volume. Here is an excellent guidebook to some of the most colorful spots in the trans-Mississippi West and to some of the most precious relics of the American heritage. It is to be hoped that those who read will be inspired to visit the sites where their nation's history was made, and to renew their knowledge of the men of both races who laid down their lives to preserve a way of life. Those who do so will become better citizens in a republic where devotion to the American ideal is once more necessary to the preservation of our civilization.

RAY ALLEN BILLINGTON
Northwestern University

Foreword

The sources of history are many, involving written documents and physical remains. This volume deals with the great "outdoor archives" of American history as found in historic sites and structures. A visitor at one of these places may stop time at a great moment of history and look with increased understanding into the past. No amount of reading can ever supplant the vivid imagery and feeling of identity with the past which one contact with the site itself will evoke.

Historians and archaeologists of the National Park Service, after comprehensive field work, prepared the basic studies from which this volume has been drawn. The studies were reviewed by the Consulting Committee, composed of eminent historians, architects and archaeologists not otherwise connected with the Park Service, and also by the Advisory Board on National Parks, Historic Sites, Buildings, and Monuments. The findings of the National Survey of Historic Sites and Buildings, achieved through this process, are made available to the public by means of this volume.

The Survey's purpose is the evaluation of places important in United States history and prehistory. Some sites and buildings may be considered for addition to the National Park System. Others, also of outstanding importance, may be designated Registered National Historic Landmarks, showing that they have exceptional value for commemorating and illustrating America's heritage. The Secretary of the Interior will upon request provide engraved certificates and bronze markers for Registered National Historic Landmark properties, attesting to their value and encouraging the community and the owner to respect their integrity. Many other places of general interest have been included in the volume, selected from the large number of sites considered by the Survey.

We believe that this book will be of widespread interest, especially to travelers, historians, students and preservation groups. "The old order changeth, yielding place to new," but, important as this progress is, it should not result in the thoughtless destruction of sites and buildings of great historic value. We hope earnestly that this volume may focus attention on, and stimulate further activities in, the safeguarding and interpretation of an important segment of our heritage.

CONRAD L. WIRTH
Director
National Park Service

SOLDIER AND BRAVE

PART I

Military and Indian Affairs:

The Historical Background

As the nineteenth century dawned on the trans-Mississippi West, the Indians who peopled its plains, mountains and deserts unknowingly stood on the threshold of disaster. A tide of white explorers, fur traders and settlers was rolling westward. Within a century it would engulf all tribes, appropriate all but a fraction of their vast domain, and leave the survivors a way of life often grotesque in its mixture of the old and the new. Their brethren east of the great river were already being pushed out of their homes by the advancing frontier. West of the Mississippi, except for Indians in Spanish New Mexico and California who had already experienced something of what was to come, only the occasional visit of a French or Spanish trader kept them from forgetting that white men even existed.

True, two significant gifts from the white man had already appeared in the West. The horse, filtering up through successive tribes from the Spanish borderlands, revolutionized an older way of life and by 1800 had made nomadic hunters of virtually all but the Pueblos and the coastal fish eaters. This transformation of a

[1

hitherto sedentary people wrought not only a new economy, but also a whole new social, ceremonial and material organization. Many of the Indians who confronted the nineteenth-century American had inhabited their areas for a long time; however their culture, because of the horse, was of quite recent vintage. The second gift, the gun, had by 1800 demonstrated its enormous utility in war and the hunt to the Plains tribes, but had yet to find its way into the hands of very many Indians. For horses the Indians were now beholden to no alien race; for guns and for a third "gift," liquor, they were soon to form a fatal dependence upon the white man.

Behind and often ahead of the official explorers—Lewis and Clark, Zebulon Pike, Stephen H. Long—came the roving fur trappers. They fanned out through the wilderness and afforded the western Indian his first long look at the whites. Generally the Indian liked what he saw, for the trappers in fact "went Indian," adopting many Indian tools, techniques, customs and values. But they also gave him a blurred glimpse of the manners and customs of white men. Both free and company trappers roamed the West until the early 1840's, but by then the fur business was coming to be dominated by the fixed trading post relying on the Indian to do the actual fur gathering.

At the trading post Indian and white met for the first time on the latter's own ground. Here the Indian was able to indulge in and quickly developed a fondness for alcohol, a weakness noticed and capitalized on by rival fur companies, who made it their chief weapon in the competition for the Indian's pelts and cooperation. The end result of this practice brought misfortune to tribe after tribe, for the Indian, unlike the white man, did not have the tolerance to alcohol that the latter had developed over centuries of use. Here, too, more significantly, the white man's trade goods —guns, kettles, pans, cloth, knives, hatchets and other useful items—revolutionized the Indian's material culture and thus bound him subserviently to the intruders. Thereafter, even in time of war with the whites, he looked to them for a large variety of manufactures that he had come to regard as essential.[1]*

Despite occasional armed clashes, the trapper-traders and the

* Superior numbers refer to a section of notes beginning on page 245.

Indians dwelt compatibly side by side. Neither was bent on dispossessing or remaking the other. Already, however, some of the western tribes had begun to feel the pressures generated by the advancing line of white settlement, for crowding upon them came the native peoples dispossessed of their homes in the East.[2]

The "Permanent Indian Frontier"

In the early decades of the nineteenth century, Americans demanded with increasing persistence that something be done about the Indians who lived east of the Mississippi River. White settlers coveted Indian land, and the hostility of the tribes of the Old Northwest and Old Southwest during the War of 1812 led to a widespread conviction that Indians and whites could not live together in peace. A solution popularly advocated was to move all eastern tribes to the plains west of the 95th meridian. Secretary of War John C. Calhoun laid this plan before Congress in 1825, and it became the policy of the administration of President James Monroe.

The Monroe policy was expanded and clarified by legislation enacted by Congress during the presidency of Andrew Jackson. The Indian Removal Act of 1830 strengthened the President's authority to effect removals. An act of 1832 created the post of Commissioner of Indian Affairs in the War Department. A comprehensive regulatory code, the Indian Trade and Intercourse Act of 1834, defined as "Indian Country" all land west of the Mississippi River not embraced by the borders of Louisiana, Arkansas and Missouri, and barred from the region all whites not licensed by the Government. Later, in 1838, Congress constituted "Indian Territory," roughly modern Oklahoma and part of Kansas, as a permanent home for the dispossessed people from the East. It was hoped that a "Permanent Indian Frontier," guarded by a line of military posts, would separate the Indians forever from the whites.

Since the United States had long regarded Indian tribes as sovereign though dependent nations—"domestic dependent nations" according to a Supreme Court decision in 1831—treaties had to be concluded with the eastern tribes. The treaties guaranteed protection en route to their new homes, resettlement aid, land ownership in perpetuity, a degree of self-government, and even representation in Congress. Few of the promises were kept. Inefficiently and often with great suffering to the Indians, United States troops escorted almost eighty thousand people to the Indian Country between 1825 and 1842.

Prominent among the immigrant Indians were the Five Civilized Tribes—Creek, Cherokee, Choctaw, Chickasaw and Seminole —who settled in what is now eastern Oklahoma. They had lived in the southeastern United States and shared among themselves a similar culture and history. Already they had decided to pattern themselves after the white man, and in fact they came to resemble him very much in economic, political and social forms. The people of the Civilized Tribes became sedentary farmers and businessmen even though land remained in tribal ownership. They were literate, and saw important benefits in schools and Christian churches. They devised a political system based on United States constitutional principles. The Cherokees even boasted an alphabet, invented by Sequoyah.

Despite their affinity for each other, the Five Civilized Tribes soon found themselves at odds with one another and with their neighbors over landownership. Conflicting treaty guarantees and errors in government boundary surveys created intertribal friction that threatened, on many occasions, to burst into open warfare. To restore peace, the Government sent soldiers to the Indian Country. They built Forts Gibson and Towson in 1824, Forts Leavenworth and Washita in succeeding years, in present Oklahoma and Kansas. Together with Fort Snelling, Minnesota, on the north, and Fort Jesup, Louisiana, on the south, these forts guarded the "Permanent Indian Frontier."

The troops helped to prevent hostilities, and a common threat from the west also tended to minimize dissension among the Five Civilized Tribes. The Kiowas, Comanches, Cheyennes, Wichitas, Osages and lesser tribes, natives of the Indian Country, resented the newcomers, and in 1834 made war upon their unwelcome neighbors. Unable to defend themselves against such formidable aggressors, the newly settled Indians called upon the Great White

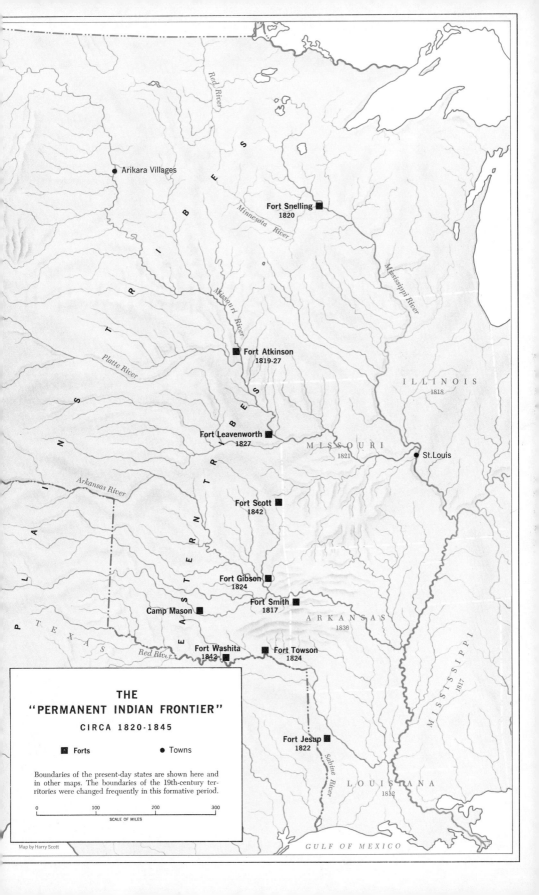

THE
"PERMANENT INDIAN FRONTIER"

CIRCA 1820-1845

■ Forts   ● Towns

Boundaries of the present-day states are shown here and in other maps. The boundaries of the 19th-century territories were changed frequently in this formative period.

0   100   200   300
SCALE OF MILES

Map by Harry Scott

● Arikara Villages

Fort Snelling
1820

Fort Atkinson
1819-27

Fort Leavenworth
1827

Fort Scott
1842

Fort Gibson
1824

Fort Smith
1817

Camp Mason

Fort Washita
1843

Fort Towson
1824

Fort Jesup
1822

St. Louis

ILLINOIS
1818

MISSOURI
1821

ARKANSAS
1836

MISSISSIPPI
1817

LOUISIANA
1812

GULF OF MEXICO

Red River

Minnesota River

Missouri River

Mississippi River

Platte River

Arkansas River

Red River

Sabine River

PLAINS   TEXAS

EASTERN TRIBES

WESTERN TRIBES

Father for help. An expedition of dragoons marched west from Fort Gibson to find and make peace with the Plains Indians. Fever took the lives of Brigadier General Henry Leavenworth and 150 men, but under Colonel Henry Dodge the command continued its march. On the north fork of Red River, Dodge finally met several bands of Kiowas, Comanches and Wichitas, and per-

Interior of reconstructed stockade of Fort Gibson, Oklahoma. National Park Service photograph.

suaded them to send delegates to Fort Gibson for peace talks. As a result, a treaty with the Indians of the southern Plains was concluded the following summer at Camp Mason, intended to bring peace to the region.

The treaty failed to pacify the Plains Indians, however. As was often to be shown in succeeding years, a scrap of paper and a few trinkets and promises could not cancel valid reasons for hostility. Nor could the weak garrisons of Fort Gibson and its sister posts bring harmony to the Indian Country. Treaties and soldiers both failing, it appeared that the Five Civilized Tribes would have to work out their own salvation.

They met in a series of intertribal councils during the early 1840's, to accomplish this. Here the "civilized" Indians convinced delegates from the untamed tribes that trade would profit them more than warfare. By means of these councils and the lucrative commerce that followed, the Five Civilized Tribes came to enjoy reasonably amicable relations with the nomads of the prairie. The latter, moreover, were now feeling the first pressures of the white advance, and were beginning to perceive in it a more serious threat than any posed by the immigrant Indians.

The Plains Indian Barrier

Before 1840 the Plains Indians had only occasional contacts with the Americans. On the southern Plains, Kiowas and Pawnees often harassed traffic on the Santa Fe Trail, and Comanches made life dangerous for settlers in a large part of Texas. These tribes, with the Arapahoes, Cheyennes and Wichitas, had parleyed with Colonel Dodge in 1834 and concluded in ineffective treaty with the United States in 1835. Wandering traders now and then visited these people in their villages.

On the northern Plains, Sioux, Cheyennes, Blackfeet, Shoshonis, Crows and others conferred with official explorers and enjoyed close relations with traders and trappers. The unpredictable Arikaras along the Missouri River in present South Dakota, however, turned hostile to American fur interests in the early 1820's. Sedentary Indians living in earth lodges, the Arikaras were one of the most powerful tribes of the Upper Missouri in the early nineteenth century. Lewis and Clark visited them without incident in 1804 and 1806 but, as fur trappers began to move up the Missouri in growing numbers, the Arikaras grew increasingly unpredictable. Early in 1823 William H. Ashley's fur brigade, about ninety strong, was treacherously attacked at the Arikara villages and lost thirteen killed and eleven wounded before withdrawing. General Henry Leavenworth marched up from Fort Atkinson (present Nebraska) with a strong force of 220 regulars, 120 mountain men and 400 to 500 Sioux allies, to punish the

Arikaras. At the Arikara villages he fought the first large-scale battle between United States troops and Plains Indians. Although he restored some of the goods stolen from Ashley, he mismanaged the attack on the villages and inspired the Arikaras with contempt for the prowess of white men.

A second expedition, two years later, had more success. With 475 soldiers, Colonel Henry Atkinson and Indian Agent Benjamin O'Fallon marched up the Missouri to the mouth of the Yellowstone, negotiated treaties with twelve tribes and accomplished much toward instilling a friendly attitude in the Indians and promoting the fur trade. O'Fallon had established the Upper Missouri Indian Agency at Fort Atkinson in 1819 and worked to keep peace among these tribes and to insure their co-operation with the trappers and traders. In 1832 the Arikaras moved upstream and settled with the Mandans. A smallpox epidemic beginning in 1837 reduced both Mandans and Arikaras to impotence, but in the meantime the main fur trading route had been shifted temporarily from the Missouri to the Platte due to the hostility of both the Arikaras and the Blackfeet, farther up the Missouri.

These military actions were but passing episodes. Trappers, traders and an occasional missionary remained the principal points of contact between the Plains tribes and the Americans, and did little to alter the impression each had of the other. Neither regarded the other as a threat. To the Americans, the Plains tribes were chiefly objects of romantic curiosity. To the Indians, the Americans, in all their numbers and technological proficiency, existed principally as improbable inhabitants of the world described by the imaginative trappers.

All of this changed in the decade of the 1840's. The myth of the Great American Desert crumbled beneath the feet of thousands of pioneers tramping westward over the Oregon and Santa Fe trails to fulfill America's "Manifest Destiny." The first immigrants headed for Oregon, soon to become part of the United States. Others were destined for California. The Mormons trekked west to found "New Zion" in the Great Salt Lake Valley. Missionaries came in greater numbers, accomplishing their most spectacular, if temporary, success in the Pacific Northwest. Following

Fort Laramie, Wyoming, depicted in 1837 by A. J. Miller. Courtesy of Walters Art Gallery. Copyright

the Mexican War the lands and wealth acquired from Mexico lured forth many more emigrants.

The emigrant trails first breached, then destroyed the "Permanent Indian Frontier." Pioneers and forty-niners, streaming across the Indian homelands, feared for their lives and demanded protection in transit. In response, the Federal Government had by 1850 moved its military forces west to confront the Indian. In

Exterior view of Fort Hall, Idaho, in 1849. Signal Corps reproduction. National Archives.

the short space of a decade the western tribes, in the minds of the American people, had merged into a barrier, stretching from Canada to Mexico, that interfered with the continental destiny that Americans perceived for their nation.

Even with four-fifths of its strength in the West, the United States Army was still too small to give adequate protection to travelers. In an effort to combat more effectively the Indian's advantage of maneuverability, a new unit, the Regiment of Mounted Riflemen, was organized specifically to police the Oregon Trail. Fort Kearny was built on the Platte River in 1849 to help guard the trail. Forts Laramie (Wyoming), Hall (Idaho) and Vancouver (Washington), formerly fur posts, were acquired and converted into military stations. But the garrisons were too small to be effective. To the south the story was the same, where after 1851 another Fort Atkinson (Kansas) and Fort Union (New Mexico) stood watch on the Santa Fe Trail.

To clear the paths of expansion, policymakers resorted to diplomacy. All tribes were to be moved either to the north or south of the Oregon Trail and assembled in two large colonies. This project was assigned to the Bureau of Indian Affairs, which in 1849 was transferred from the War Department to the newly created Department of the Interior. Officials of the Indian Bureau set out to conclude a series of treaties that, through a policy of concentration, was expected to open safe corridors across the continent.

The first compact was signed near Fort Laramie, midpoint of the Oregon Trail, on September 17, 1851. By threats and promises of annuities, government commissioners induced chiefs of several tribes, most importantly the Sioux, Northern Cheyenne, Arapaho and Crow, to agree to withdraw to clearly defined areas in Dakota, Montana and eastern Colorado, and to cease making war on one another. To clear the Santa Fe Trail, emissaries of the United States met at Fort Atkinson, Kansas, on July 27, 1853, with Kiowas, Comanches and Kiowa-Apaches, and promised annuities in return for guarantees of safe passage for travelers on this vital artery of commerce and travel. In 1854 the treaty agents turned to the small tribes of eastern Kansas and Nebraska. A series of treaties extinguished their title to these lands and moved them to Indian Territory. The way was now presumed to be open for the organization of Kansas and Nebraska Territories, and for the construction of a transcontinental railroad.

Despite all their hopes, the treatymakers were to be disappointed. More and more it became apparent that, by forming two concentrations of Indians, they had unwittingly created new problems instead of solving old ones, and they were to find that making treaties with the Indians was one thing, enforcing them another.

War on the Plains

Expanding areas of settlement, along with the trails that bore an ever greater volume of traffic, all of which the treaties were

General William S. Harney. Undated Signal Corps photograph. National Archives.

supposed to protect, were profoundly disruptive to the Indians' pattern of existence. No longer could they pursue freely the major source of their livelihood, the bison, in its seasonal migrations, and in fact they seemed constricted almost everywhere they turned. Inevitably, many Plains warriors refused to abide by treaties made either without their knowledge or without their consent. Occasional forays against a wagon train or an isolated cabin produced plunder and personal prestige. Such coveted prerogatives were not easy to give up. Everywhere the story was essentially the same.

The Treaty of 1851 kept the northern tribes generally quiet until, in 1854, Lieutenant John L. Grattan was sent from Fort Laramie with a small detachment of soldiers to investigate the killing of a cow belonging to a Mormon immigrant. The young officer managed his assignment badly, killing an innocent squaw, and the indignant Sioux retaliated by wiping out every man of the detachment. Several raids on traffic along the Oregon Trail followed, and relations between Indians and whites steadily deteriorated to the point that, next year, Colonel William S. Harney led a punitive expedition against the Sioux.

This was the first major clash between United States soldiers and Sioux Indians. Harney, with twelve hundred men, discovered the Brûlé Sioux village of Little Thunder in Bluewater Creek Valley just above its junction with the North Platte. By a circuitous route, the dragoons entered the valley above the village and advanced downstream, while Harney and the infantry marched up the valley from the Platte. Attacked from two directions, the Indians scattered, but not before the troops inflicted severe casualties—eighty dead, five wounded, and seventy women and children captured. Harney's loss was four killed and seven wounded. The rest of the Sioux, and the Northern Cheyennes, managed to avoid his command. The expedition went to Fort Laramie and then marched through the heart of the Sioux country to the Missouri River, where they spent the winter of 1855–56. This campaign ended serious trouble with the Sioux until the Civil War weakened frontier defenses.

Convinced that the whites would never abandon the "Great Medicine Road," as they called the Oregon Trail, bands of Sioux and Northern Cheyennes withdrew from areas adjacent to the trail. Depredations here diminished but peace did not come to the northern Plains. The Sioux pushed north and west against the less powerful Crows, beginning a war that lasted for twenty years. The Crows steadily retreated, leaving the Sioux in possession of all of present southern Montana east of the Bighorn River.

Hostilities had broken out to the south, on the Texas frontier, at about the same time as violence had erupted in the north. Raiding in Texas had long been a favorite practice of the Kiowas and Comanches, who resided in Indian Territory but made periodic excursions southward. The Great Comanche War Trail, which they usually followed, extended all the way from Indian Territory (Oklahoma) into Mexico. Between 1836 and 1845 the

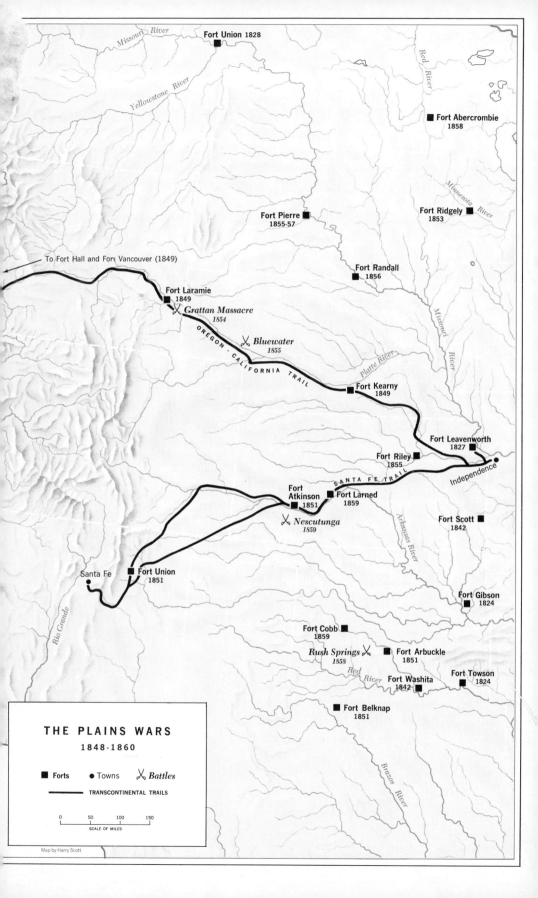

Fort Union 1828

Missouri River

Yellowstone River

Red River

Fort Abercrombie
1858

Minnesota River

Fort Ridgely
1853

Fort Pierre
1855-57

Fort Randall
1856

Missouri River

To Fort Hall and Fort Vancouver (1849)

Fort Laramie
1849

✗ Grattan Massacre
1854

✗ Bluewater
1855

OREGON - CALIFORNIA TRAIL

Platte River

Fort Kearny
1849

Fort Leavenworth
1827

Fort Riley
1855

Independence

SANTA FE TRAIL

Fort Scott
1842

Fort
Atkinson
1851

Fort Larned
1859

✗ Nescutunga
1859

Arkansas River

Santa Fe

Fort Union
1851

Fort Gibson
1824

Fort Cobb
1859

Rio Grande

Rush Springs ✗
1858

Fort Arbuckle
1851

Fort Towson
1824

Red River

Fort Washita
1842

Fort Belknap
1851

Brazos River

THE PLAINS WARS

1848-1860

■ Forts　　● Towns　　✗ Battles

━━━ TRANSCONTINENTAL TRAILS

0　　50　　100　　150
SCALE OF MILES

Map by Harry Scott

Republic of Texas made progress in punishing the raiders and imbuing them with restraint. Following the admission of Texas to the Union in 1845, the United States fell heir to its Indian problem just as the Comanches and Kiowas began raiding with new vigor.

The powder magazine at Fort Belknap, an original structure, now houses a small chapel. National Park Service photograph.

To protect settlers on the Texas frontier, the Government constructed a line of forts in 1848–49. Including Forts Graham, Worth, Gates, Croghan, Inge and Duncan, the chain extended more than eight hundred miles. Such an enormous area could not be defended effectively with the meager forces assigned to it, and it soon became necessary to erect another line of posts two hundred miles to the west, in order to keep pace with the rapidly advancing frontier. On this outer chain of posts, built between 1850 and 1852, Forts Belknap, Phantom Hill, Chadbourne, McKavett and Clark, and also Camp Cooper, stood guard. Both lines were occupied, and an attempt was made to coordinate one with the other in an elastic defense system. (Map following p. 24.)

In spite of the construction of these forts, and the Fort Atkinson Treaty, Indian depredations steadily mounted until the citizens of Texas again demanded action. Accordingly, in the spring of 1858, with a fervor reminiscent of the days of the Republic, Texans united with the Army in a determined campaign against the enemy. The first strike occurred on May 12, 1858, when a group of Texas Rangers, with a party of friendly Indian scouts, destroyed a Comanche village and inflicted heavy losses on its inhabitants. Skirmishes continued throughout the summer, but the big blow came in the fall of 1858.

The Comanches, under Bull Hump, had come north from Texas to discuss peace with the military authorities at Fort Arbuckle, Indian Territory, and were camped at the Wichita villages at Rush Springs. The officers at Arbuckle, however, had neglected to give information of Bull Hump's intentions to Captain Earl Van Dorn, who was bivouacked about a hundred miles away at Camp Radziminski, a temporary post on Otter Creek. Learning of the presence of the Comanches, Van Dorn, with four hundred troopers of the 2nd Cavalry and 135 Indian allies from Texas, made a rapid thirty-six-hour march to Rush Springs and attacked Bull Hump's camp. In a hard-fought battle which involved some friendly Wichitas as well as the Comanches, the troops killed 56 warriors, burned 120 lodges and captured 301 ponies. Five soldiers were killed, including a lieutenant, and Van Dorn was severely wounded by an arrow through the lung. Van Dorn surprised another band of Comanches the following spring, fifteen miles south of Fort Atkinson, Kansas, and in the Battle of Nescutunga almost annihilated their village.

Such aggressive measures forced the Indians to divide into smaller bands for survival. Many fled to the safety of the Staked Plains of eastern New Mexico and the Texas Panhandle, while those remaining near the more populated areas of Texas and Indian Territory curtailed their activities.

In newly organized, strife-torn Kansas, where growing numbers of whites were settling, a rash of misunderstandings and unprovoked killings on both sides prodded the Southern Cheyennes into a state of intermittent war. In 1857 several military columns took the field to punish the Cheyennes. One, under Colonel E. V.

Sumner, located a Cheyenne village on Solomon Fork in western Kansas. The Indians, secure in the belief that a supernatural power protected them, drew up to receive the cavalry. Sumner ordered a saber charge, and the disconcerted warriors fled pre-

General Edwin V. Sumner. Matthew Brady Collection, Signal Corps reproduction. National Archives.

cipitously with slight loss. The troops burned 171 lodges and destroyed eight to ten tons of dried meat.

For the moment, at least, the Army had gained the upper hand and the tribes of the southern Plains had been thrown off balance. But the guns of Fort Sumter had scarcely been silenced by Confederate batteries before war cries again echoed across the Plains.

The Plains During the Civil War

When the troops of the Regular Army marched away to eastern battlefields in 1861, they left the frontier virtually stripped of protection. Some tribes took almost immediate advantage of the absence of the "long knives." Others reacted only a little more slowly.

On the northern Plains the Spirit Lake Massacre of 1857 was a significant portent of future violence but, although the Sioux and Cheyennes raided periodically, the big explosion did not come until 1862. In August of that year the Santee Sioux of Minnesota went on the warpath under Chief Little Crow. After killing the whites at their Lower Sioux agency, Little Crow's warriors swept up and down the Minnesota River Valley slaughtering perhaps as many as eight hundred settlers and soldiers. Refugees from the valley flooded Fort Ridgely, below the agency, and New Ulm, a German settlement farther down the valley.

Sending a courier to Fort Snelling for reinforcements, Captain John S. Marsh left a skeleton guard at Fort Ridgely and set out for the agency with forty-five men and an interpreter. Near the agency an overwhelming force of Indians fell on the small command and, in the running fight back to the fort, killed half of the men including Marsh. More refugees poured into the fort. About 180 men, both civilians and volunteer soldiers, manned the defenses when about four hundred Sioux attacked in the early afternoon of August 20, 1862. With artillery and rifle fire, the defenders beat off successive charges that day and on August 22, when Little Crow led an attacking force of approximately eight hundred. Both first and second lines of defense were breached, but the Indians could not take the fort itself and, with heavy casualties, finally gave up and withdrew.

While the main body of warriors attacked Fort Ridgely, about a hundred raided New Ulm. There were approximately fifteen hundred persons in the town, from whom Judge Charles E. Flaundrau organized a defending force of no more than 250 indifferently armed men. After burning some houses the Indians withdrew but, on the twenty-third, having failed to take Fort Ridgely, 650 warriors moved to attack New Ulm. They drove Flaundrau's men from the outskirts and occupied outlying houses. Fighting raged back and forth throughout the day. Finally, Flaundrau and fifty men charged, drove the Indians from the buildings, and burned them. Without this shelter, the Sioux

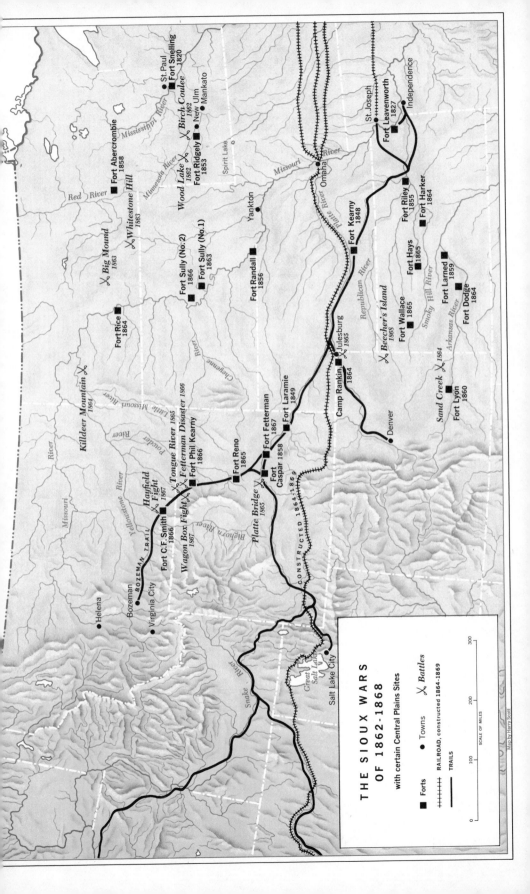

THE SIOUX WARS
OF 1862-1868

with certain Central Plains Sites

■ Forts   ● Towns   ✗ Battles

┼┼┼┼ RAILROAD, constructed 1864-1869

──── TRAILS

SCALE OF MILES

0   100   200   300

Map by Harry Scott

lost interest and departed. In New Ulm about thirty-four settlers were killed and sixty wounded; 190 buildings in New Ulm were put to the torch. Indian losses are not known.

As soon as news of the Little Crow outbreak reached St. Paul, the governor commissioned Henry Hastings Sibley a colonel in the state militia with orders to put down the uprising. Sibley assembled such volunteer troops as had not been sent to support the Union cause in the Civil War, and advanced up the Minnesota River, arriving at Fort Ridgely with fourteen hundred men on August 27. On September 3 Sibley came to the relief of a force of two hundred volunteer soldiers under Major Joseph R. Brown that had been besieged for thirty-one days by a large band of Sioux at Birch Coulee, losing thirteen killed and over three times as many wounded. The Indians withdrew, and on September 18 Sibley moved up the river against them.

Little Crow arranged an ambush near Wood Lake, but on the morning of the twenty-third the trap was sprung prematurely, before Sibley's army could march into it. In the ensuing Battle of Wood Lake Little Crow was decisively defeated and driven from the field with perhaps thirty killed and many wounded. This action ended the Minnesota uprising, although many of the Sioux, including Little Crow and the other principal leader, Inkpaduta, fled westward into Dakota rather than surrender.

Sibley imprisoned fifteen hundred warriors at Fort Snelling and Mankato, and tried them before a military court. Of the 307 sentenced to die, President Lincoln pardoned nearly all. Thirty-eight were publicly hanged at Mankato in December; Little Crow was killed by settlers the following year.

The Santees who had eluded Sibley's troops and fled to Dakota joined forces with the Teton Sioux. In the spring of 1863 Sibley, now a brigadier general, gave pursuit and spent the entire summer campaigning. On July 24 he surprised about three thousand Sioux who were hunting buffalo near Big Mound, in present North Dakota. The party was made up of friendly Sissetons and Inkpaduta's hostile renegades. A parley was arranged but was disrupted when one of Inkpaduta's warriors shot and killed a military surgeon. At once the two sides began fighting. The Indians fought tenaciously to cover the retreat of their families, and the battle was a running action in which thirteen Indians were killed. Reinforced by Teton Sioux, the fugitives turned on their pursuers at Buffalo Lake on July 26 and at Stony Lake on July 28.

Execution of thirty-eight Sioux Indians, Mankato, Minnesota, December 26, 1862. From a lithograph. Collections of the Library of Congress.

They were defeated in both encounters. Sibley followed them to the Missouri River and then returned to Minnesota.

Brigadier General Alfred Sully had intended to unite in a joint campaign with Sibley, but his advance up the Missouri River was delayed by low water. Sully reached the area of Sibley's operations in late August, and marched eastward from the Missouri. On September 3, near Whitestone Hill, his advance guard surprised Inkpaduta and his people, but the guard was in turn surrounded by an overwhelming force of about 950 warriors. Inkpaduta delayed the final attack so that his warriors could paint themselves for battle, believing the destruction of the small detachment was certain. But this gave Sully and the main command time to reach the site. The Indians promptly began to retreat; however, many were caught in a pocket from which there was no escape. After bitter fighting, Sully's men counted three hundred Indians dead on the field and about 250 women and children captured. Their own casualties were twenty-two killed and fifty wounded.

Sully wintered on the Missouri River near present Pierre, South Dakota. In the spring of 1864 he opened a campaign against Inkpaduta with 2200 volunteer cavalry and artillery. Inkpaduta had about sixteen hundred warriors, both Santee and Teton Sioux, and he decided to engage Sully in an open fight. He posted his force at the south base of Killdeer Mountain and battle was joined on July 28. The Indians gave way before Sully's assault. With about a hundred dead and wounded, they fled from the field. Sully captured and burned their village. He then marched through the North Dakota badlands to the Yellowstone River and, with the Sioux coalition disbanded, passed down the Yellowstone and Missouri Rivers to Fort Rice, south of present Bismarck.

The campaigns of Sibley and Sully inflamed the Sioux, Cheyennes and Arapahoes west of the Missouri River, and hostilities along the Platte River, related below, added further to the unrest. In the summer of 1865 the Government sent a sizable force under Major General Patrick E. Connor into the Powder River country of present Wyoming. Operating in three columns, the Powder River Expedition marched great distances and endured severe hardship but fought only one engagement. On the headwaters of the Tongue River one of the columns surprised an Arapaho village and dealt the inhabitants a costly defeat. Otherwise, because of lack of coordination between the columns, the campaign was a dismal failure. By annoying but not intimidating the Indians, it aroused them to strike back.

Uniting for a great war expedition against the Oregon Trail, three thousand Sioux, Cheyenne and Arapaho warriors descended upon a military outpost at Platte Bridge, where the trail crossed the North Platte River. On the north side of the river, on July 26, the warriors ambushed a troop of Ohio cavalry under Lieutenant Caspar Collins riding out to escort an approaching wagon train. The troops managed to cut their way back to the bridge, but Collins and four men were killed. The Indians next turned on the wagon train and slew a sergeant and nineteen soldiers. The military post at Platte Bridge was then named Fort Caspar, and the city that grew up there took the same name although with different spelling.

The Southern Cheyennes and their allies, the Southern Arapahoes, took early advantage of the Civil War. Their hatred of the white man had fully matured in recent years, for by the late 1850's they had begun to feel the pressure of American expansion. They had responded with sporadic raiding. Sumner's aggressive campaign during the summer of 1857 brought about a restless peace, but soon hundreds of gold-seeking whites came tramping

Platte Bridge Station, Idaho Territory. Lt. Caspar W. Collins arrived at Platte Bridge Station, en route from Fort Laramie to his own station (Sweetwater), only two or three days before the fight of July 26, 1865, in which he was killed. From a drawing by Bugler C. Moellman, Co. G, Eleventh Ohio Cavalry, in 1863. Signal Corps photograph. National Archives.

across their hunting grounds, hurrying to Colorado's new "rush." The Cheyennes and Arapahoes perceived that the advancing agricultural frontier of the East and the mining settlements of the West would soon crush them.

For this reason, many Cheyenne and Arapaho chiefs believed it futile to resist the inevitable. In 1861, by the Treaty of Fort Wise, they agreed to move to the area south of the Arkansas River in eastern Colorado. Many warriors refused to accept terms they considered dishonorable, however, and showed their contempt by nearly three years of rapine and murder, raiding roads and settlements.

By the fall of 1864 the Indians had begun to tire of incessant warfare. Winter was approaching, and the prospect of fighting increasingly active volunteer troops in the biting cold of a Plains winter was an unpleasant one indeed. A Southern Cheyenne chief,

Black Kettle, approached Governor John Evans of Colorado and requested peace terms. Reflecting public sentiment accurately, the governor refused and instead decided to mount an offensive against the Indians, sensing their discouragement. Black Kettle next turned to the commanding officer of Fort Lyon, Colorado, who appears to have assured the chief that the troops at Fort Lyon would protect the Indians until peace could be arranged. Black Kettle and his people, about seven hundred Southern Cheyennes and Arapahoes, thereupon camped along Sand Creek, in eastern Colorado. Governor Evans ordered Colonel J. M. Chivington and his regiment of Colorado volunteers to seek out and annihilate the village. Chivington believed strongly in a policy of Indian extermination and lost no time in executing the order.

On the morning of November 29, 1864, Black Kettle saw the militia deploy for attack. He hurriedly raised a large American flag over his lodge, and as an added precaution displayed a white flag. It was useless. Guns blazing, the Coloradoans charged into the camp, indiscriminately slaughtering the surprised Indians—men and, reportedly, over two hundred women and children—as they emerged from their lodges. The victorious troops carried away a hundred scalps, which were proudly displayed to the approving patrons of a Denver theater.

Word of Chivington's deed spread swiftly among the Plains Indians and strengthened war sentiment everywhere. By June 1865, most of the great tribes between Canada and the Red River were on the warpath, and the handful of troops stood helplessly by in their forts while the warriors did as they wished.

Hundreds of vengeful Cheyenne and Arapaho warriors disrupted mail delivery, cut communications, and at one time so isolated Denver that only a six weeks' supply of food remained in town. With increasing boldness they focused their depredations in the area between the North and South Platte Rivers. On January 7, 1865, one of their bolder attacks fell upon Camp Rankin (later Fort Sedgwick) and the small settlement of Julesburg, an important way station on the stagecoach and freight lines to Denver. Failing to take the camp, garrisoned by a troop of the 7th Iowa Cavalry, about a thousand Cheyenne, Arapaho and Sioux warriors sacked the town, taunting the soldiers and refugees from the town who watched helplessly from the camp only a mile away. A few weeks later Julesburg was again pillaged, and this time burned. Again the small garrison dared not challenge the large war party.

Perhaps it would have been some consolation for the Union soldiers at Camp Rankin to have known that, farther south, their Confederate counterparts endured similar humiliation at the hands of Apaches, Kiowas and Comanches. As early as 1861, Mescalero Apaches ravaged southwestern Texas, and the weak Texas Frontier Regiment was unable to stop them. With equal impunity, Kiowas and Comanches burned and looted over much of western Texas. In desperation the Texans tried to negotiate, but found most of the Indians wholly unresponsive.

Texans watched with dread as large war parties roamed the Plains. The raiders were so numerous, in fact, that they confidently attacked large bodies of troops. A band of two hundred Kiowas and Comanches, for example, fell on a Confederate outpost near Fort Belknap in October 1864, and carried off seven women and children. Behind them the bodies of sixteen soldiers and civilians littered the ground.

The marauders also ranged along the eastern border of New Mexico Territory. In retaliation the Federal commander at Santa Fe, Brigadier General James H. Carleton, dispatched a punitive expedition. The ensuing Battle of Adobe Walls took place on Confederate soil, just three days before Chivington's massacre of Black Kettle's people at Sand Creek. Colonel Christopher "Kit" Carson, fresh from victories over the Apaches and Navajos of New Mexico, led the expedition, composed of 350 volunteer cavalry and infantry soldiers with seventy-five Ute and Jicarilla Apache auxiliaries. In the Texas Panhandle near an abandoned trading post named Adobe Walls, built by William Bent on the Canadian River in 1845 but soon abandoned because of Indian hostility, Carson found Chief Little Mountain's village of Kiowas and a conflict ensued with about a thousand warriors. The attackers became the besieged, however, when some two thousand Kiowas and Comanches from other camps joined in the fight. The battle raged throughout the day but Carson's force was protected in part by the ruins of Adobe Walls, and with howitzers kept the Indians at bay. At dusk the troops burned one of the Indian camps and withdrew, returning to their base at Fort Bascom, New Mexico.

Once there, Carson returned to the task of bringing peace to

Brevet Brigadier General Christopher "Kit" Carson, in Civil War uniform. Denver Public Library Western Collections.

that country. It was a formidable undertaking, for about 47,000 Indians inhabited the 300,000 square miles that made up the Territory of New Mexico. Many had a long tradition of hostility toward the white man.

War in the Southwest

Residents of the Southwest had suffered since Spanish times from Apache and Navajo raids. Particularly troublesome were the Apaches, those "tigers of the human species," as General George

Crook later described them. Their attacks on ranches, settlements and travel routes were perhaps unequaled in cunning, cruelty and skillful execution. They continued to terrorize the Southwest long after New Mexico was added to the United States in 1846.

To combat the Indians, the Government during the 1850's built a network of military outposts in the region newly won from

Fort Stanton, New Mexico. Undated Signal Corps photograph. National Archives.

Mexico. Including Forts Massachusetts, Union, Marcy, Defiance, Conrad, Stanton, Thorne, Fillmore and Webster, they extended from Colorado to the Mexican border. Two more posts, Forts Buchanan and Breckinridge, established in 1857 and 1860, policed the area acquired from Mexico by the Gadsden Purchase of 1853.

There were several notable campaigns in the 1850's, of which the most important were those of Lieutenant Colonel Philip St. George Cooke against the Jicarilla Apaches in 1854, of Colonel Thomas T. Fauntleroy against the Utes and Jicarillas in the San Luis Valley of Colorado the following year, and of Colonel B. L. E. Bonneville against the Gila Apaches in 1857. For the

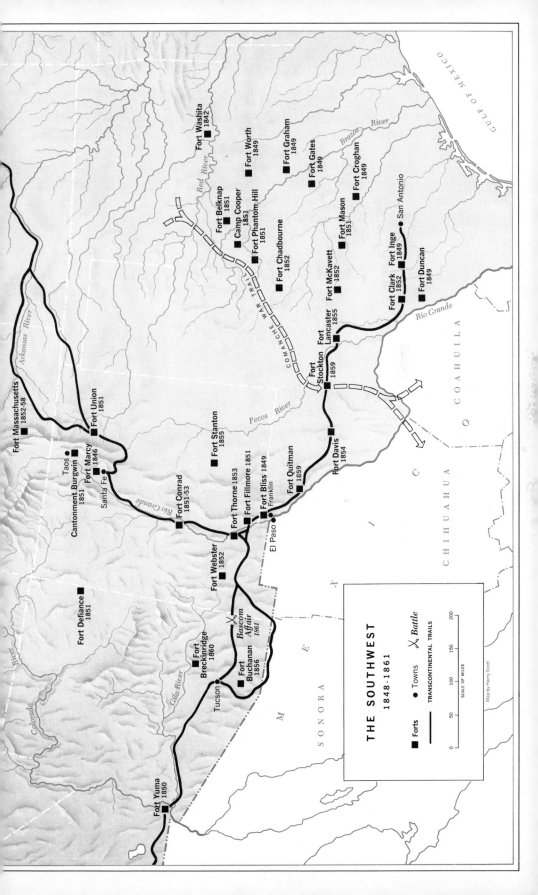

GULF OF MEXICO

Fort Washita
1842

Fort Worth
1849

Fort Graham
1849

Brazos River

Fort Gates
1849

Fort Croghan
1849

Red River

Fort Belknap
1851

Camp Cooper
1851

Fort Phantom Hill
1851

Fort Mason
1851

San Antonio

Fort Chadbourne
1852

Fort McKavett
1852

Fort Inge
1849

Fort Clark
1852

Fort Duncan
1849

COMANCHE WAR TRAIL

Fort Lancaster
1855

Fort Stockton
1859

Rio Grande

O COAHUILA

Arkansas River

Fort Massachusetts
1852-58

Fort Union
1851

Fort Stanton
1855

Pecos River

Taos ●
Cantonment Burgwin
1851

Fort Marcy
1846

Santa Fe ●

Fort Conrad
1851-53

Fort Thorne 1853

Fort Fillmore 1851

Fort Bliss 1849

Franklin

Fort Quitman
1859

Fort Davis
1854

CHIHUAHUA

Rio Grande

Fort Defiance
1851

Fort Webster
1852

El Paso ●

MEXICO

River

Fort Breckinridge
1860

Fort Buchanan
1856

Bascom
Affair
1861

Tucson ●

Gila River

SONORA

Colorado River

Fort Yuma
1850

THE SOUTHWEST
1848-1861

■ Forts   ⚔ Battle

● Towns

── TRANSCONTINENTAL TRAILS

SCALE OF MILES

0   50   100   150   200

Map by Harry Scott

most part, however, indecisive small-unit patrols and skirmishes, interrupted by an occasional meaningless treaty, characterized relations with the Apaches during the decade of the fifties.

In the 1860's relations became even worse. Early in February 1861, Lieutenant George N. Bascom attempted to arrest Cochise, the able chief of the Chiricahua Apaches, for a crime which he probably did not commit. Although the attempt failed, blood was spilled on both sides and the enraged Cochise launched a war on the Americans that was to last for more than a decade. This incident occurred in Apache Pass, the strategic passage through the Chiricahua Mountains of southeastern Arizona. The springs in Apache Pass made it a landmark on a major transportation and communication route across the Southwest. Through it traveled California-bound forty-niners, boundary commissioners, railroad surveyors and military forces. In 1858 the famed Butterfield Overland Mail Company fixed its route over the rocky slopes of the pass and built a stage station near the site of the Bascom-Cochise incident. The company's picturesque Concord stagecoaches operated for more than two years through Apache Pass, connecting St. Louis and San Francisco.

The alienation of the Chiricahuas in 1861 was untimely indeed, for a few months after the Bascom affair regular troops were ordered to the East. New Mexico and southern Arizona thus lay open not only to Indian attacks but also to Confederate invasion from Texas. When the Texan invaders arrived in the summer of 1861, they learned that Apaches did not discriminate between blue and gray. Apaches harassed the Confederates until Union volunteer troops drove the Texans out of New Mexico in the summer of 1862.

While helping to recapture Arizona and New Mexico, the California Column, led by Brigadier General James H. Carleton, swiftly received its introduction to Apache warfare. One of the first lessons in Apache methods came on July 15, 1862, when above five hundred Chiricahua and Mimbreño warriors ambushed a detachment of Californians in Apache Pass. Only by using artillery were the troops able to rout the Indians from stone breastworks commanding the water hole. To meet such threats to his line of communication through the vital pass, General

Carleton ordered Fort Bowie built at its entrance. For two decades thereafter this post was the center of operations against hostile Chiricahuas.

Two months later, having assumed command of the Department of New Mexico, Carleton opened an offensive against the

Counting Indians, at Bosque Redondo, Fort Sumner, New Mexico, about 1865. Signal Corps photograph. National Archives.

Indians. He sent Colonel "Kit" Carson and New Mexico volunteers to subdue the Mescalero Apaches of central New Mexico. By early 1863, Carson had succeeded. He placed his captives on a new reservation at Bosque Redondo, beside the Pecos River in eastern New Mexico, guarded by Fort Sumner. Meanwhile another column, under Brigadier General Joseph R. West, captured Mangas Colorado, leader of the Mimbreño Apaches, in southwestern New Mexico. Soon after his arrest the giant chieftain was killed—allegedly attempting to escape. Although West subsequently destroyed several Apache *rancherías*, Apache and Navajo depredations increased.

The outlook, however, was not entirely bleak. Kit Carson once again took the field, this time against the Navajos. He harried them throughout the summer and winter of 1863 until, reduced to near starvation, they took refuge in their favorite stronghold— Canyon de Chelly. On January 6, 1864, Carson sent his troops into the supposedly impregnable fortress, and they had little difficulty in capturing nearly seven thousand half-starved Navajos. Shortly thereafter, under military escort, the prisoners began a punishing "Long Walk" which ended, much to the chagrin of the Mescaleros, at Bosque Redondo.

By his decision to concentrate the two tribes on a single reservation, General Carleton aggravated the troubles that already beset the territory. The Mescaleros, refusing to tolerate the arrogance of the more numerous Navajos, fled from the reservation in 1865. The Navajos stayed until 1868 when, after much suffering, they were finally allowed to return to their ancestral homes. So thoroughly had Carson humbled them that they never regained their former power. The Mescaleros, after an interlude of raiding, were persuaded to settle at the Fort Stanton Agency, in Lincoln County. Before long, however, they grew dissatisfied. For the next ten years they alternately fled and returned, until Fort Stanton became virtually a replacement depot for hostile Apaches. (See pp. 201–202.)

Although Carleton's aggressive policy decreased hostilities in New Mexico, it did not intimidate the Apaches of Arizona. By the close of the Civil War most of the ranches in the Tucson area were abandoned, the town of Tubac was deserted, and everywhere the followers of Cochise and other Apache leaders lurked in ambush.

To the northwest, Overland Mail and Pony Express operations, along with the influx of miners into the Carson Valley of western Nevada, had driven the Paiute Indians of that area into open hostility in the spring of 1860. On May 7 a war party attacked a Pony Express station, killed five whites and burned the building. The miners at Virginia City, Carson City, Genoa and Gold Hill organized a volunteer punitive expedition of 105 men under Major William M. Ormsby and marched into the Paiute country around Pyramid Lake. Riding carelessly up the Truckee River Valley on

Group of Paiute Indians in Nevada. Photographed by Timothy H. O'Sullivan, 1871. U.S. Army Geographical and Geological Explorations and Surveys, under Lt. George M. Wheeler, Corps of Engineers. Collections of the Library of Congress.

May 12, the volunteers were ambushed by Paiute warriors and, after a sharp clash, were routed with a loss of forty-six killed, almost half of the force.

Reinforcements poured in from California, and by the end of May eight hundred men were under arms in Carson Valley. This force of whites, commanded by former Texas Ranger Colonel Jack Hayes, marched northward again and encountered the

Camp Douglas (later Fort Douglas), Utah, 1864. View of post headquarters and officers quarters. Signal Corps photograph. National Archives.

Paiutes on June 3 at the battlefield of May 12. After a three-hour battle in which the Indians lost twenty-five killed, they gave way and sought refuge in the mountains. Fort Churchill was established in the Carson Valley to keep watch on the defeated Paiutes.

California Volunteer soldiers under Colonel Patrick E. Connor moved still farther to the east, into Utah, in their work of protecting the Overland Mail. Having established Camp (later Fort) Douglas at Salt Lake City, Connor led a column of infantry, cavalry and artillery in January 1863 against hostile Shoshoni, Snake and Bannock Indians in northern Utah. He struck a surprise blow at the village of Bear Hunter, on Bear River, and inflicted a severe defeat on the Indians, returning to his base with sixteen dead.

Almost every part of the western frontier endured Indian attacks during the 1860's and hence was ripe for the military and political reforms of the post-Civil War period.

The First Attempts at Reform

It was imperative to regarrison, as quickly as possible after the Civil War, the seventy-two forts scattered along the frontier. The western military establishment was placed under the command of Lieutenant General William Tecumseh Sherman. About eleven thousand men—Union veterans, ex-Confederates (called "Galvanized Yankees") and soldiers-of-fortune—composed his tough little army. Even with the addition of four new regiments of cavalry in 1866, however, it was inadequate to protect the huge expanse of territory assigned it. A parsimonious Congress added to Sherman's problems, for he was expected to exhaust Civil War surpluses before ordering new material. Forced to use obsolete weapons and equipment, his understrength command found it impossible to protect the mounting tide of postwar migrants.

It therefore became necessary for all westbound wagon trains to provide for their own defense. By so doing they released many troops to protect construction parties of the Union Pacific Railroad, then pushing west into Nebraska. Sherman was convinced that the railroad would be the lifeline of his army, an artery along which troops could be rushed in a fraction of the time previously required. Such tactical considerations, however, were but a few of the vexing problems that the general faced. Certain forces were working to curtail the influence of the Army in Indian affairs.

During the Civil War the Army had been in complete charge of hostile Indians. After the war the precise definition of "hostile Indians" came under close scrutiny. Critical examination stimulated disagreements over exactly where and when military control of the Indians should begin and end. On the one hand the War Department, contemptuous of lax and often corrupt civilian management, demanded a restoration of its former primacy in all Indian affairs. On the other hand the Interior Department defended its supremacy and cited the military's failure to bring peace by means of the "mailed fist." Humanitarians entered the fray, and with their support the Interior Department staved off the Army's bid for control. This problem of authority was of basic importance, but it was only one of several issues debated in the postwar period.

The treaty system and the policy of trying to concentrate Indians in large areas also came under fire from legislators and humanitarians, who offered a torrent of suggestions for reform of Indian policy. Among them was a system of small reservations. Another was individual land allotments for each Indian. These and many other ideas were in harmony with a growing belief that the Indian could be conquered only by kindness. But even as such debates began to rage in and out of Congress, Sioux and Northern Cheyenne scalping knives were shaping future Indian policy.

The discovery of gold in the mountains of western Montana in 1862 triggered a rush to the diggings of Bannack, Virginia City, Helena and Bozeman. The most direct route to the scene of the discoveries was blazed in the same year by John Bozeman and John M. Jacobs. It lay along the eastern flank of the Bighorn Mountains and linked the Oregon Trail near present Casper, Wyoming, with Bozeman, Montana. The new trail could be used throughout the year, but it lay through the heart of the hunting grounds that the Sioux had recently seized from the Crows. In 1865, at Fort Sully, a peace commission headed by Major General S. R. Curtis concluded treaties with representatives of some of the Sioux tribes. In return for yearly annuity issues, the Indians promised to stay clear not only of the established overland route, but also of any other roads "hereafter to be established." The commissioners, however, had signed up only a few unimportant leaders of tame bands along the Missouri River, not the people who really mattered. Red Cloud, Man-Afraid-of-His-Horses, and other chiefs in the Powder and Bighorn range to the west had no intention of letting travelers pass unmolested.

In the spring of 1866, as miners began to push up the Bozeman Trail believing that the treaties guaranteed their safety, another commission arrived at Fort Laramie with the task of obtaining the signatures of the chiefs who roamed the Bozeman Trail country. Red Cloud and others came in to talk over the matter and to receive the usual presents. In the midst of the council, however,

Fort Reno, Wyoming. From a photograph taken in 1866. Signal Corps reproduction. National Archives.

Colonel Henry B. Carrington and the 18th Infantry marched into Fort Laramie. When Red Cloud learned that Carrington's mission was to build forts along the Bozeman Trail, he angrily withdrew from the conference and in effect declared war on all invaders of his country.

Carrington built or improved and garrisoned three posts along the trail. Fort Reno was at the crossing of the Powder River, the successor of Fort Connor, which had been established in 1865 by General Connor's Powder River Expedition. Fort Phil Kearny, on Little Piney Fork of Powder River, near its confluence with Big Piney Fork, was laid out in July. Fort C. F. Smith was located at the crossing of the Bighorn River. During the summer and winter of 1866, Sioux and Northern Cheyenne warriors all but closed the Bozeman Trail to travelers, and even heavily guarded supply trains had to fight their way through to the forts. The forts themselves endured constant harassment, and almost every wagon train hauling wood for fuel and construction had to fight off Sioux warriors. As described by the leading historians of the Bozeman Trail:

There was never a day, never an hour, but that the Indians attacked or would have attacked if not properly watched; or would have raided if they had found an opportune moment any or all of the three forts. Eternal vigilance was not only the watchword, but the living necessity. Horses were stampeded, emigrant outfits raided—more often for the guns and ammunition than the killing of people. The soldiers were killed at every opportunity, for they represented the hated forts.[3]

Sioux efforts focused on Fort Phil Kearny, Carrington's headquarters. Because the Indians were so numerous, and because his little command was poorly armed, the colonel remained on the defensive. Several of the younger and more impetuous officers held this attitude in contempt. Prominent among them was Captain William J. Fetterman, who boasted that he could ride through the whole Sioux Nation with eighty men. On December 21, 1866, a Sioux war party attacked the wood train near the fort, and Colonel Carrington sent Captain Fetterman to its relief with eighty officers and men. Although cautioned not to cross Lodge Trail Ridge, where he would be out of sight of the fort, Fetterman let a small party of Indians decoy him beyond the ridge and into an ambush prepared by Red Cloud. Hundreds of warriors overwhelmed the little command and annihilated it to the last

Fort C. F. Smith, Montana, 1867. Signal Corps reproduction. National Archives.

man. Following this disaster John "Portugee" Phillips made an epic 236-mile midwinter ride to Fort Laramie for help. In the five months from August 1 to December 31, 1866, the Sioux and allied Cheyennes killed 154 persons at or near Fort Phil Kearny, wounded twenty more, and killed or captured nearly seven hundred head of livestock. They made a total of fifty-one hostile demonstrations.[4]

In the summer of 1867 the Sioux and Cheyennes agreed to wipe out both Fort Phil Kearny and Fort C. F. Smith. But in typical Indian fashion a disagreement arose which divided their formidable numbers into two factions, each to attack the fort of its choice.

On August 1, 1867, one of these large war parties fell upon a detail of a lieutenant, nineteen soldiers and six civilians working in a hayfield 2½ miles from Fort C. F. Smith. They took refuge in a log-and-brush corral and were able to withstand the Sioux attack all day long, being equipped with newly issued breech-loading rifles. The lieutenant, Sigmund Sternberg, was killed early in the fight but one of the civilians, Al Colvin, who had been an officer during the Civil War, assumed command. The Indians suffered very heavy casualties in fierce assaults on the small position, but even fire arrows failed to dislodge the whites. The Indians withdrew late in the afternoon, ending the "Hayfield Fight."

The other force of warriors, led by Red Cloud himself, reached its objective, Fort Phil Kearny, the next day. They discovered a detachment of twenty-six infantrymen, under Captain James Powell and Lieutenant John C. Jenness, guarding civilian woodcutters on Piney Island, about five miles from the fort. Most of the civilians succeeded in reaching the fort in safety, but four were trapped with the soldiers in a hastily improvised circular barricade formed of the boxes removed from the running gear of fourteen wagons. The troops had been armed recently with the new breech-loading rifles—a costly surprise for the Sioux. Six times in four hours the warriors charged the wagon boxes, but each time they were thrown back with severe casualties. Reinforcements finally arrived from the fort with "wagon guns," which quickly dispersed the Indians with a few shells.

The Hayfield and Wagon Box Fights, although exacting a modicum of revenge for the Fetterman disaster, did not deter the hostile tribes, whose forays steadily increased until the following spring. To the south, in Nebraska and Kansas, Cheyennes and Arapahoes terrorized Union Pacific construction crews and traffic on the Smoky Hill Trail to Denver. A large expedition under Major General Winfield S. Hancock in the summer of 1867 failed

U.S. Indian Peace Commissioners at Fort Laramie, 1868. Left to right: Generals A. H. Terry, W. S. Harney and W. T. Sherman; Sioux woman; Commissioners N. G. Taylor, S. F. Tappan and General C. C. Augur. Signal Corps photograph. National Archives.

to intimidate them. Still farther south, Kiowas and Comanches plundered the Texas frontier.

Destructive and costly Indian wars, combined with the growing sentiment for reform, led to the formation of a special peace commission in 1867. On October 21, 1867, the commission met with tribes of the southern Plains and concluded the Medicine Lodge Treaty, by which the Indians agreed to cease fighting and withdraw to lands set aside in western Indian Territory. Part of this land had been seized from Indians of the Five Civilized Tribes who had sided with the Confederacy in the Civil War and had thus, reasoned Federal officials, forfeited their title.

At Fort Laramie on April 29, 1868, the commissioners bowed
to the demands of Red Cloud and agreed to close the Bozeman
Trail and abandon its protecting forts. For their part, the Sioux
and Northern Cheyennes promised to settle on a reservation near
the Missouri River, but insisted on retaining the Powder River

U.S. Indian Peace Commissioners at Fort Laramie, 1868, shown in Council
Tent with Sioux chiefs Red Cloud and Thunderman. Signal Corps photograph. National Archives.

country as unceded hunting grounds. As soon as the troops withdrew from Forts Reno, Phil Kearny and C. F. Smith, the following August, the jubilant Sioux hurried to burn the hated forts.

Yet these treaties failed to solve the Indian problem or to bring
peace to the Plains. Treaties, tools of civilized man, were not
sufficient to bind down the Indian in his less regimented, less in-
hibited way of life. The Cheyennes and Arapahoes immediately
returned to the warpath. Their destructive potential was greatly
augmented when, in August 1868, a band of warriors bluffed
Lieutenant Colonel Alfred Sully into handing over a large supply

of new guns and ammunition. Delighted with their windfall, the Indians spread over the Plains to test their gifts on white targets.

In September a company of about fifty frontiersmen enlisted for Indian duty by Major George A. Forsyth rode out of Fort Wallace, Kansas, on the trail of a large war party of Sioux and Cheyennes led by Roman Nose, Pawnee Killer and other chiefs. On September 16 the Indians, estimated to number over a thousand, turned on their pursuers, who entrenched on a small island in the Arikara Fork of the Republican River, in northeastern Colorado. The Indians made repeated charges, but were each time repulsed with heavy losses on both sides. During the nine-day siege that followed, volunteers worked their way through the Indian cordon and reached Fort Wallace for help. The defenders held out and the Indians retreated when a relief column approached. Lieutenant F. W. Beecher was killed in the action, which became known as the Battle of Beecher's Island.

Meanwhile, Major General Philip H. Sheridan began organizing a cold-weather campaign that he hoped would trap the tribes in their winter encampments. He planned to have columns from Fort Bascom, New Mexico; Fort Lyon, Colorado; and Fort Larned, Kansas, converge on western Indian Territory (Oklahoma). After they had driven the adversary into the valley of the Washita River, the Fort Larned column would administer the *coup de grâce*. Before moving his columns, Sheridan ordered from the area of operations all Indians who claimed to be peaceful. Old Fort Cobb was reactivated to provide them refuge, and Colonel W. B. Hazen put in charge of the agency. The way was now cleared for the offensive.

Departing from Fort Larned early in November 1868, the 7th Cavalry under Lieutenant Colonel George A. Custer began its march southward. Establishing a base of operations (Camp Supply) in northwestern Indian Territory, Custer pressed forward in a raging blizzard. At dawn on November 27 the troopers, their band blaring the regimental battle song, swept down from three directions into the valley of the Washita toward the Cheyenne camp of Black Kettle, who had witnessed a similar scene at Sand Creek four years earlier. The startled Indians poured from their lodges in panic, only to meet the fire of cavalry carbines. Some

two hundred Cheyennes were killed and wounded, with Black
Kettle among the dead. But Custer had found only one of several
villages that lined the Washita. Large groups of fresh warriors
appeared on hills overlooking the field. He burned the Cheyenne camp, slaughtered the pony herd, and withdrew hastily.

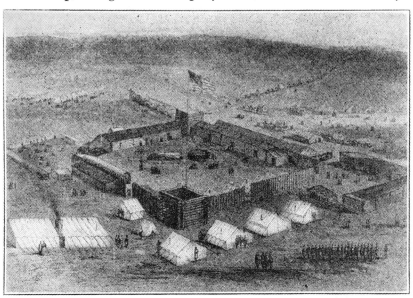

Camp Supply, Oklahoma. Undated Signal Corps reproduction. National
Archives.

In an engagement on Christmas Day, Major A. W. Evans and
the Fort Bascom column smashed a Comanche village at the
Battle of Soldier Spring, in the Wichita Mountains a short distance south of the Washita battleground. By demonstrating that
the troops would fight in the winter when the Indians preferred
to be left alone, the Battles of Soldier Spring and the Washita
dealt a heavy blow to Indian morale.

Many survivors of these engagements escaped to the Staked
Plains, from which they continued to raid on a somewhat reduced
scale. Others chose less remote areas, only to be ferreted out by
Sheridan's pursuing columns. His troops were thus occupied
throughout the winter and spring of 1869. The final action took
place in the summer of that year. Tall Bull and his Cheyenne "Dog

Soldiers" had been plundering the settlements of Kansas and east-ern Colorado. Major E. A. Carr went in pursuit, guided by "Buf-falo Bill" Cody, with five troops of the 5th Cavalry and 150 Pawnee scouts under Frank and Luther North. They surprised Tall Bull's camp at Summit Springs, Colorado, on July 11, 1869. In the battle that ensued, against a loss of one soldier wounded, the Indians lost fifty warriors killed, including Tall Bull, and 117 captured.

All but a few of the Southern Cheyennes were rounded up and escorted to Fort Cobb, where it was hoped they would cause no further trouble. But this was not to be. The hard-won ascendancy that the Army had attained over the southern Plains Indians was about to be nullified by an ever-growing spirit of beneficence that culminated in President U. S. Grant's "Peace Policy."

The Peace Policy

In the years immediately following the Civil War reformers had clamored for an end, on the one hand, to harsh military policies of Indian control and, on the other, to lax and often fraudulent civilian management. Their philosophy of conquest by kindness had influenced the formation of the Peace Commission of 1867 and the conclusion of the Fort Laramie and Medicine Lodge Treaties. This doctrine found expression in official policy when Ulysses S. Grant came to the presidency in 1869.

During his two terms in the White House, several policy inno-vations were introduced that revolutionized Indian management. Not least among them was renunciation of the treaty system. After years of argument, reformers finally convinced legislators that Indian tribes should be treated, not as sovereign nations, but as wards of the United States. In 1871 Congress demonstrated its agreement by passing a bill that prohibited any future treaties with Indian tribes. Thereafter relations were defined in executive agreements, which were actually treaties in all but name.

In the same year the concentration policy was replaced by one which required a new system of small reservations. At such places the Indian was to be furnished with every necessity, thus advanc-ing him toward ultimate assimilation into white society. Such

care and kindness, however, were condemned by still other reformers, who stressed individual land allotments as the only solution of the Indian problem. Pampering with government doles,
they contended, would keep the Indian dependent upon his
white benefactors and make him less likely to become a self-
reliant citizen. Allotment of land in severalty would be put to the
test someday, but in the meantime the small reservation held the
limelight.

While debates continued over these issues, President Grant attempted innovations of his own. He appointed a Board of Indian
Commissioners, composed of eminent philanthropists serving
without pay, to advise the Indian Bureau on formulation of policy
and also to try to purge the annuity-procurement system of corruption. The Bureau, however, usually chose to ignore the recom-
mendations of the Board, and thereby insured its impotence.
While the Board struggled to make itself heard, another of
Grant's experiments was also losing ground.

In 1869 the Chief Executive decided to appoint church-
nominated men as Indian agents. He hoped thus not only to end
corruption on the reservation level, but also to provide the
Indians with examples of morality. The Quakers were the first
denomination assigned reservations under the new system. The
southern Plains were selected as a testing ground for the "Quaker
Policy," and the gentle Friends fell heir to some of the fiercest
tribes in the West.

Illustrating the problems they faced and their failure to solve
them was the experience of Quaker Agent Lawrie Tatum. At Fort
Cobb, Indian Territory, on July 1, 1869, he took charge of the
Kiowas and Comanches, shortly to be moved to the newly erected
Fort Sill. Among his charges was the Kiowa Chief, Satanta, who
five years before had led an attack on Fort Larned, Kansas, which
resulted in the killing of a sentry and capture of the horseherd.
The audacious Satanta sent word to the post quartermaster that
the horses were inferior, and that he hoped the Army would provide better stock for him in the future. At Fort Sill Tatum attempted immediately to transform his nomadic wards into
peaceful farmers. His recalcitrant flock construed his solicitude
as weakness, however, and continued their depredations in Texas.

They had little fear of punishment, for the Peace Policy forbade Army interference on the reservations unless requested by the agent. And since Tatum refused to believe that his charges were guilty the Fort Sill reservation became a "city of refuge" where the Kiowas and Comanches could find protection after each raid. Their boldness grew in proportion to their success and they defied the Army to stop them. But their ardor was dampened in 1871 by an unexpected turn of events.

General view of Fort Sill, Oklahoma, in the 1890's. Quartermaster's Photo Album. National Archives.

In May of that year a large Kiowa war party under Satanta, Big Tree and Satank wiped out a wagon train near Jacksboro, Texas. Unknown to the Indians, General William T. Sherman was on a tour of inspection in this very area, and only by a few hours did he escape a similar fate. Everywhere examples of Kiowa and Comanche destruction caught his eye and strengthened his determination to see the Indians punished.

Consequently, when the Kiowa chiefs bragged at Fort Sill of their exploit, they were arrested at once and sent to Texas for an unprecedented civil trial. This heretofore unseen facet of the Peace Policy aroused a great deal of public interest. Not a little

Big Tree, Kiowa chief, imprisoned at Fort Sill, Oklahoma, in 1871. Signal Corps photograph. National Archives.

chagrin was evident among the Kiowas who, although threatening reprisals, noticeably decreased their raids during the winter of 1871–72. They were further shocked when Satanta and Big Tree were sentenced to death (Satank was shot and killed while trying to escape en route to the trial). Later, however, Federal officials brought enough pressure on the governor of Texas to have the sentences of Satanta and Big Tree commuted to life imprisonment.

While the Kiowas eagerly awaited the outcome of the trial, their Comanche friends did not curtail activities. They continued to plague Texas with a rash of raids until even Agent Tatum was forced to acknowledge the guilt of his wards. He reluctantly called on the Army to punish them, but in so doing incurred the displeasure of his more idealistic superiors. Discouraged, Tatum resigned his post. The Army welcomed an opportunity to punish the Indians, but its small force could do little more than teach them that the Fort Sill reservation was no longer a haven.

Meanwhile, humanitarian groups worked diligently for the release of Satanta and Big Tree. Just as they were making their influence felt, an unexpected event momentarily checked progress. Public sentiment was aroused in opposition to lenient treatment of Indians by an uprising in the Pacific Northwest.

On November 29, 1872, a company of soldiers attempted to arrest Captain Jack, a Modoc leader who, two years earlier, had murdered another Indian and with some followers had fled from their Oregon reservation. The attempt precipitated a battle between the soldiers and Indians, and Captain Jack retreated with his band into the natural fortress of northern California's Lava Beds. Here, amid caves, chasms, cinder cones and masses of lava rock twisted into almost every conceivable shape, he and his determined warriors, never numbering more than seventy-one, stood off for five months a force of four hundred regular and

Captain Jack. Undated Signal Corps photograph. National Archives.

volunteer troops, later augmented to more than a thousand, led
by Lieutenant Colonel Frank Wheaton.

Next a peace commission which included the department commander, Brigadier General E. R. S. Canby, tried to negotiate. On

Brigadier General E. R. S. Canby, just before his death in 1873 at the hands
of the Modocs. Signal Corps photograph. National Archives.

April 11, 1873, the commissioners entered the Lava Beds t
under a flag of truce with the fugitives. After a brief exch
words the Modocs treacherously murdered General Ca
another commissioner. The rest of the commission man.
escape.

Colonel Alvin Gillem took command of the encircling
His men brought up mortars and shelled the Modoc strongh.
and then for three days they fought their way forward throu
the lava flow. When finally captured, the stronghold was emr.
Although the Modocs escaped here, they were later defe

nearby Dry Lake. Captain Jack and three other leaders, who escaped again, were captured a few weeks later and went to the gallows for murder. The rest of the band was sent to a reservation in Kansas and the Pacific Northwest settled down to several years of peace.

The entire nation was stunned by the murder of General Canby, but when the story disappeared from the front pages humanitarians increased their agitation for the release of Satanta and Big Tree. Finally, responding to this pressure, the Federal Government induced the governor of Texas to free the prisoners. They promptly displayed their gratitude by resuming depredations. Once again the Peace Policy had been tested and found wanting.

Strict adherence to the Peace Policy had produced a serious division of authority between military and civil officials. Such an arrangement played havoc with Indian administration, and as usual the Indian suffered. The system failed to benefit either his physical or his spiritual well-being. Denominational agents had not proved the paragons of morality that had been predicted.

Panorama of lava beds from Army Signal Station at Tule Lake, during Modoc Campaign, 1873. Signal Corps photograph. National Archives.

Moldy flour and rancid meat continued to be items of issue at Indian agencies, and unscrupulous agents still coined small fortunes at the expense of their wards.

The food was often of inferior quality, and frequently there was not enough of it. The Medicine Lodge and Fort Laramie Treaties had authorized a mere three-dollars-a-month food allowance for each Indian, on the assumption that agency rations would be supplemented by hunting. But the southern Plains had become the scene of probably the greatest slaughter of wildlife in history. Between 1872 and 1878 the repeating rifles of professional hunters of buffalo accounted for no less than seven and a half million of these animals, so essential to Indian life. Obviously, under the existing system, the Indian must steal or starve.

It is not surprising, then, that reservations were hotbeds of discontent and resentment. Pampered on the one hand and abused on the other, the Indian had little reason either to love or to respect his Federal overlords. He therefore sought to rid himself of their yoke by force of arms.

The Last of the Plains Wars

While the Indians of the southern Plains resisted United States domination, the demands for Army intervention increased. The debate was revived over which government agency should control the Indians. Although the military never regained complete jurisdiction over the tribes, it did win authority in July 1874 to attack hostile Indians on their reservations. This shift of policy was occasioned apparently by realization that the frontier once more faced a full-scale war. Only a month earlier a large band of warriors had opened an offensive that developed into the Red River War of 1874–75.

In the summer of 1874 the Kiowas and Comanches, prodded by some Southern Cheyennes, attempted to rid the Texas Panhandle of the hated buffalo hunter. Isitai, a dynamic young Comanche medicine man, encouraged a strong war party of perhaps as many as seven hundred warriors to move against a group of twenty-eight hunters camped one mile from the scene of Kit Carson's battle of ten years earlier, at Adobe Walls. The whites took refuge in two stores and a saloon, and for several days held off the besieging Indians with accurate rifle fire. Reinforcements began to arrive from other hunting parties and the Indians at length withdrew. Buffalo hunting, however, declined sharply in this area for the next few months.

A month after the Adobe Walls fight, the Interior Department gave in to Army demands for a free hand to punish the Indians. Preparatory to his proposed campaign, General Sheridan ordered all professedly friendly Indians to report to their agencies for registration. A severe drought delayed his plans until late summer, when forty-six companies of cavalry and infantry finally took the field. Columns from Fort Union, New Mexico, Fort Sill and Camp Supply, Indian Territory, and Forts Concho and Griffin, Texas, began to close in on the Staked Plains.

Oddly enough, one of the first clashes in the Red River War took place on a reservation. Lieutenant Colonel John W. Davidson and four troops of the 10th Cavalry were dispatched from Fort Sill to help the infantry guard at the Wichita Agency at Anadarko keep order. The generally submissive Wichitas were being stirred up by Kiowas and Comanches, many of whom had avoided the required registration and were bent on violence. When the troopers tried on August 22, 1874, to enforce orders for the disarming of all the Indians, they resisted. Two days of skirmishing followed during which six civilians were killed and four soldiers wounded, after which most of the Kiowas and Comanches escaped westward to join other fugitives on the Staked Plains.

West of Anadarko, near the Antelope Hills, the first of the fourteen major engagements of the Red River War was fought. A column under Colonel Nelson A. Miles, moving south from Camp Supply, encountered a band of warriors on August 30. After a sharp battle his cavalry, ably supported by Gatling guns, forced the Indians to withdraw to the Staked Plains. The troops pursued. But after a grueling chase, during which some of the soldiers opened their veins in search of moisture, the chase was abandoned.

A month later, following an audacious three-day siege of an

Army wagon train, the Indians suffered another reverse. This time it was at the hands of Colonel Ranald S. Mackenzie and the 4th Cavalry, out of Fort Concho. On September 27, Mackenzie discovered a large encampment of Comanches in Palo Duro Canyon, a gash in the Staked Plains southeast of present Amarillo, Texas. After a perilous descent into the canyon, Mackenzie's troopers charged the village. The surprised inhabitants scattered to shelter on the slopes of the canyon and returned the fire so effectively that Mackenzie had to pull back. Before retreating, however, he burned the village and its provisions and took with him fourteen hundred ponies, which he later slaughtered. The Battle of Palo Duro Canyon badly crippled the Comanches and sapped their morale.

Sheridan's other columns, meanwhile, were having similar adventures. Their relentless pursuit during October and November 1874 so discouraged the Indians that many drifted east to surrender at the agencies, although these columns too won no overwhelming victories. As in the Washita campaign, mopping-up operations continued for several more months but finally ended in 1875 when the last fugitives gave up. In that same year Satanta was again sent to Huntsville prison in Texas, where he committed suicide. Seventy-four Kiowas, Comanches and Southern Cheyennes regarded as troublemakers were imprisoned at St. Augustine, Florida.

Although it was one of the most comprehensive campaigns ever prosecuted against Indians in the United States, the Red River War produced few casualties on either side. It was the sort of campaigning that General Sheridan viewed as the most effective and humane—relentless pursuit that kept the enemy always off balance, always on the move, always tormented by insecurity. Such tactics so hurt Indian morale that surrender was but a question of time. Except for occasional depredations by renegade bands, the Red River War won permanent peace for the southern Plains. Kiowas, Comanches, Cheyennes and Arapahoes retired to their reservations in Indian Territory and submitted themselves to the dictates of the Indian Bureau. But the last warrior of the southern Plains had scarcely been herded back to his reservation when more trouble threatened, again in the north.

Two Sioux leaders, American Horse and Red Cloud. Photographed in 1891 by Grabill, of Deadwood, South Dakota. Collections of the Library of Congress.

Following conclusion of the Fort Laramie Treaty in 1868 most of the Sioux, including Red Cloud, had settled in the country set apart as the Great Sioux Reservation—present South Dakota west of the Missouri River. To manage the affairs of these Indians, several agencies were built along the Missouri River. The most important, however, were Red Cloud and Spotted Tail Agencies,

Fort Benton, Montana, about 1854. From a tinted lithograph drawn by John Mix Stanley. U.S. Pacific Railroad Explorations and Surveys, 47–49th parallels. Collections of the Library of Congress.

in northwestern Nebraska south of the Black Hills. Nearby Fort Robinson guarded them.

Many Sioux and Cheyennes, instead of going to the reservation, elected to live in the unceded hunting grounds centering on the Powder River, west of the Black Hills and south of the Yellowstone River. Prominent among them was the Hunkpapa Sioux medicine man, Sitting Bull. These Indians continued to make war on the Crows. They demonstrated their contempt for the Fort Laramie Treaty by attacking isolated settlements and travelers in western Montana, and by contesting the advance of surveying crews mapping a route for the Northern Pacific Railroad.

Gradually, during the early 1870's, this country was ringed by military posts. Forts Robinson, Laramie and Fetterman lay to the south. The Missouri River forts—Randall, Sully, Rice, Lincoln, Stevenson and Buford—lay to the east and north. To the northwest were Forts Benton, Ellis and Shaw. The Army could at any time converge from several directions on the bands in the unceded country.

In 1874 an expedition under Lieutenant Colonel George A. Custer entered the Black Hills, Sioux territory protected by the Treaty of 1868, and confirmed the presence of gold. Living up to treaty commitments, the Army barred prospectors from the Hills. Public demand forced the Government to withdraw this protection, however, and in 1876 a few chiefs were induced to sign an agreement selling the Black Hills to the United States.

Throughout 1875 hundreds of Sioux, incensed at the invasion of the Black Hills, left their agencies and joined non-reservation Indians in the Powder River country of Wyoming and Montana. Sitting Bull, Crazy Horse and other Sioux and Cheyenne chiefs vowed to resist further white advances. The Indian Bureau ordered them to report to the agencies by January 31, 1876, or be driven in by the Army. This ultimatum precipitated another Indian war.

Brigadier General George Crook advanced north from Fort Fetterman, Wyoming, in March 1876, discovered an Indian trail on the sixteenth, and sent six troops of the 2nd and 3rd Cavalry under Colonel Joseph J. Reynolds to find the village to which the trail led them. At dawn on the seventeenth in the Powder River Valley, Reynolds located and charged the village,

General view of Fort Ellis, Montana. Undated Signal Corps photograph. National Archives.

Sitting Bull. Signal Corps photograph. National Archives.

commonly thought to have been that of Crazy Horse. The surprised Indians poured out of their lodges and fled in panic to the bluffs above the valley. Recovering from their fright, they occupied the commanding heights and poured a deadly fire into the troops below. Reynolds burned most of the village and, with the captured Indian ponies, hastily withdrew his command. The Indians harassed the retreat and recaptured all their ponies that night. Crook's force was reunited again but, discouraged by their setback, by the shortage of supplies, and by the bitter cold and deep snow, they returned to Fort Fetterman to refit. Crook later initiated a court-martial of Reynolds, charging misconduct and abandonment of the dead and a wounded man to the Indians, but the colonel was allowed to retire from the Army without trial.

Following the failure of this first expedition, General Sheridan planned a three-pronged offensive to force the Indians back to their reservations. While Colonel John Gibbon marched eastward from Fort Ellis, in western Montana, Brigadier General Alfred H. Terry and another column marched westward from Fort Abraham Lincoln in Dakota. Crook and his troops planned to complete the envelopment by a march northward again from Fort Fetterman. The plan was fated to suffer grave reverses before final victory was won.

Crook was the first to suffer. The Sioux and Cheyennes had united in one vast camp on the Little Bighorn River, where they learned from scouts of Crook's approach down Rosebud Creek.

General George A. Custer, about 1865. Signal Corps reproduction. National Archives.

Custer, standing with fringed sleeves, among a group of other officers of the 7th Cavalry and visitors. Left to right: Lt. James Calhoun,* 7th Cavalry; Mr. Sweet (son of Leonard Sweet of Chicago, guest of the Custers); Capt. Stephen Baker, 6th Infantry; Boston Custer* (brother of General Custer); Lt. W. I. Edgerly, 7th Cavalry; Miss Watson; Capt. Myles W. Keogh,* 7th Cavalry; Mrs. James Calhoun (General Custer's sister); Mrs. George A. Custer (nee Elizabeth Bacon); Custer,* Dr. H. O. Paulding, M.C., U.S.A.; Mrs. A. E. Smith; Dr. G. E. Lord,* M.C., U.S.A.; Capt. T. B. Weir, 7th Cavalry; Lt. W. W. Cooke,* Adjutant, 7th Cavalry; Lt. R. E. Thompson, 6th Infantry; Misses Wadsworth of Chicago (guests of the Custers); Capt. Thomas W. Custer,* 7th Cavalry; Lt. A. E. Smith,* 7th Cavalry. Those starred were killed in the fight on the Little Bighorn River. Taken in 1875 at the Little Heart River near Fort Lincoln, Dakota Territory. Signal Corps

Crazy Horse thereupon led a force of about fifteen hundred warriors forth to stop him. In the hard-fought Battle of the Rosebud on June 17, 1876, Crook's army drove the attackers from the field but suffered such heavy losses that the general felt compelled to withdraw once more, this time to a supply depot on Goose Creek, near present Sheridan, Wyoming. This action prevented Crook from joining forces with Terry.

While Crook retreated, Terry and Gibbon met on the Yellowstone at the mouth of the Rosebud. Riding with Terry was the flamboyant Custer and his 7th Cavalry, eager to repeat his success of the Washita campaign. An opportunity offered itself when the 7th was dispatched to reconnoiter along Rosebud Creek. As Custer and his troopers rode out of sight, all were confident that they could more than match any Indians they met.

On June 25, 1876, Custer located the huge Indian village on the banks of the Little Bighorn and decided to attack at once. He divided his command, seven hundred strong, into three battalions. With one, Major Marcus A. Reno charged the upper end of the camp. He was thrown back across the river and forced to dig in on the high bluffs that line the east bank of the stream. Captain Frederick W. Benteen and a second battalion, which had been sent on a scout to the west, joined Reno. Custer meanwhile rode north and then west to attack the lower end of the village. He encountered overwhelming numbers of Indians and fought a defensive action along the crest of a ridge paralleling the river across and downstream from the village. The battle probably lasted no more than an hour. All five companies, 230 or more men, died at the hands of swarms of warriors. Not one soldier escaped. Reno and Benteen managed to beat off repeated assaults for two days, until the approach of Generals Terry and Gibbon on June 27 frightened the Indians into calling off the fight and moving off to the south.

Exactly what happened after Custer led his battalion into the valley of the Little Bighorn is not certain. An aura of mystery surrounds the annihilation of Custer and the five troops that he personally led. It is an enigma that spurs students of military history to infinite speculations over exactly why and how Custer met such a catastrophe. But one thing is certain. By suffering one of the worst defeats in the history of the Indian wars, he won for himself and his regiment an immortality that no victory, however brilliant and decisive, could have achieved.

Instead of pressing their advantage, the victorious Indians scattered across eastern Montana while the Army sent additional troops into the field to join in pursuing them. The 5th Cavalry under Colonel Wesley Merritt was ordered to join General Crook. Learning that eight hundred to a thousand Cheyenne warriors from the Spotted Tail and Red Cloud Agencies were leaving to join Sitting Bull's victorious Sioux, Merritt headed them off. On July 17, 1876, on Warbonnet (or Hat) Creek, he engaged them in a spirited battle and drove them back to the agencies. In this fight "Buffalo Bill" Cody was reputed to have killed Chief Yellow Hand in hand-to-hand combat, an episode that novelists and publicity agents turned into a legend. Recent scholarship suggests that, instead of Yellow Hand, Cody killed a subchief named Yellow Hair, and not in hand-to-hand combat.

In August the forces of Crook and Terry were united, but this army was too unwieldy now that the Indians had scattered in small parties. Terry therefore returned to Fort Lincoln, and Crook headed south for the Black Hills, in a famous "starvation march." On September 8 the advance guard, under Captain Anson Mills, came upon a band of Sioux under American Horse camped on Rabbit Creek near Slim Buttes, north of the Black Hills. Mills charged and captured the village, although he was greatly outnumbered, and then hung on until Crook came to his support. Crazy Horse was camped nearby and tried to help American Horse, but was not in time. American Horse and several warriors were trapped in a cave but surrendered after the chief received a mortal wound. Although losses were slight on both sides, Slim Buttes was one of the first setbacks suffered by the Sioux in 1876. Crook continued on to the Black Hills and the summer campaign ended.

Terry had left Colonel Nelson A. Miles to police the line of the Yellowstone and try to prevent the escape of the Indians to Canada. Crook returned to Fort Fetterman but was back in the field by late November. Receiving word of the winter camp of

Soldier on stretcher, wounded in the Battle of Slim Buttes, South Dakota, September 9, 1876. Signal Corps photograph. National Archives.

Dull Knife's Cheyennes, in a canyon on the Red Fork of Powder River, Crook sent out his cavalry under Colonel Ranald S. Mackenzie of the 4th Cavalry. At dawn on November 25 Mackenzie burst into the sleeping camp of Cheyennes and after severe fighting drove them, scantily clad, into the surrounding hills. After burning the camp and its contents he withdrew. Most of the Indian refugees who survived, without food, clothing or shelter, made their way with great suffering to the village of Crazy Horse and surrendered with him the following spring. Mackenzie's loss was one officer and four men killed, twenty-five wounded; the Indians left twenty-five dead on the field.

To the north, Miles was also having success. He captured about two thousand Sioux in October and sent them to the reservation. Despite blizzards and extreme cold he remained in the field. On January 7, 1877, he camped beside Tongue River on the southern flank of the Wolf Mountains. Next morning Crazy Horse led his eight hundred or more warriors in a surprise attack on the military camp. Miles had howitzers disguised as wagons, however, and with exploding shells he quickly repulsed the attack. The Indians took refuge on bluffs overlooking the camp. The infantry assaulted the bluffs, supported by the artillery, and the warriors broke off the engagement and withdrew under cover of a snowstorm. Most of this group soon gave up at Fort Robinson.

By the spring of 1877 most of the Indian coalition that had overwhelmed Custer had been persuaded or forced to surrender. Only Lame Deer's band of Miniconjou Sioux and Sitting Bull's Hunkpapa Sioux remained at large. Early in May Colonel Miles set forth from his cantonment at the mouth of Tongue River (see Fort Keogh, pp. 192–93) and marched up the Rosebud. On May 7 he surprised and surrounded Lame Deer's camp on Lame Deer Creek, a tributary of the Rosebud. After a brief skirmish Lame Deer surrendered, but his son refused to lay down his rifle, and in a scuffle with soldiers it went off. Lame Deer, fearing that he was to be murdered, seized his rifle and fired at Miles, but killed his orderly instead. Renewed fighting broke out in which fourteen Indians (including Lame Deer and his son) and four soldiers were killed. The Miniconjous were subdued and sent back to their reservation.

Fort Buford, North Dakota, viewed looking south. From a painting not identified. Signal Corps reproduction. National Archives.

Gradually, the remaining bands came to see the futility of resistance and turned themselves in at their agency, where they were disarmed and fed. Only Sitting Bull and about four hundred Hunkpapas eluded the Army. They escaped to Canada and lived under British rule until 1881 when, hungry and reduced in numbers by defections, they crossed the border and surrendered at Fort Buford.

The power of the northern tribes had been broken forever. Occasional small raids continued for some time yet, but except for a brief Sioux uprising in 1890 they never regained their former magnitude. Like their brethren to the south, the northern tribes now became reservation Indians. The Army had not yet finished their subjugation, however, when another crisis flared—in the Pacific Northwest.

The Mountain Wars

While Colonel Miles was rounding up the remnants of Lame Deer's Sioux in May 1877, a disturbance arose in the mountains to the west that was the first act in what was to be a remarkable epic. The Nez Percé Indians of northeastern Oregon, under their able leader Chief Joseph, were resisting Army attempts to move them to a small reservation in Idaho. Their resentment over this was brought to a head at the time of the murder by several of Joseph's warriors of some settlers on the Salmon River. Brigadier General Oliver O. Howard was sent with more than five hundred soldiers from Fort Lapwai to enforce their removal, and to make the arrests.

Chief Joseph deployed his warriors, two hundred strong, in White Bird Canyon, with some drawn up in line and the rest hidden in the brush on one side. Captain David Perry and two troops of the 1st Cavalry rode down the canyon toward the Nez Percé village at its mouth and attacked the main line. Attacked vigorously on its flank by the concealed warriors, Perry's command retreated in disorder up the canyon, leaving thirty-seven dead behind them. This action, on June 17, was followed by triumphs for Chief Joseph on July 1 and 12. They marked the begin-

Fort Lapwai, Idaho, from a painting by Lt. R. H. Fletcher, 21st Infantry, made about 1875. Signal Corps reproduction. National Archives.

ning of the Indians' heroic fighting retreat across the Bitterroot Mountains in a vain effort to find a haven in Canada. Having inflicted heavy casualties on his pursuers, Joseph started over the rugged Lolo Trail across the Continental Divide, although impeded by a large number of women and children. General Howard's infantry and artillery were soon hopelessly outdistanced, unable to keep pace.

In two and a half months the Nez Percés retreated two thousand miles, either dodging or defeating the two thousand troops trying to subdue them. Surprise attacks failed to produce the panic usual to Indians and others under such circumstances. On August 9, for instance, Colonel John Gibbon and elements of the 7th Infantry intercepted Joseph at the Big Hole River. A dawn attack drove the Indians from their camp, but they rallied and forced the troops back to higher ground. Gibbon's men withstood a costly siege throughout the day but that night Joseph withdrew, continuing his race for a Canadian sanctuary. Time and again during this period the Nez Percés rallied around their great leader, beat off attackers and resumed their flight toward Canada. Despite sound tactics, however, Joseph was finally cornered. A column led by Colonel Miles, after a swift march from Fort Keogh, found him camped on Snake Creek in the Bear Paw Mountains of northern Montana, only about forty miles from the Canadian border. Miles struck on September 30, 1877. Although taken by surprise, the Nez Percés beat off the assault, inflicting 20 percent casualties on the troops. Miles then surrounded the Indians. The next day General Howard and his column arrived, and after a five-day siege Chief Joseph surrendered, ending the most remarkable chase in the history of the Indian wars.

The following year, 1878, the Northwest was the scene of an-

Chief Joseph of the Nez Percés. Undated Signal Corps photograph. National Archives.

Sketch of Big Hole Battlefield by Granville Stuart, May 11, 1878. Courtesy of the Montana Historical Society.

other disturbance. In the spring the Bannocks of Idaho left the Fort Hall Reservation and began plundering white settlements and ranches. Joined by a few Paiutes, Umatillas and Cayuses, they carried their operations into Oregon. After a series of skirmishes with soldiers, they were defeated by General Howard at Birch Creek, Oregon, in July, and returned to the reservation.

Far more serious was the outbreak the next year at White River Agency in northwestern Colorado. With the possible exception of the Ghost Dance outbreak of the Sioux in 1890, the Meeker Massacre at White River Agency was the most violent expression of Indian resentment of the reservation system and the policy behind it. Forced to settle on a reservation in western Colorado by a treaty concluded in 1873, the nomadic Utes resisted the attempts of Agent N. C. Meeker to make them farm, raise stock and send their children to school. In September 1879 they rose in revolt. Meeker called for military help when he was assaulted by a subchief during a petty quarrel. When the Indians learned that troops were on the way they attacked the agency, burned the buildings, killed Meeker and some of his employees, and took the white women captive. Then they set forth to do battle with the soldiers.

Quartermaster's storehouse, stables and shops at Fort Keogh, Montana, in the 1890's. Quartermaster's Photo Album. National Archives.

"The Surrender of Chief Joseph," by Frederic Remington. Signal Corps reproduction. National Archives.

Utes at White River Agency, Colorado, identified as "promoters and participants" in the Meeker Massacre. Signal Corps photograph. National Archives.

Major T. T. Thornburgh and three troops of cavalry, about 150 men, marched south from Fort Fred Steele, Wyoming, in response to Meeker's appeal. They were ambushed by Ute warriors at Milk Creek, on the north edge of the White River Reservation, on September 29, 1879. The major was killed and Captain J. Scott Payne, succeeding to the command, corralled the supply train and went on the defensive. A messenger was able to slip out with a call for reinforcements. Payne fought off the besieging Utes until October 5, when Colonel Wesley Merritt and about 350 men, both cavalry and infantry, arrived to lift the siege. The Army lost thirteen men killed and forty-three wounded in the Battle of Milk Creek but the revolt collapsed, with the result that several of the Ute leaders were sent to prison and the tribe was placed on a new reservation in Utah.

Lasting peace had come at last to the northern and southern Plains, and also to the Northwest with the settlement of the Ute and Bannock difficulties. Public interest now focused on the one part of the frontier still to be conquered.

The Desert Wars

When the Civil War ended, Arizona was still engrossed in an Apache war, despite the aggressive measures of General Carleton. Arizonans repeatedly petitioned for increased military protection, but to no avail. Incensed at all Indians and angry at governmental neglect, some embittered citizens of Tucson took matters into their own hands. A band of about three hundred Aravaipa Apaches under Eskiminzin had surrendered to Lieutenant Royal Whitman at Camp Grant and was encamped five miles from the post, under his protection. A mob from Tucson descended upon the camp on April 30, 1871, killed eighty-five or

General George Crook in the field with his favorite riding mule, "Apache," and two Apache scouts, Dutchy at left and Alchiseo. Undated Signal Corps photograph. National Archives.

Indian Agent John P. Clum, with Diablo and Eskiminzin, at San Carlos Agency, 1875. Signal Corps photograph. National Archives.

more adults, almost all women, and carried twenty-nine children into captivity. The Camp Grant Massacre, although generally receiving the approbation of westerners, did much to confound the efforts of Peace Policy representatives then in the territory. Treaty agents now found the Apaches more reluctant than ever to trade their freedom for the apparent insecurity of reservation life.

While the peace commissioners tried unsuccessfully to overcome the stigma of Camp Grant, Lieutenant Colonel George

Crook took command of the Department of Arizona on June 4, 1871. In anticipation of a punitive campaign against the Apaches, he reorganized his little army. His plans were forestalled, however, by the arrival of still another peace representative, General Howard, who surprised Crook with amazing success. With the assistance of Thomas J. Jeffords, a close friend of Cochise, How-

Five Apache Indians wearing leg-chains. Wittemann Collection, Library of Congress.

ard persuaded the aging Chiricahua to quit fighting and settle on a reservation at Sulphur Springs, west of Apache Pass.

Other Apaches were less amenable, and increased depredations evoked still louder demands for military action. Ignoring the Peace Policy, Crook converged troops on the Tonto Basin of central Arizona, the haunt of the Apache-Mojaves, or Yavapais. During this campaign Captain W. H. Brown, with two troops of the 5th Cavalry and thirty Apache scouts, won the Army's most striking victory in the long history of Apache warfare. At dawn on December 28, 1872, he surprised a band of more than a hundred Yavapais at a cave deep in the recesses of Salt River Canyon. The trapped Indians refused to surrender, and in the ensuing fight some of Brown's men shot at the roof of the cave and deflected a deadly fire into the defenders. Other troops completed the destruction by rolling boulders over the cliffs above. About seventy-five Indians were killed.

These aggressive measures so lowered the morale of the Yavapais that, on April 6, 1873, they made peace at Camp Verde. Crook was rewarded by promotion to brigadier general. While he remained in command of the department Arizona enjoyed a respite from serious Apache troubles. He was transferred to the north in 1875 and, whether coincidentally or not, the Apaches again grew restive.

The decade 1876–86 was characterized by continual Apache raids in the Southwest, and by two major outbreaks. The Indians had been herded to reservations where agents doled out a meager fare and unscrupulous traders sold inferior whiskey. The most important agency was San Carlos, on the Gila River, where plans of the Indian Bureau called for all Apaches to be concentrated. Labeled "hell's forty acres" by one observer, it was noted for its unhealthy location, overcrowded condition and dissatisfied inhabitants. A few renegade bands refused to go to the reservation, and for ten years they terrorized southern Arizona and New Mexico and the settlements of northern Mexico. The size of these war parties fluctuated, for they drew recruits from the reservation. When weary of raiding, or when troops pressed too closely, they gave themselves up and returned to the reservation, only to start anew when agency life again grew irksome.

Troops based at Forts Apache, Thomas, Grant, Bowie and Huachuca, Arizona; or Forts Bayard and Stanton, New Mexico; and at Forts Bliss, Davis, Quitman and Concho, Texas, campaigned ceaselessly against the Apaches. It was arduous and frustrating duty. Climate and geography aided the enemy, and the Apaches were skilled·at avoiding engagements where the odds were not overwhelmingly in their favor. For soldiers in the Southwest, the Apache wars consisted chiefly of endless marches under the desert sun, with very rarely a chance to come to grips with the foe.

Irrigation ditch under construction at San Carlos, Arizona. "O" and "X" mark 10th Cavalry Lts. Seward Mott (died March 11, 1887, from injuries inflicted by an Indian a few days after this picture was taken) and J. B. McDonald (in charge of the ditch). Signal Corps photograph. National Archives.

Issuing rations to Apaches at the San Carlos Indian Agency, Arizona, 1895. Signal Corps photograph. National Archives.

Geronimo. Photograph copyrighted in 1904 by Gerhard Sisters, St. Louis. Collections of the Library of Congress.

Twice during the decade the pace of raiding approached the scale of major war. In 1879, with more than a hundred Warm Springs and Mescalero Apache warriors, the Warm Springs leader Victorio struck time and again in New Mexico, Chihuahua and western Texas. When cornered he skirmished with soldiers, Texas Rangers and citizens' posses, but always managed to escape. Columns from Fort Davis and other Texas posts marched ninety thousand miles in the Victorio campaign. In October 1880 Mexican troops finally trapped Victorio in Chihuahua and in the ensuing battle he was killed. A remnant of his followers, under the aged and rheumatic Nana, escaped to the Sierra Madre, where they later joined forces with another wily Apache leader, Geronimo.

Following the death of Cochise in 1874, Geronimo grew in stature among the Chiricahuas, who had been moved from their reservation near Fort Bowie to one adjoining San Carlos on the north, near Fort Apache. In June 1881 trouble flared again, although it was not of Geronimo's making. A White Mountain Apache medicine man, Nakaidoklini, began preaching a new religion, blending pagan and Christian elements, foreshadowing the more widespread Ghost Dance religion of 1889–91. His mystical teachings and prophecies created great excitement among the Indians of the White Mountain Reservation. The agent called upon the Army for help and Colonel Eugene A. Carr, commanding nearby Fort Apache, was ordered to arrest Nakaidoklini.

On August 30 Carr led eighty-five cavalrymen and twenty-three Apache scouts to the camp of the medicine man on Cibecue Creek and took him into custody. The command moved down the creek two and a half miles and made camp for the night. At five o'clock that evening about a hundred heavily armed warriors, followers of Nakaidoklini, attacked Carr's troops. Some of the enlisted Indian scouts were affected by the religion. They re-

General Eugene A. Carr, taken here as Colonel of the 6th Cavalry. Undated Signal Corps photograph. National Archives.

Camp (or Fort) Apache, Arizona, in 1873. Photographed by Timothy H. O'Sullivan. U.S. Army Geographical and Geological Explorations and Surveys, under Lt. George M. Wheeler, Corps of Engineers. Collections of the Library of Congress.

volted, shooting down Captain E. C. Hentig and joining the attackers. During the struggle Nakaidoklini was killed by his guard. Carr's men repulsed the assailants but next morning, while Carr was still in the field, they joined with other disaffected bands and attacked Fort Apache. The garrison successfully withstood the assault and the Indians withdrew, later to surrender.

Partly as a result of the unrest created by the death of Nakaidoklini, a party of fifty-four warriors under Nantiatish left the Fort Apache Reservation in July 1882, raided San Carlos Agency and the settlements of the Tonto Basin, and ascended the Mogollon Rim at the head of the East Verde River. From the top they could see pursuing cavalry under Captain Adna R. Chaffee, and next day, July 17, they arranged an ambush in a deep canyon seven miles north of the rim. Chaffee's Apache scouts unmasked the trap and, his single troop reinforced by four more troops, he

Pedro, "captain" of a band of Coyotero Apaches, in his "Washington costume," Camp Apache, Arizona, 1873. Photographed by Timothy H. O'Sullivan. U.S. Army Geographical and Geological Explorations and Surveys, under Lt. George M. Wheeler, Corps of Engineers. Collections of the Library of Congress.

dismounted and formed a skirmish line on the brink of the canyon opposite the enemy. Posting one troop as base of fire to pin down the Indians across the gorge, he sent the rest in two flanking columns to get across the canyon and strike the Apaches in both flanks. The columns succeeded, and the surprised Indians were cut to pieces and scattered in all directions. They left twenty-one dead on the field and took with them many wounded, five of whom later died. The troops lost one scout and one enlisted man killed, two officers and five men wounded.

The Chiricahuas had not participated in either of these incidents, but they apparently feared that the Army's retaliation would not discriminate between guilty and innocent. Under

Geronimo and other leaders, about seventy-five Chiricahuas fled the agency and escaped to Mexico, avoiding the pursuing columns.

Two years of increased raiding followed. As usual the Army guarded water holes along the border and trusted that relentless pursuit and hardship would discourage the raiders. Despite the bleak outlook, the winter of 1882 brought some reassurance. On September 4 General Crook resumed command of the department. Immediately he inspected the deplorable conditions on the Apache reservations. Because of the Peace Policy, the crippling division of authority between military and civilian officials still

Four Apache braves, ready for the trail, Camp Apache, Arizona, 1873. Part of a wickiup (shelter) is seen on the right. Photographed by Timothy H. O'Sullivan. U.S. Army Geographical and Geological Explorations and Surveys, under Lt. George M. Wheeler, Corps of Engineers. Collections of the Library of Congress.

Typical Apache country—entrance to Cochise's stronghold at the summit of the Dragoon Mountains, Arizona, 1883. Signal Corps photograph. National Archives.

existed. Poor management by the Indian Bureau and the unrestricted use of liquor had played havoc with reservation discipline. Crook assigned several young officers to the agencies in hopes that their influence would bring order out of chaos.

He then turned to the hostiles. The United States and Mexico had signed an agreement that pledged mutual cooperation in tracking down renegade Apaches. Determined to take full advantage of this arrangement, Crook sent several detachments of Apache scouts into Mexico, commanded by white officers. Although unable to force decisive battles, they did, by their persistence, show the fugitives that the Sierra Madre no longer afforded sanctuary. By the spring of 1884 most of the renegade Chiricahuas had agreed to return to their reservations, much to the relief of the citizens of Arizona.

It was premature, however, for the Apache reservations still simmered with unrest. Only a spark was needed for hostilities to begin anew. Tiswin, the potent native liquor, provided the ignition. Violence flared again in May 1885, when 190 tiswin-saturated Chiricahuas, led by Geronimo, Natchez (son of Cochise), Nana and others, fled Fort Apache and headed for Mexico. They eluded the cavalry sent to intercept them and continued to do so as they raided all summer.

Illustrating the supreme difficulties their method of fighting presented the Army were the activities carried on by a single band of only eleven hostiles. Starting in November 1885 these raiders, in less than four weeks, traveled more than twelve hundred miles, wore out 250 horses, murdered thirty-eight people, and made good their escape to Mexico, although dismounted twice during this time.

Again Crook sent detachments of Apache scouts south of the border. Again persistence won out. No great victories were achieved this time either, but constant pursuit finally compelled the renegades to meet in conference with Crook at Canyon de los Embudos, Mexico, on March 25, 1886. They surrendered to him, but en route to Fort Bowie they went on a mescal spree and broke for the Sierra Madre. Their defection brought such a storm of criticism, both public and official, that Crook asked to be relieved of his command.

General Nelson A. Miles and his staff, in South Dakota about 1890. Signal Corps photograph. National Archives.

He was replaced on April 12, 1886, by Brigadier General Nelson A. Miles. Miles promptly revamped his supply system and erected twenty-seven heliograph stations on high peaks in Arizona and New Mexico. Large reinforcements made it possible for the new commander to organize "pursuing commands" instead of the detachments of Apache scouts, in whom he placed little faith. In spite of such innovations, Miles' hard-working army made scant progress against the hostiles until the fall of 1886. Then, largely because of the efforts of Lieutenant Charles B. Gatewood, Geronimo and Natchez were induced to surrender. Gatewood, with two Apache scouts, went into the Apache camp near Fronteras, Mexico. The Indian leaders insisted on talking with General Miles before laying down their arms and, escorted by Captain H. W. Lawton's command, they moved north and camped near the mouth of Skeleton Canyon, a favorite Apache haunt in the Guadalupe Mountains. General Miles rode down from Fort Bowie, sixty-five miles to the northwest. Geronimo and

After the surrender: "The Last of the Renegades," 1886, at Fort Bowie, Arizona. Above, the squatting Apache's moccasins are badly worn from the strenuous pursuit by the troops. Cut Nose Squaw is at the extreme left; her nose was removed by the Indians because of misbehavior. Below, center, left to right, Natchez and Geronimo, the latter wearing an alpaca coat he bought for fifty cents and a twelve-dollar pair of boots, both purchased at Bowie after his arrival. Members of the Fourth Cavalry band are at the right. Signal Corps photographs. National Archives.

Natchez surrendered here on September 3 and 4, 1886. They were promptly sent to Fort Marion, Florida, for imprisonment, and peace came to the frontier.

The Reservation System

In a matter of two decades, 1865 to 1885, the Indian had been progressively denied the two things essential to his traditional way of life—land and game. In their stead, as the Army subjugated one tribe after another, the Government substituted the reservation and the dole.

At first the reservation system was simply an expedient. The problem was to clear the paths of expansion. The solution was to corral the Indians on a parcel of land that (as yet) no one else wanted, and there keep them reasonably content by regular issues of food and clothing.

But the reservation system assumed quite a different shape during the decade of the eighties. Abolition of the treaty system in

Annuity goods for Indian prisoners of war at Fort Randall, South Dakota, April 17, 1882. Collections of the Library of Congress.

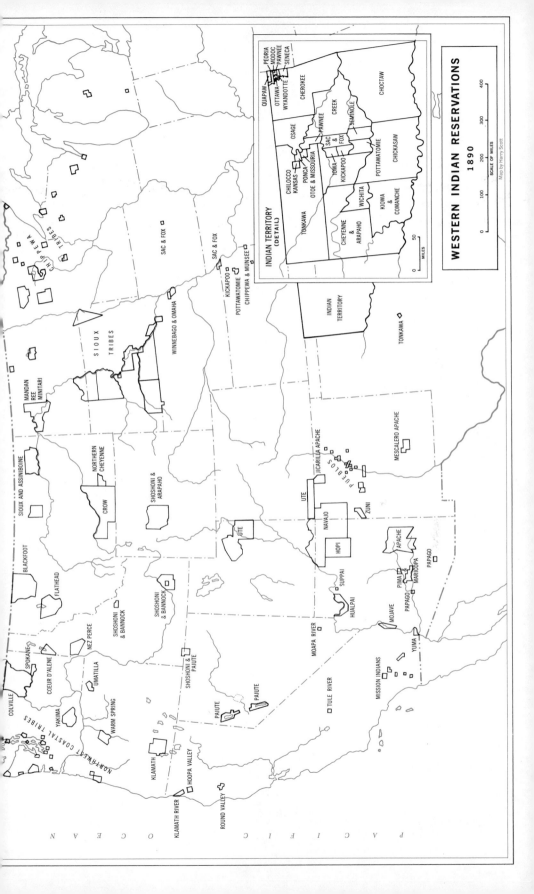

WESTERN INDIAN RESERVATIONS
1890

Map by Harry Scott

SCALE OF MILES

0   100   200   300   400

INDIAN TERRITORY
(DETAIL)

PEORIA
MODOC
PAWNEE
SENECA
QUAPAW
OTTAWA-
WYANDOTTE
CHEROKEE
CHOCTAW
OSAGE
PAWNEE
CREEK
SEMINOLE
CHILOCCO
KANSAS
PONCA
OTOE & MISSOURIA
SAC
&
FOX
POTTAWATOMIE
CHICKASAW
TONKAWA
IOWA
KICKAPOO
WICHITA
KIOWA
&
COMANCHE
CHEYENNE
&
ARAPAHO

0   50   100
MILES

COLVILLE
SPOKANE
COEUR D'ALENE
NEZ PERCE
UMATILLA
WARM SPRING
YAKIMA
NORTHWEST COASTAL TRIBES
KLAMATH
HOOPA VALLEY
KLAMATH RIVER
ROUND VALLEY

BLACKFOOT
FLATHEAD
SHOSHONI
& BANNOCK
SHOSHONI & BANNOCK
SHOSHONI &
PAIUTE
PAIUTE
PAIUTE

SIOUX AND ASSINIBOINE
CROW
NORTHERN
CHEYENNE
SHOSHONI &
ARAPAHO
UTE
UTE

MANDAN
REE
MINITARI

SIOUX
TRIBES

CHIPPEWA
TRIBES

WINNEBAGO & OMAHA

SAC & FOX

SAC & FOX

KICKAPOO
POTTAWATOMIE
CHIPPEWA & MUNSEE

INDIAN
TERRITORY

TONKAWA

PUEBLOS
JICARILLA APACHE
NAVAJO
ZUNI
HOPI
MESCALERO APACHE

SUPPAI
HUALPAI
MOAPA RIVER
MOJAVE
YUMA

APACHE
MARICOPA
PIMA
PAPAGO
PAPAGO
PAPAGO

TULE RIVER
MISSION INDIANS

PACIFIC   OCEAN

1871 had deprived the tribes of even the small comfort of theoretical sovereignty. Thus, when they came to the reservation, fresh from military conquest and dependent upon the largess of the Great Father, they were undeniably wards of the Government and subject to its will. In the eighties this will derived largely from the theories of a growing number of Indian reform organizations which wielded increasingly potent influence on national legislators and administrators. And the reformers expressed the almost universal conviction of enlightened Americans that the solution of the Indian problem lay in transforming the Indian, as rapidly as possible and by compulsion if necessary, into a God-fearing tiller of the soil enjoying the blessings of Christianity, education, ownership of land in severalty, and national citizenship. Reformers and like-minded officials used the reservation system as the instrument for attempting this program. Thus, in the end, the reservation system brought with terrible force the social convulsion that had been foreshadowed by the collapse of the "Permanent Indian Frontier."

On the reservation the Indian found himself suddenly overwhelmed by the civilizing process. It took the form of a concerted campaign to root out the old and inculcate the new. Indian policemen and Indian courts, controlled by the agent, ironically provided the compulsion. When they failed, withholding of rations ordinarily produced a surface illusion of the desired conformity.

All facets of Indian life came under fire. Because tribal communalism stood in the way of change, the attack centered on the basic social, economic and political institutions of the tribe, many of which, indeed, had already lost their meaning in the transition from nomadic to sedentary life. "Every man a chief," announced the Government, and urged the people to abandon their camps, throw away their lodges, spread out over the reservation, build cabins and ignore the traditional leaders. A list of "Indian offenses" outlawed fundamental social and religious customs. The list included the Sun Dance, the foundation upon which the Plains Indian had built his whole theological edifice, and the many practices of the medicine man.

Other whites helped the agent. They were a far different breed than the easygoing, fun-loving trappers of old. The "practical

One Apache and ten Pueblo children, newly arrived at Carlisle Barracks, Pennsylvania. Photograph by J. N. Choate, undated. Collections of the Library of Congress.

farmer" tried to teach farming to a people who did not want to farm, on land that for the most part was not suitable for farming anyway, using techniques that were ill-adapted to the soil and climate. The schoolteacher tried to teach unwilling children of unwilling parents the "useful arts" of civilization, but these arts had little real meaning in the reservation environment. Off-reservation boarding schools, patterned after the military model of Carlisle Indian School in Pennsylvania, proved much more effective—until the child returned to the reservation and found no place for himself in either white or Indian society. Missionaries tried to substitute Christianity for a paganism that had developed as a functional part of Indian culture. Here the Indians were often receptive to the new but also unwilling to surrender the old. To the Indians, the trader was frequently the only entirely agreeable white man on the reservation. He furnished them with useful manufactures without eternally carping about their barbarous habits.

The severalty movement was central to the reform program. Give the Indian his own individual title to the soil, reformers held, and virtually all other problems would automatically solve themselves. The Indian would become a responsible, self-supporting citizen just like any white citizen. The severalty movement culminated in the Dawes Act of 1887, which provided for the allotment of reservation lands, generally in 160-acre parcels, to the individual native residents. In the Dawes Act eastern reformers and western land boomers met on common ground, for severalty meant that all reservation lands not needed for allotments might be thrown open to white settlement. The great majority of western Indians resisted allotment, yet vast tracts of surplus reservation land were opened to settlement before allotment programs got under way.

The loss of surplus land created enormous resentment on the part of the Indian. Worse, after the Indian had finally bowed to the inevitable and accepted allotment, he found himself imprisoned by a vicious and unfamiliar system that forced him ever lower on the economic scale. Despite legal safeguards the patented land found its way relentlessly, by one subterfuge or another, into

Boys in uniform at Carlisle Barracks, Pennsylvania. Photograph by J. N. Choate, undated. Collections of the Library of Congress.

Indian School at Keams Canyon, Hopi Indian Reservation, Arizona. Undated Signal Corps photograph. National Archives.

white ownership. The remaining land was endlessly subdivided through inheritance. Allotments that, even in the beginning, were too small for economic efficiency when devoted to crop-raising were transformed into clusters of tiny patches on which the heirs eked out the barest subsistence.

In spite of all objections, however, the policies of the 1880's, founded on the sincerely idealistic dreams of the severalty advocates, prevailed in general until 1934. Only then did hope revive for the Indian.

The End of Hostilities

For the Indian, a decade of exposure to the frenzied activity of the reservation program served mainly to blend twisted remnants of the old life with a few frayed strands of the new. Frustration, bitterness and impotence characterized most of the tribes. Bleak prospects for the future combined with nostalgic memories of the past to produce a state of mind particularly susceptible to a Messianic fervor that swept the western reservations in 1889 and 1890. A strange mixture of Christianity and paganism, the Ghost

Dance religion promised a return of the old order and the disappearance of the white race. Wild "Ghost Dances" attended the movement. Although they did not necessarily imply violence, they nevertheless alarmed whites living near the reservations by displays of unbridled emotions. Among the Oglala Sioux the religion took on a militancy that frightened the new and inexperienced agent into calling for military protection.

In November 1890 troops came to the Sioux reservations. For a time it looked as if the trouble might be settled without bloodshed. But on December 29 at Wounded Knee, near Pine Ridge Agency, soldiers of Colonel James W. Forsyth's 7th Cavalry tried to disarm Big Foot's band of Miniconjou Sioux, who had fled from the Cheyenne River Reservation. In a scuffle over a rifle, between soldiers and an Indian, the rifle went off and fighting broke out. Hotchkiss guns placed nearby immediately went into action and in the brief contest that followed both sides suffered heavy

Interior of barrack, Fort D. A. Russell, Wyoming, in the 1890's. Quartermaster's Photo Album. National Archives.

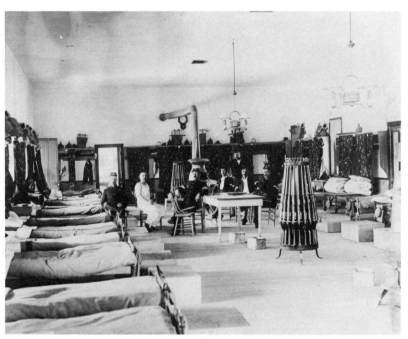

"Villa of Brûlé." Large camp of Brûlé Sioux near Pine Ridge Agency. Photographed by Grabill of Deadwood, South Dakota, probably in January 1891. Collections of the Library of Congress.

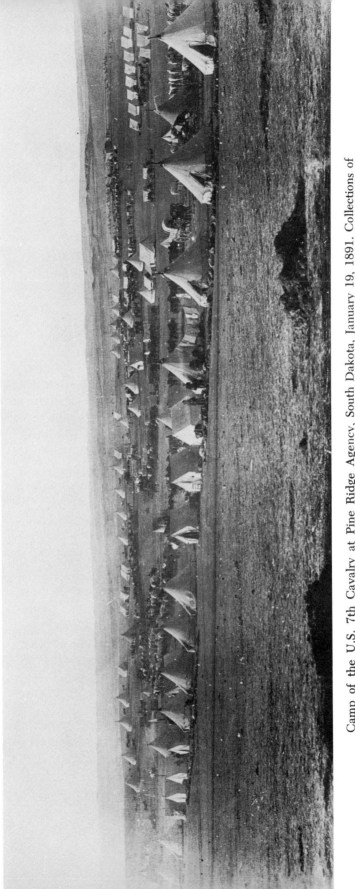

Camp of the U.S. 7th Cavalry at Pine Ridge Agency, South Dakota, January 19, 1891. Collections of the Library of Congress.

Return of Casey's Scouts from the Battle of Wounded Knee, winter, 1891. Their commander, Lt. Edward W. Casey, was killed on January 7. Signal Corps photograph. National Archives.

casualties. Many Indian women and children, caught in the line of fire, lost their lives. Big Foot's band was utterly crushed. Other chiefs scattered, and maneuvering continued for about a month, but the Indians saw the futility of resistance and at length surrendered.

Quartermaster Sergeant's Quarters, Fort Washakie, Wyoming, in the 1890's. Fence made of barrel staves. Quartermaster's Photo Album. National Archives.

Although a few stray renegades plagued some areas of the West for another decade, the Battle of Wounded Knee marked the close of the Indian wars. In the same year, 1890, the Census Bureau discovered that a distinct line of settlement could no longer be traced on the map. It was appropriate, and perhaps not entirely coincidental, that the last vestige of the Indian barrier vanished together with the frontier of settlement. The Indian barrier had been one of the most powerful of the forces guiding the course of frontier history. It had influenced significantly the advance and development of the miner's frontier, the cattleman's frontier and the farmer's frontier. It had affected transportation and communication and the growth of towns and cities. It passed away at the same time as the frontier, but the heritage that remains is both vivid and meaningful.

PART II

Survey of Historic Sites
and Buildings

A PROFUSION of historic sites illustrating nine-teenth-century military and Indian affairs has survived in the western United States. In fact, only the miner's frontier exceeds the present subject in number of sites with tangible remains still in existence. As a result of the recent surge of popular interest in the West, inspired by motion pictures, television, books and magazine articles, the historic sites of the Indian wars have become prominent landmarks on the itineraries of vacationing Americans.

Army forts that defined the advancing frontier account for the majority of sites. West of the Mississippi River, almost two hundred forts with visible remains may be listed and located. Some are marked only by mounds of earth covering building foundations. Others offer the visitor a virtually complete picture of the Army's frontier outpost. Between these two extremes are scores of forts with adobe or stone ruins in various stages of disintegration. Because the Plains Indian posed the greatest barrier to the westward movement, most of the forts are to be found in the Plains and Rocky Mountain states. Logically, they are concentrated

[91

along historic routes of transportation and communication such as the Missouri, Yellowstone, Platte, Arkansas, Rio Grande and Gila Rivers; the Oregon, Santa Fe, Smoky Hill and Bozeman Trails; and the Northern Pacific, Union Pacific, Kansas Pacific, and Southern Pacific Railroads.

Battlefields where Indians and soldiers clashed are also numerous. The sites of almost fifty major engagements, located mostly in the Plains states, may be identified. At many the natural setting remains unimpaired, and the student has little difficulty locating key positions and visualizing the action. A few have been destroyed by farming or ranching operations. Most of the battle sites have been marked by Federal, state or local agencies, and some have been set aside as historical monuments.

The Indian was not conquered by military means alone. Other methods also proved effective. Agencies, missions and trading posts are historic sites that exemplify this other part of the story. A number of agencies with structures dating from the late nineteenth century are scattered about the West, the best examples being in Oklahoma, the Dakotas and Montana. Good remains of nineteenth-century Indian missions may be seen in Kansas, Idaho, the Dakotas, Montana and the Pacific Northwest. The trading post, together with the ritual of Indian trading, is still vividly displayed on the Navajo Reservation of Arizona and New Mexico.

Aridity and, until recently, sparsity of population have combined in the West to reduce the threat of nature and man to historic sites. The threat has nevertheless been serious and with the increasing westward shift of population, it is growing even more so. Most forts were built of adobe. When the Army moved out, local settlers customarily stripped them for building materials. Deprived of roofs, doors and windows, the adobe walls were left exposed to the elements. Today, as a result, the sites of many forts are marked by melting adobe ruins that disintegrate more and more each year. Stone forts were less vulnerable to the ravages of wind and rain, but they too yielded building material— stone blocks already quarried and shaped—to ranchers or farmers of the surrounding country. Today, however, the ruins of stone forts are generally more imposing than those of adobe forts.

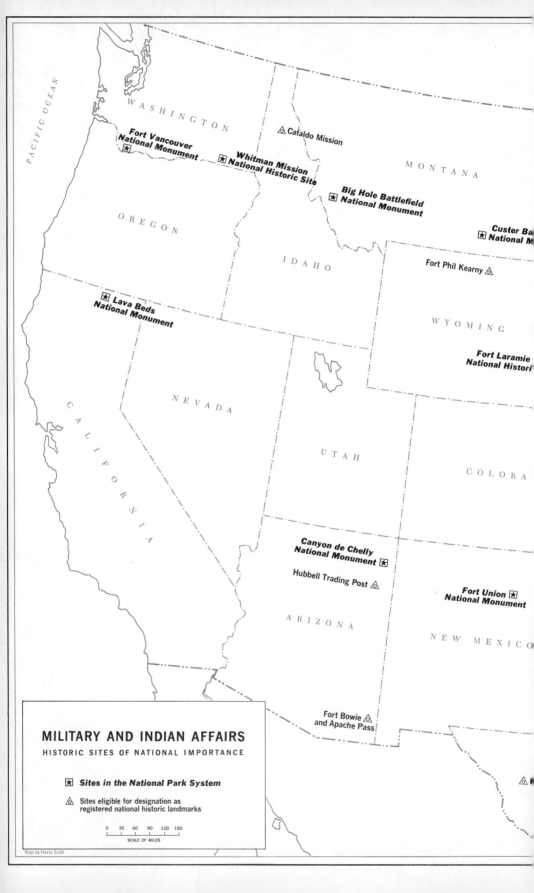

PACIFIC OCEAN

WASHINGTON

△ Cataldo Mission

MONTANA

Fort Vancouver National Monument ⊠

Whitman Mission National Historic Site ⊠

Big Hole Battlefield National Monument ⊠

OREGON

Custer Ba ⊠ **National M**

IDAHO

Fort Phil Kearny △

⊠ **Lava Beds National Monument**

WYOMING

NEVADA

Fort Laramie National Histori

CALIFORNIA

UTAH

COLORA

Canyon de Chelly National Monument ⊠

Hubbell Trading Post △

Fort Union ⊠ **National Monument**

ARIZONA

NEW MEXICO

△

Fort Bowie △ and Apache Pass

MILITARY AND INDIAN AFFAIRS

HISTORIC SITES OF NATIONAL IMPORTANCE

⊠ **Sites in the National Park System**

△ Sites eligible for designation as registered national historic landmarks

0 30 60 90 120 150
SCALE OF MILES

Map by Harry Scott

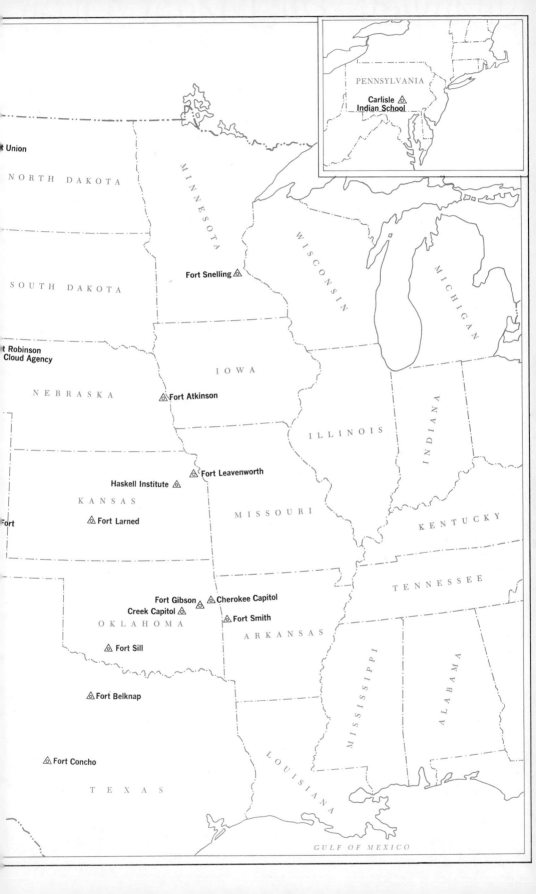

PENNSYLVANIA

Carlisle
Indian School

t Union

NORTH DAKOTA

MINNESOTA

WISCONSIN

MICHIGAN

Fort Snelling

SOUTH DAKOTA

t Robinson
Cloud Agency

IOWA

NEBRASKA

Fort Atkinson

ILLINOIS

INDIANA

Fort Leavenworth

Haskell Institute

KANSAS

MISSOURI

KENTUCKY

ort

Fort Larned

TENNESSEE

Fort Gibson   Cherokee Capitol
Creek Capitol

OKLAHOMA

Fort Smith

ARKANSAS

Fort Sill

MISSISSIPPI

ALABAMA

Fort Belknap

Fort Concho

TEXAS

LOUISIANA

GULF OF MEXICO

Some sites escaped destruction by continuing use. The Army still uses Forts Huachuca, Bliss, Sill, Leavenworth and Riley. The Indian Bureau still maintains agencies at Lame Deer (Montana), Pine Ridge (South Dakota), Standing Rock (North Dakota) and elsewhere. Some sites have survived by finding other uses. The city of San Angelo, Texas, engulfed Fort Concho, and some buildings survived as private residences and parts of commercial establishments. A similar fate overtook Camp Verde, Arizona, and Fort Stockton, Texas. Indian agencies moved into Fort Apache, Arizona, and Fort Simcoe, Washington; and an Indian school into Fort Wingate, New Mexico. The State Game Farm took over the agency complex at the headquarters of the Cheyenne-Arapaho Reservation in Oklahoma. A dude ranch now uses the old buildings at Fort Clark, Texas; a cattle ranch those of Fort Larned, Kansas.

Probably the greatest destruction of sites in recent years has resulted from the flood control and irrigation programs of the U.S. Army Corps of Engineers and the Bureau of Reclamation. When the Missouri River Basin Project is completed along the main stem of the Missouri River, much of the valley will be subject to inundation between Yankton, South Dakota, and the North Dakota–Montana boundary. The sites of many forts, agencies and missions will be lost. In Oahe Reservoir alone, one battle site, four military posts and seven missions will be endangered. The National Park Service and the Smithsonian Institution have carried out historical and archaeological studies to salvage as much history as possible in the reservoir areas.[5]

Against the dangers to survival must be balanced the efforts of Federal, state and local preservationists to save the historic sites of the Indian wars. The National Park Service preserves and interprets Fort Laramie, Wyoming, Fort Union, New Mexico, and the sites of the battles at Captain Jack's Stronghold in California, and at Big Hole and the Little Bighorn in Montana. The United States Army preserves and interprets the historical values of Forts Sill, Huachuca, Bliss, Riley and Leavenworth.

Many of the western states maintain historical societies or other agencies that have taken an active interest in preserving or marking sites discussed here. Wyoming owns, in whole or part, the sites of Forts Bridger, Reno and Phil Kearny, and two battlefields. Seven forts and one battlefield in North Dakota are in state ownership. At Fort Garland the State Historical Society of Colorado preserves and interprets a typical nineteenth-century frontier outpost. Kansas maintains four Indian missions, and Minnesota owns seven noteworthy sites. The Oklahoma Historical Society has conducted a state survey of historic sites and has supervised an extensive highway-marking program. The state park system includes Fort Gibson and Sequoyah's Home. Texas also is surveying its historic sites, and Fort Griffin is maintained as a state park. Fort Churchill is part of the Nevada State Park System, and Fort Simcoe has been leased to the Washington State Parks and Recreation Commission by the Yakima Indians. California preserves Forts Tejon and Humboldt, and the Yuma Tribal Council has recently interested the California Division of Beaches and Parks in developing Fort Yuma as a state historical monument.

In the following pages the more important historic sites associated with nineteenth-century military and Indian affairs are evaluated. The first group are units of the National Park System; the second, sites judged to possess "exceptional value" when measured by the criteria (see appendix) and thus eligible for designation as Registered National Historic Landmarks; the third, sites of sufficient importance to merit attention but not considered nationally important when measured by the criteria; and the fourth, sites of marginal importance examined by the field historians in the course of their studies and travels.

A. Sites in the National Park System

The principal aim of the National Survey of Historic Sites and Buildings is to identify nationally important historic sites that are not units of the National Park System, but no survey of historic sites would be complete without mention of historic areas in the Park System. The sites briefly described below are those areas administered by the National Park Service that have primary or secondary associations with nineteenth-century military and Indian affairs. Further information about a particular area may be obtained by writing directly to the Superintendent.

1. Canyon de Chelly National Monument, Arizona

Location: Apache County, 46 miles north of Ganado; address: Chinle, Arizona

Canyon de Chelly National Monument preserves several hundred prehistoric Indian ruins tucked away in the recesses of some of the nation's most spectacular canyons. As a secondary value, it contains the scenes of Kit Carson's decisive though almost bloodless victory over the Navajo Indians in 1864, described on p. 27.

Today, within the Monument, Navajo families live a simple pastoral life much as they did in Kit Carson's time. Their hogans dot the level canyon floor at the base of red sandstone cliffs which rise vertically as high as eight hundred feet. Flocks of sheep graze in the canyon and on the rims. At the historic trading post adjacent to Monument headquarters, Navajos from the surrounding area trade blankets, wool and piñon nuts for merchandise.[6]

Canyon de Chelly, "Camp Beauty," 1873. Photographed by Timothy H. O'Sullivan of the U.S. Army Geographical and Geological Explorations and Surveys, under Lt. George M. Wheeler, Corps of Engineers. Five lateral canyons branch off from the main gorge in this area. The canyon walls here are 1000 to 1200 feet high. Collections of the Library of Congress.

2. Lava Beds National Monument, California

Location: Siskiyou County, 30 miles southeast of Klamath Falls, Oregon; address: Tulelake, California

Following the outbreak of hostilities between soldiers and Modoc Indians in the autumn of 1872, the Modoc leader, Captain Jack, led a small band of his people to the natural fortress now contained in Lava Beds National Monument. The bloody struggle that followed is described on pp. 43–45.

Lava Beds National Monument embraces 46,000 acres of lava flow. It draws attention primarily for its scientific values. Within the Monument boundaries are Captain Jack's Stronghold, where the Modocs took refuge; the site of the Army base camp; the site of Canby's murder; and the sites of the principal engagements of the campaign.[7]

3. Big Hole Battlefield National Monument, Montana

Location: Beaverhead County, 12 miles west of Wisdom on State Highway 43; address: Superintendent, Yellowstone National Park, Wyoming

Big Hole Battlefield National Monument commemorates one of the series of actions, described on pp. 59–61, in the Nez Percé War

Navajo man and woman, in Canyon de Chelly, 1873. Photographed by Timothy H. O'Sullivan of the U.S. Army Geographical and Geological Explorations and Surveys, under Lt. George M. Wheeler, Corps of Engineers. Collections of the Library of Congress.

Custer Battlefield, Montana. View toward the Little Bighorn River. White grave markers in middle distance show route taken by some of Custer's men away from the river. Wooden cross in foreground bears legend, "Here fell Custer, June 25, 1876"; white stone markers all read, "U.S. Soldier, 7th Cavalry, fell here, June 25, 1876." Undated Signal Corps photograph. National Archives.

of 1877. Chief Joseph was resisting confinement in a reservation, and attempting to gain a refuge in Canada. The Monument comprises 200 acres of land in the vicinity of the battlefield, but not the site of the Indian encampment or the scene of the fiercest fighting. The natural setting remains little changed, and traces of trenches used by the troops may still be seen.[8]

4. Custer Battlefield National Monument, Montana

Location: Bighorn County, 3 miles southeast of Crow Agency; address: Crow Agency, Montana

Of all the battles between Indians and soldiers, "Custer's Last Stand" is the best known. On June 25, 1876, along the bluffs and ridges overlooking the Little Bighorn River, Lieutenant Colonel George A. Custer and the 7th Cavalry sustained the most spectacular defeat suffered by U.S. troops in the history of the Indian wars. A full description of the affair is on pp. 53–56.

The central feature of Custer Battlefield National Monument is the ridge along which the heaviest fighting took place. White marble headstones mark the approximate places where each man of Custer's battalion died. On the west slope, at the north end of the ridge, a cluster of about fifty headstones marks the site where Custer and the remnant of his command made the famous "last stand." Just above this group, on top of the ridge, stands a granite shaft bearing the names of the soldiers killed in the engagement; their bodies are buried in a mass grave beneath it. A detached area, four miles to the south and accessible by road, includes the scene of Reno's two-day battle on the bluffs. A monument and restored entrenchments mark this battlefield. A visitor center and museum, and a National Cemetery containing burials from many of the Indian battles of the northern Plains, may be visited here also.[9]

5. Fort Union National Monument, New Mexico

Location: Mora County, 8 miles north of U.S. Highway 85 at Watrous; address: Watrous, New Mexico

As a result of the Mexican War, the United States acquired the "Spanish Southwest" and with it the Indian problem that had

Fort Union, New Mexico, in September 1866. Plaza of the Mechanic's Corral, Quartermaster's Depot. Signal Corps photograph. National Archives.

plagued its people since earliest times. The Army therefore laid out a system of forts that blanketed New Mexico and southern Arizona. One of the most important posts was Fort Union. Erected in 1851 on the eastern frontier of New Mexico, near the junction of the Mountain and Cimarron branches of the Santa Fe Trail, Fort Union became the major supply depot of the southwestern military frontier and one of the most active bases of operations against hostile Indians. From 1851 to 1875, troops stationed at the fort were constantly in the field guarding the Santa Fe Trail, scouting, patrolling and skirmishing with Ute, Jicarilla Apache, Mescalero Apache, Navajo, Kiowa and Comanche raiders, and participating in major offenses against these tribes. Fort Union also played a significant role in repelling the Confederate invasion of New Mexico in 1862. With the coming of the railroad in 1879 Fort Union began to lose its importance. It was finally abandoned in 1891.

Fort Union National Monument preserves the eroding adobe ruins of the sprawling post and quartermaster depot that took shape during the 1860's. The original Fort Union, built of logs in 1851, has long since disappeared. On its site, now a detached section of the Monument, the Army later built the Fort Union Arsenal, whose ruins may be seen across the valley from the main post. Adjacent to the main post is the massive star fort, an earthen fortification built in 1861 to halt the Confederate thrust at New Mexico. Ruts of the Santa Fe Trail may be identified readily in the vicinity. A museum and visitor center interpret the Fort Union story.[10]

6. Fort Vancouver National Monument, Washington

> *Location: Clark County, city of Vancouver; address: Vancouver, Washington*

Fort Vancouver became a U.S. Army post in 1849, following the acquisition of Oregon by the United States, after serving for twenty years as the headquarters for the Hudson's Bay Company in the Pacific Northwest. In 1849 Lieutenant Colonel W. W. Loring led the Regiment of Mounted Riflemen in a march over the Oregon Trail and placed garrisons at Forts Kearny, Laramie and Hall to protect immigrants. Fort Vancouver became Loring's headquarters and the western anchor of this defense system. Dur-

Ruins of Fort Union, New Mexico. National Park Service photograph.

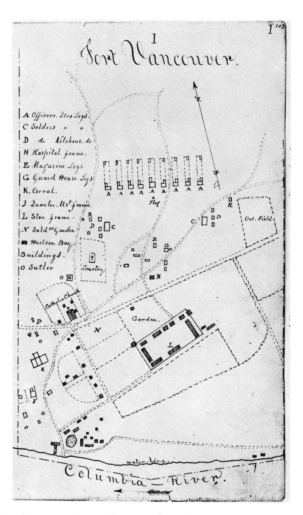

Plan of Fort Vancouver, Washington, from "Report on the Department of the Pacific in 1854," by General Joseph K. F. Mansfield. War Department Records. National Archives.

ing the 1850's the fort served as the base for several campaigns against hostile Indians of Oregon and Washington, and from 1849 throughout the period of the Indian wars housed the department headquarters that administered military affairs in the Pacific Northwest.

Located within the city limits of Vancouver, Fort Vancouver National Monument contains the site of the original fort, which burned during the 1860's. Although the interpretive program

Fort Vancouver, Washington Territory, viewed from the northwest, showing many of the buildings identified in the plan opposite. Large building in left center is the Catholic Church, with the cemetery stretching up the slope to the left and the sutlery within stockade beside it. Officers' quarters are at top left, with soldiers' quarters and kitchens the large buildings in the left background. The white building just beyond the church is the hospital and the large stockade on the right encloses the Hudson's Bay Company store and other buildings. From a tinted lithograph, drawn by Gustave Sohon about 1855. U.S. Pacific Railroad Explorations and Surveys, 47–49th Parallels. Collections of the Library of Congress.

Visitors at Whitman Mission National Historic Site, Washington, pause at the Great Grave, marked by the slab, which commemorates the victims of the Cayuse massacre of 1847, and the monument to William H. Gray, buried here also, who aided the Whitmans to establish their mission. On the hilltop is the Whitman Memorial Shaft erected in 1897. National Park Service photograph.

focuses primarily upon the Hudson's Bay Company fur-trade story, the area, together with Vancouver Barracks, still an active Army installation, also illustrates the role of the Army in the conquest and settlement of the Pacific Northwest.[11]

7. Whitman Mission National Historic Site, Washington

Location: Walla Walla County, U.S. Highway 410, 6 miles west of Walla Walla; address: Walla Walla, Washington

At Whitman Mission National Historic Site the National Park Service preserves the site of the famous Waiilatpu Mission and interprets its story against the background of the American missionary effort which exerted so great an influence on the ultimate

104]

Fort Laramie in 1863. From a drawing made by Bugler C. Moellman, 11th Ohio Cavalry. Signal Corps reproduction. National Archives.

"Old Bedlam," about 1874. The wing at the left no longer exists. This structure was used at various times as officers' quarters, post headquarters and social center. It is the oldest surviving building and has been restored carefully inside and out and refurnished in the period of about 1866. Fort Laramie National Monument, Wyoming. National Park Service photograph.

View of restored buildings across the parade ground. "Old Bedlam" is nearest on the left, officers' quarters and sutler's store center, and cavalry barracks between the trees. Fort Laramie National Monument, Wyoming. National Park Service photograph.

occupation and acquisition of the Pacific Northwest by the United States. The Waiilatpu Mission was founded in 1836 among the Cayuse Indians near Fort Walla Walla by Marcus and Narcissa Whitman. For eleven years the missionaries labored with indifferent success to Christianize the natives and teach them to become farmers. The effort created unrest, jealousy and distrust among the Indians, and finally led to the massacre in which Whitman lost his life in November 1847.

Whitman Mission National Historic Site comprises about ninety-eight acres of the mission grounds. It contains the "great" grave where the massacre victims are buried, the Whitman Memorial Shaft and the foundation ruins of the mission buildings. A small temporary museum houses artifacts uncovered by archaeological excavations at the site, until a new visitor center is completed.[12]

8. Fort Laramie National Historic Site, Wyoming

*Location: Goshen County, 3 miles southwest of U.S. High-
way 26 and the town of Fort Laramie; address: Fort
Laramie, Wyoming*

First established as a fur-trading house in 1834, Fort Laramie was
purchased by the Government in 1849 and as a military post continued to be important in the history of the northern Plains. After
the Treaty of 1851 was concluded near Fort Laramie, bringing
the Sioux and other Plains tribes into official relations with the
United States, the fort was the focal point of long, costly wars
with the Sioux and Cheyennes down through the 1870's, as described in Part I. The garrison led a routine existence in the 1880's
until the fort was abandoned in 1890.

At Fort Laramie National Historic Site the National Park
Service preserves the surviving features of the military period and
is carrying out a program to restore standing buildings and related
portions of the grounds. Certain older structures provide glimpses
of the fort scene as early as 1849. Remains of twenty-one historic
buildings may be viewed. Surviving original structures include
the guardhouse, hospital, officers' quarters and cavalry barracks.
Partially restored buildings include the sutler's store, commissary
storehouse, bakery, and "Old Bedlam," the first military structure
and long the administrative and social center of the post. A small
museum in the cavalry barracks displays artifacts of Fort
Laramie.[13]

B. Sites Eligible for the Registry of National Historic Landmarks

The historic sites in this group have been judged to meet the criteria of "exceptional value" (reproduced in the appendix) and therefore to possess importance to the nation for commemorating and illustrating the history of the United States. As historic sites of national importance, they have been declared by the Secretary of the Interior to be eligible for inclusion in the Registry of National Historic Landmarks. Some have already been designated Registered National Historic Landmarks, and others will receive the designation upon application of the owners. A few have been proposed for addition to the National Park System.

Ruins of Fort Bowie, Arizona. National Park Service photograph.

After the surrender: some of Geronimo's renegade Apaches at Fort Bowie, Arizona, 1886. The large house in upper left with the French roof is the commanding officer's quarters. Signal Corps photograph. National Archives.

Fort Bowie, Arizona. Fort Bowie guarded strategic Apache Pass through the Chiricahua Mountains of southeastern Arizona and played a key role in twenty-five years of war with the Apaches. This photograph was taken about 1890. Courtesy National Archives.

1. Fort Bowie and Apache Pass, Arizona

Location. Cochise County, 15 miles south of town of Bowie.

Ownership and Administration. Fort Bowie is situated on privately owned land. Much of the surrounding land is in public ownership subject to grazing lease. The public land is administered by the Bureau of Land Management, Department of the Interior.

Significance. Fort Bowie commanded the eastern entrance to Apache Pass, which with its isolated springs was a landmark to travelers traversing the Chiricahua Mountains. The fort was established on July 28, 1862, by the brigade of California volunteers under Brigadier General James H. Carleton, in the campaign described on pp. 25–26. (See also pp. 68 ff.) For the next twenty-four years, until the end of the Apache wars, Fort Bowie was the hub of military operations against the Chiricahua Apaches led by

Cochise, Geronimo and Natchez. With Geronimo's capture and exile in 1886 peace was restored, and the fort entered its final chapter, which ended with its abandonment in 1894.

The events that occurred in Apache Pass and at Fort Bowie, or which through close association are illustrated by these sites, spanned half a century. In large measure they controlled the pattern of frontier development in southern Arizona during the nineteenth century.

Present Appearance. The fort built by the California volunteers in 1862 stood on a hill dominating the strategic springs. It has eroded badly and only the foundations and some fragments of adobe wall are still visible. This fort was replaced in 1868 by a larger post a few hundred yards to the east, on a slope below Bowie Peak. The ruins of the later fort are more impressive. Walls in varying stages of disintegration mark practically all the buildings. The stone corrals are virtually intact, and the water system is easily definable. The post cemetery is located west of the earlier fort. Well-preserved traces of the Butterfield Trail may be seen still at various points throughout the pass, and a pile of rock rubble north of the cemetery marks the site of the Butterfield stage station. The historical setting of Apache Pass has been only slightly impaired by roads and ranching activity.[14]

2. Hubbell Trading Post, Arizona

Location. Apache County, Navajo Route 3, 1 mile west of Ganado.

Ownership and Administration. Owned by the heirs of John Lorenzo Hubbell and administered as an active trading post by Mrs. Roman Hubbell.

Significance. For four centuries the Indian trade was one of the dominant influences shaping the course of North American history. The Indian trader early became the most influential point of contact between Europeans and aborigines. He achieved an ascendancy over the tribes unequaled by any other white. After the collapse of the Indian barrier the trader gravitated to the reservation and continued to function in his traditional role. He helped to evolve an economy adapted to reservation life, transmitted the material culture of the white man to the Indians, and fulfilled a paternalistic function as the Indians adjusted to the new conditions being thrust upon them. These activities made the trading post one of the most important institutions on the reservation, and also contributed to the two policy objectives that the Government pursued through the reservation system—to control and to civilize

Still an active trading center, the Hubbell store captures the flavor of the Navajo trade at the turn of the century. National Park Service photo.

the Indians. Trade on the Navajo Reservation in Arizona and New Mexico not only manifested the characteristics of trade elsewhere, but in fact carried them to their sharpest expression. More clearly than any other site on the Navajo Reservation today, the Hubbell Trading Post delineates these characteristics.

The Hubbell Trading Post was the most important single trading post in the history of Navajo trading. This distinction rests, first, upon its unbroken history of eighty years. It is now the oldest continuously operated business on the reservation and in northern Arizona. With an uninterrupted chain of ownership, it enjoyed a rare opportunity to maintain a uniformly high reputation. The distinction rests also upon its position as parent to a chain of Hubbell enterprises that blanketed a large part of the reservation, for its policies were those of all Hubbell posts. The distinction rests, finally, upon the eminence of John Lorenzo Hubbell, founder of the original store in 1878 and owner of it until his death in 1930. One of the first traders on the reservation, he influenced the character of trade and traders for more than fifty years. He participated in the evolution of a native economy adapted to conditions of the reservation, and in the transition in native material culture that occurred between 1870 and 1920. The origin and development of Navajo craftwork as a profitable industry owe much to his influence, which reached large areas of the reservation through the network of Hubbell posts.

Present Appearance. The significance of the Hubbell Trading Post lies also in its preservation today of the trading post of yesterday. There have been few changes since the present post and house were built in the 1890's to replace an earlier, smaller structure. The long stone trading post, with its wareroom, storeroom, office, and blanket room, appears much as it did in Hubbell's time, and much as other Navajo posts looked. The original massive counters still dominate the storeroom. The office furniture is that of half a century ago. Old firearms, Indian craftwork, paintings and rugs adorn the rug room. The rambling adobe hacienda in which Hubbell lived and entertained retains its atmosphere. The walls of the long living room and the bedrooms are covered with artwork, photographs and Indian artifacts. Shelves laden with books line the walls. Navajo rugs lie everywhere. The home conveys graphically the manner in which the Hubbells and other early traders lived. The barn and utility buildings, mostly of stone, round out the complete picture of the old-time trading post. At the Hubbell Trading Post, the visitor at once understands the pattern of the Navajo trade, the type of man who conducted it, and the kind of life he lived.[15]

3. Fort Smith, Arkansas

Location. Sebastian County, city of Fort Smith.

Ownership and Administration. This site was authorized by Congress in 1961 for addition to the National Park System contingent upon acquisition of necessary land. At this writing it is owned and administered by the city of Fort Smith.

Fort Smith, Arkansas. Viewed from across the Arkansas River. From a tinted lithograph, about 1853, by Heinrich B. Möllhausen, artist with the U.S. Pacific Railroad Survey, 35th Parallel. Collections of the Library of Congress.

Significance. When the normal pattern of westward movement had resumed, in 1817 after the second war with England, an expedition including Major Stephen H. Long of the Topographical Engineers arrived at the junction of the Arkansas and Poteau Rivers in Missouri Territory. There, just east of the Osage Indian boundary line, on a rocky bluff named by French traders "La Belle Pointe," a log fortification was built by the expedition commander, Major William Bradford, called Cantonment (later Fort) Smith. When completed, the fort included a number of wooden buildings with sturdy stone foundations. Two-story blockhouses stood at the alternate angles, the whole being approximately 132 feet square.

The establishment of Fort Smith filled a pressing need. The Cherokees had begun crossing the Mississippi River in 1809 and were encroaching on Osage land. Constant vigilance was necessary to prevent intertribal warfare. Force was occasionally required here, as elsewhere along the frontier, to keep the westward-moving settlers from occupying Indian lands. Although four companies of the 7th Infantry were sent to reinforce the garrison in 1822, Indian depredations continued. In April 1824 the Fort Smith garrison was moved westward to the mouth of the Verdigris River, where the troops established Fort Gibson. Only a token force was left at Fort Smith, which soon fell into decay. A second fort was established at Fort Smith in July 1838, because of the spread of white settlers in the Southwest. The new site was a short distance east of the first fort, and the buildings were of brick and stone—the latter quarried from the outcroppings at Belle Pointe. Work was halted within five years, after several buildings had been completed, but troops continued to be stationed there until 1871.

In that year the United States Criminal Court for the Western District of Arkansas was moved from Van Buren to Fort Smith and housed in one of the old fort buildings. Judge Isaac C. Parker was appointed in March 1875 to head the court, which had jurisdiction over 74,000 square miles in Arkansas and Indian Territory. During his twenty-one years on the bench Judge Parker gained a national reputation for his efforts to bring law and order to a lawless frontier. During this time about 13,500 cases were docketed in his courtroom, varying from theft of government timber to murder. About 9500 defendants were convicted, and eighty-eight died on the scaffold that stood nearby. Mute testimony to the rigors of Parker's task is afforded by the record, which shows that sixty-five of his deputy marshals were slain in the line of duty.

Present Appearance. There are no surface remains of the first fort at Belle Pointe. The quarries used in constructing the second are visible, however, and a shantytown section called Coke Hill was recently cleared in a program for creating a municipal park. A small part of the site, a corner of the fort, has been destroyed by erosion. The remainder is providing a fruitful field for archaeological excavations, in progress in 1962 but not reported as this is written. Preliminary archaeological work has already located the stone foundations believed to have supported the walls of the first fort. Railroad tracks of the Frisco and Missouri Pacific Railroads, together with the passenger and freight stations of these two lines, lie immediately adjacent to the site, separating it from the site of the second fort.

Of the second fort there are two important remains. The old commissary building, a large stone structure immediately behind the Frisco Railroad station, was built in 1839 to serve as the northwest bastion of the second fort. It was used by the military until 1871 and now houses a museum. The old Federal Building, half of it built in 1840 as a barracks for troops, is a block southeast of the commissary. It housed soldiers until 1871, and the Federal Court and jail from 1872 to 1887. The courtroom where Judge Parker presided from 1875 to 1887 has been restored to its original appearance. This two-story brick building is in two parts. The old half was used by the Army and by Judge Parker; the new was added in later years.[16]

4. Bent's Old Fort, Colorado

Location. Otero County, State Highway 194, 8 miles northeast of La Junta.

Ownership and Administration. This site was authorized by Congress in 1960 for addition to the National Park System contingent upon acquisition of additional land. At this writing five acres, containing the site of the main fort, is owned by the State of Colorado and administered by the State Historical Society. Adjacent acreage is privately owned, through which access is had from the highway.[17]

Significance. Although deriving its chief historical values from its role as a fur-trading post, as a way station on the Santa Fe Trail, and as a base for the conquest of New Mexico during the Mexican War, Bent's Old Fort also served as the principal point of contact between whites and the Indians of the southern Plains— Kiowas, Comanches, Cheyennes, Arapahoes and lesser tribes. Opened for business in 1833 by Charles and William Bent, the adobe "castle" on the Arkansas operated until 1849, when William Bent abandoned the old fort and erected a new one farther down the river. Bent's Fort rivaled Fort Laramie, Wyoming, and Fort Union, North Dakota, as a center of activity on the Great Plains.

Throughout its twenty-one years, Bent's Fort was the central agency of cultural transmission for the southern Plains tribes. The Indians came to trade and to indulge in the amusements of the trading post. Here, under the influence of the paternal William Bent, who married into the Southern Cheyenne tribe, many of them gained their first knowledge of the ways of the white man. They acquired by trade the items of white manufacture that revolutionized their material culture.

Bent's Old Fort was also a point at which the southern Plains tribes were brought into official relations with the United States. Beginning with an expedition of dragoons under Colonel Henry Dodge in 1835 (see pp. 6, 219), military commands occasionally paused at Bent's Fort to talk peace with the Indians and to distribute presents and peace medals to the chiefs. In 1846 Bent's Old Fort was named the Upper Platte and Arkansas Agency, with Thomas Fitzpatrick as agent. His activities among the Indians of his vast domain led to the conclusion in 1851 of the Fort Laramie Treaty and in 1853 of the Fort Atkinson Treaty. Annuities were distributed to the tribes along the Arkansas River from Bent's Old Fort and, later, Bent's New Fort.

Although the old fort was abandoned in 1849 and the new fort taken over by the Army in 1857, the influence of the Bent brothers and their offspring persisted among the southern Plains tribes, especially the Cheyennes, for many years afterward. On occasion

Bent's Old Fort, Colorado. Drawing by Lt. James W. Abert, 1846. National Archives.

the Bents played a decisive role in guiding the direction of Indian affairs.

Present Appearance. Bent's Old Fort was originally a 24-room adobe structure with two corner bastions arranged around a quadrangle. Dimensions were 170 feet on two sides, 150 and 168 on the other two. Disgruntled because the Army refused to buy the post, William Bent abandoned and partially burned it in 1849 and the adobe walls gradually disappeared. In the early 1950's the site was excavated by Dr. Herbert Dick under the auspices of the State Historical Society of Colorado. The project revealed most of the ground plan. His findings, together with detailed documentary evidence, yield a comprehensive picture of what the fort once looked like. Low adobe walls have been constructed which outline the original foundation.[17a]

5. Cataldo Mission, Idaho

Location. Kootenai County, U.S. Highway 10, 20 miles east of Coeur d'Alene.

Ownership and Administration. Boise Diocese of the Catholic Church.

Significance. Jesuit missionary fathers in 1848 began to construct the Old Mission of the Sacred Heart, deep in the wilderness of the Oregon country. Built with primitive tools by Indian labor under the direction of an Italian-born priest, Cataldo or Coeur d'Alene Mission showed the influence of the Greek revival in architecture, then in favor in the East. Of noted architectural significance, the mission also contributed importantly to the settlement of the Pacific Northwest. Cataldo Mission is the oldest building in Idaho, having been completed in 1853.

The Flathead–Nez Percé group which went to St. Louis in 1831, which incited the Protestant missionary movement in Oregon, was followed by other delegations asking for "black robes"

The outlines of Bent's Old Fort, Colorado, as revealed by archaeological excavations. State Historical Society of Colorado.

Cataldo or Coeur d'Alene Mission, Idaho. U.S. Pacific Railroad Explorations and Surveys, 47–49th Parallels, about 1854. From a tinted lithograph by John Mix Stanley. Collections of the Library of Congress.

to teach them. The Indians had learned of prayer and of black-robed priests from Catholic Iroquois who lived among them. The Bishop of St. Louis sent first the now-famous Father Pierre Jean DeSmet, who traveled west with the fur caravan of 1840. In succeeding years he selected sites and built several missions, and other priests joined him in the work. The first site of the Cataldo Mission was destroyed by floods. During a later visit to the Coeur d'Alene Indians Father DeSmet chose the present site of the Mission of the Sacred Heart.

In 1846 a temporary chapel of bark was erected on the hill site selected for the permanent mission. On this hill, in 1848, Father Anthony Ravalli began construction of the mission building. The church was in use by 1849, and was formally opened in 1852 or 1853. Constructing this edifice was a feat of skill and ingenuity. Apart from several broadaxes, an auger, some rope and pulleys, and a pocket knife, there were no tools, nor any draft animals to haul building materials. For workmen Father Ravalli had two

Brothers and a band of Indians. He drew plans for a church some ninety feet long, forty feet wide and thirty feet high, and the plan was followed faithfully.

Trees were sawed with an improvised whipsaw. Crude trucks were made to which the Indians were harnessed, and in this fashion rocks for the foundation and logs for uprights and rafters were obtained. Wooden pegs fitted into auger holes served as nails. Willow saplings were used to lace beams together, and these were closely interwoven with rope made from twisted wild grass. Over the whole was spread adobe mud from the river bank, making the walls about eight inches thick. Three altars and a baptismal font were built inside. Statues were carved from logs, and Indian dyes were used for decoration. Two paintings have survived, one representing heaven and the other hell. The building was unaltered until its restoration in 1928–30, except for the walls, which were lined with clapboards in 1865.

The Cataldo Mission was built by Jesuit missionaries in the Idaho wilderness in 1848. National Park Service photograph.

The Interior of Cataldo Mission was restored to its original appearance in 1928. National Park Service photograph.

The Jesuits labored at the Sacred Heart Mission from 1846 to 1877. During this time the mission Fathers revolutionized the life of the Indians. Originally organized in small, nomadic bands that had acquired horses, they had not hesitated to hunt buffalo on the Plains territory held by the hostile Blackfeet. Under Jesuit guidance, however, many of the Indians settled near the mission and became farmers, although some Coeur d'Alenes joined the foray against Colonel E. J. Steptoe's expedition in 1858. The teachings of the Jesuits were probably in part responsible for the refusal of the Coeur d'Alenes to join Chief Joseph in the Nez Percé War of 1877.

The construction in 1861–62 of the Mullan Road, designed to link the heads of navigation of the Missouri and Columbia Rivers, antagonized some of the tribes along its route. Believing that Cataldo Mission exercised a moderating influence on the Indians, Lieutenant John Mullan urged the Jesuits not to abandon it. The mission served as a base camp for labor crews working on the road and, after its completion, as a rest point for travelers.

In 1877 the Indians were moved to a reservation, and the mission activities to DeSmet, Idaho.

Present Appearance. Over the years the outbuildings disappeared and the church fell into disrepair. In 1928, through the combined efforts of service clubs in Kellogg, Coeur d'Alene and Spokane, the mission church was repaired and restored as nearly as possible to its original condition. The work was completed in 1930. Today the mission is in excellent condition, and provides a remarkable example both of the primitive methods used in construction and also of the handsome architectural results that were obtained. A caretaker's residence adjoins the mission, and the caretaker opens the church for the inspection of visitors. Once each year the Mass is celebrated in the church.[18]

6. Fort Larned, Kansas

Location. Pawnee County, U.S. Highway 50N, 6 miles west of Larned.

Ownership and Administration. Ten acres, all in private ownership, comprise the site. The Fort Larned Historical Society, Larned, Kansas, administers part of the site.

Significance. One of the most active military posts in Kansas during the 1860's, Fort Larned was significant as a way station on the Santa Fe Trail, as a base of military operations against hostile Indians of the central Plains, and as a center for the administration of these tribes by the Bureau of Indian Affairs. First established in 1859 and called "Camp on Pawnee Fork," it was soon named Camp Alert. In 1860, at a new site three miles farther west, a lasting sod-and-adobe post was built and named Fort Larned. In the early 1860's, Fort Larned was the northern anchor of the line of forts that defined the southwestern military frontier. This line extended south from Fort Larned through Fort Cobb, Indian Territory, Forts Griffin, Concho, McKavett and Clark, Texas, to Fort Duncan, on the Rio Grande.

As a military center Fort Larned played an important part in the Plains War of 1863–64, as a base for Major General Winfield S. Hancock's unsuccessful expedition in 1867, and as a key post in the war of 1868–69, which was highlighted by Custer's defeat of Black Kettle on the Washita. (See pp. 20–21, 35, and 37–38.)

Throughout the 1860's Fort Larned was also an administrative center for peaceful attempts at managing the Plains Indians.

From 1861 to 1868 officials of the Indian Bureau issued annuities here to tribes that had signed the Fort Wise Treaty of 1861. In 1864 the fort became the agency for the Kiowas and Comanches, and the following year for the Cheyennes, Arapahoes and Kiowa-Apaches. Attracted by the opportunities thus found at Fort Larned, traders flocked to the post and it became an important center of trade, much of it illicit. The agency at Fort Larned was abolished in 1868, and the tribes were moved to new reservations in Indian Territory.

The last important function of the post was to provide protection for construction workers on the Santa Fe Railroad. After the completion of the line through Kansas the fort was abandoned in 1878.

Fort Larned, Kansas. Substantial stone buildings afford facilities for ranching operations and museum space for displays relating to the history of the fort. Cliff Studios, Larned, Kansas.

Present Appearance. Beginning in 1865, substantial stone buildings largely replaced the earlier sod-and-adobe construction. Nine of these stone buildings are still standing, used in part as the headquarters of an extensive ranching enterprise and in part to house museums maintained by the Fort Larned Historical Society. Three large silos, together with surrounding plowed fields and stock-feeding lots, intrude somewhat on the historical setting, but otherwise the scene is unimpaired. The officers' quarters, with minor modifications of the original construction, now serve as residences for ranch personnel. The two barracks, designed to quarter two companies each, together with the quartermaster office and storehouse, were converted into barns after the fort was abandoned, but are now used as museums. The workshops, bakery and storehouses of the Army, subsequently used for ranch purposes, are now also part of the fort exhibit. Buildings maintained by the Fort Larned Historical Society are open to the public.[19]

7. Fort Leavenworth, Kansas

Location. Leavenworth County, east edge of Leavenworth.

Ownership and Administration. United States Government, Department of Defense, Department of the Army.

Significance. Fort Leavenworth was established in 1827 to help protect caravans on the Santa Fe Trail. During the 1820's and 1830's, it occupied the center of the line of forts that marked the "Permanent Indian Frontier." This line extended from Fort Snelling, Minnesota, through Forts Leavenworth, Gibson and Towson, to Fort Jesup, Louisiana. Fort Leavenworth played a major role in the Indian wars of the central Plains, in the Mexican War and in the Civil War. Later it achieved a notable record as a training center and a school for advanced military instruction. It has been in continuous military use for more than a century and a third, and today remains one of the most important Army installations in the United States.

As a frontier fort, Leavenworth attained its greatest significance in the three decades before the Civil War. Strategically located on the Missouri River near the starting points of the Oregon and

Fort Leavenworth then and now. On the east side of the parade ground stand, from left to right, the Rookery (c. 1834), and the twin Syracuse Houses (1855), and the Dragoon Barracks, torn down in 1903 and replaced by the Surgeon's residence. U.S. Army photographs.

Santa Fe Trails, the fort served as base for several important expeditions to the Plains. From here Captain Bennet Riley led the first military escort of caravans over the Santa Fe Trail in 1829; Colonel Henry Dodge marched up the Platte River to the Rocky Mountains and returned by the Santa Fe Trail in 1835; Colonel Stephen W. Kearny in 1839 led the largest Regular Army mounted force assembled to that date into the Cherokee country; and, under the same officer, dragoons went to South Pass and the Rockies in 1845. Because of its location Fort Leavenworth was also, from 1827 to 1839, headquarters of the Upper Missouri Indian Agency, which administered all tribes of the Upper Missouri and northern Plains. It was thus the scene of many conferences and treaty councils between United States officials and tribal delegations.

When the Mexican War broke out, Colonel Kearny organized the "Army of the West" at Fort Leavenworth. Kearny marched over the Santa Fe Trail, conquered New Mexico without bloodshed, and went on to the Pacific Coast to aid in the subjugation and occupation of California. Soon after the Territory of Kansas was organized in 1854, Fort Leavenworth became a temporary territorial capital and was therefore associated with the strife of "bleeding Kansas." In the Civil War, too, it assumed military significance in the western campaigns, and was twice threatened by Confederates.

The frontier had advanced beyond Fort Leavenworth by the end of the Civil War. The post nevertheless continued to fulfill essential if less dramatic functions. To support operations farther west, it served as an ordnance arsenal from 1860 to 1874 and as quartermaster depot for the Military Division of the Missouri from 1874 to 1878. In 1881 the school for infantry and cavalry officers was founded at Leavenworth; in 1901 it became the General Service and Staff School and later the Command and General Staff College. A military prison was established here in 1875.

The passing of the frontier left Fort Leavenworth untouched, unlike many other western posts. It became one of the Army's permanent and well-established installations. During both world wars many thousands of men and officers advanced their military educations here. As home of the Command and General Staff College, it still carries on its educational tradition.

Present Appearance. Although several notable historic structures survive at Fort Leavenworth, modern buildings are mixed indiscriminately with the old, thus impairing the historic scene. The more important historic structures include:

1. The Rookery. Built not later than 1834 and enlarged in 1879, it was the quarters of Governor Andrew Reeder, first territorial governor of Kansas, in 1854.

2. No. 611 Scott Avenue. This was built as a residence for the post sutler and occupied from 1841 to 1862 by Hiram Rich. A second story was added later.

3. Summer Place, east side of parade ground. Known as the "Syracuse Houses," these two structures are adjacent to each other and identical in design. They were built in 1855 as officers' quarters and were supposed to house two captains each.

4. No. 1 Scott Avenue. Built in 1861 as a residence for the commandant of the ordnance arsenal, this house is now the residence of the commanding officer of Fort Leavenworth. It has undergone considerable reconstruction.

5. Headquarters buildings, Sherman Avenue. A complex of buildings, two of which were built in 1859 and others later, these now serve as post headquarters.

6. Nos. 20–22 Summer Place. Built about 1837 as a residence for the commanding officer, it is now a double officers' quarters.

7. Old Post Headquarters Building, Kearny Avenue and McPherson. Built in the late 1870's, it was originally the Cavalry and Infantry School of Application. It now houses the Army National Bank and administrative offices of the Nike Battalion.

In addition to these, Fort Leavenworth has a museum of military equipment emphasizing modes of transportation.[20]

8. Haskell Institute, Kansas

Location. Douglas County, city of Lawrence.

Ownership and Administration. U.S. Government, Department of the Interior, Bureau of Indian Affairs.

Significance. Established in 1884, Haskell Institute was one of the first schools modeled after the Carlisle Indian School in

Pennsylvania, and over the years attained an importance second only to it. Unlike Carlisle, Haskell still serves today as a key unit in the Federal Indian School system.

The educational system that began to take shape in the 1880's was based on the conviction that the solution to the Indian

Keokuk Hall, a boys' dormitory, was built in 1884 and is the oldest building at Haskell Institute, Kansas. National Park Service photograph.

problem lay in "civilizing" the Indian. This meant, among other things, teaching the Indian a trade so that he could support himself like a white man, and inculcating in him the values and customs of the white man. Partly through a carefully devised educational system, it was argued, this objective could be attained. Many reformers believed that the off-reservation boarding school provided the best vehicle because it removed the Indian youth from the influences of the reservation. The program of Haskell and its sister institutions, therefore, was designed to train the student in manual arts and in the attitudes that made up the "civilization" of nineteenth-century America. Although it is debatable whether this program was good for the Indian or successful in achieving its purpose, there can be little doubt that it exerted a profound influence upon the course of Indian history during the closing decades of the nineteenth century and the opening decades of the twentieth.

The school opened in 1884 with only 22 pupils, but at the end of the second year 220 students, representing thirty-one tribes, were enrolled. By 1906 attendance had risen to 921 students from sixty tribes living in almost every state and territory where there were Indians. In the early years both elementary education and vocational training were stressed, but after the turn of the century, when conditions and policy began to change, academic courses gradually overshadowed vocational courses. Although agriculture, handicrafts and home economics continued to be taught, the Haskell curriculum came more and more to resemble that of standard elementary and junior high schools. Today Haskell offers a four-year high school course supplemented by some vocational and preprofessional training.

Present Appearance. Haskell Institute today looks much like a typical small American college. Although most of the buildings now standing were built after 1910, several structures have survived to recall the earlier years of the school's history. They include Keokuk Hall, a boys' dormitory built in 1884; the hospital, erected in 1886 and now housing employees; Winona Hall, a girls' dormitory built in 1899; and Hiawatha Hall, a girls' gymnasium, built in 1898.[21]

9. Fort Snelling, Minnesota

Location. Hennepin County, junction of State Highways 55 and 100, South Minneapolis.

Ownership and Administration. Historic Fort Snelling, including the site of the Indian village on the Mississippi River bottoms, the site of the Indian agency, and related structures, covers 2500 acres of which the state has recently acquired three hundred. Five hundred ninety acres, containing the site of most of the original fort, are owned by the United States and administered by the Veterans Administration. Most of the remaining 1600 acres are in private ownership.

Significance. Americans turned their attention again toward the western frontier after the War of 1812. Three military posts were built between 1817 and 1819—Forts Snelling (Minnesota), Atkinson (Nebraska) and Smith (Arkansas). These posts were to protect the frontier from Indians, to promote the fur trade and to clear the way for settlement. During the 1820's, as eastern tribes

Old round tower and prison building, Fort Snelling, Minnesota, in the 1890's. Quartermaster's Photo Album. National Archives.

began to be removed to the West, the concept of a "Permanent Indian Frontier" gained prominence. More military posts were established, so that by 1830 a well-defined "military frontier" helped to set off the "Permanent Indian Frontier." From north to south, the military line was based on Forts Snelling, Leavenworth (replacing Atkinson in 1827), Gibson (replacing Smith in 1824), Towson and Jesup. These were the most important forts until the frontier moved to the Plains and jumped to the Pacific in the 1840's.

Fort Snelling alone, the northern bastion of this military frontier, guarded a vast arc of territory extending from the Great Lakes to the Missouri River. For more than a third of a century it was the most northwesterly military installation in the United

States. Although few expeditions used it as a base of operations against Indians, Fort Snelling exerted a powerful influence upon the region and by its very presence contributed to clearing the way for settlers.

The territory drained by the Upper Mississippi River, west of the river, was acquired as part of the Louisiana Purchase of 1803, and plans for a fort in the region were drawn up immediately. Not until August 1819, however, did Lieutenant Colonel Henry Leavenworth arrive with troops at the mouth of the Minnesota River. Construction began at this place the following summer, directed by Colonel Joseph Snelling, but was not finished until July 1823. Originally called Fort Saint Anthony, the name was changed after completion to Fort Snelling.

In conjunction with the fort, Indian Agent Lawrence Taliaferro established the St. Peters Agency nearby for the resident Sioux and Chippewa Indians. Both agent and troops were constantly occupied trying to prevent warfare among the various tribes. During the 1820's the Sioux and Chippewas had violent conflicts. In 1826 strife broke out among the Winnebagos near Prairie du Chien. Troops from Fort Snelling quelled it, but were called upon again in 1840 and succeeding years to pacify these Indians. Expeditions were sent also to the international boundary to prevent French-Canadian hunters from crossing the border to hunt buffalo. In 1849 infantry from the fort joined dragoons from Fort Gaines (later Fort Ripley) to investigate troubles in Iowa. One result of this expedition was the founding of Fort Dodge near the present city of that name.

Abandoned in 1857, Fort Snelling was reactivated in 1861 and saw considerable activity during the Sioux uprising of 1862, described on pp. 16 f., 189 f. It was declared a permanent post at this time. But the locus of conflict between Indians and soldiers shortly thereafter shifted farther west, to the Dakotas and later to Montana and Wyoming. Fort Snelling played a supporting role in these conflicts, and in 1881 became headquarters of the Department of Dakota, which included Minnesota, the Dakotas and Montana.

For eighty-five years following 1861 Fort Snelling served as a regional training center for troops, a function that became particularly important during World Wars I and II. In 1946 the Army abandoned the fort and transferred it to the Veterans Administration.

Present Appearance. Located on a plateau commanding the Minnesota and Mississippi Rivers, Fort Snelling occupies an impressive setting. Bridges, streets and urban expansion, however, have impaired the historic scene. The state is reducing the intrusions as much as possible by placing the highway system underground.

Surrounded on three sides by the modern Fort Snelling, the site of the original fort still contains four of the original sixteen buildings listed in the completion report of August 1824: the quarters of the commanding officer, officers' quarters, the hexagonal tower and the round tower. Of these structures, the hexagonal tower has undergone the least alteration. The officers' quarters were remodeled extensively in 1904 and bear little resemblance to the original. In 1957 and 1958 archaeological excavations were undertaken at the site by the Minnesota Historical Society. They revealed the foundations of several early structures, including the powder magazine, schoolhouse, sutler's store, hospital, shops, cistern, and a portion of the original walls of the fort.

Some 320 acres associated with the original fort, comprising bottom lands and bluffs near the fort and surrounding the round tower, have been released by the Veterans Administration to the General Services Administration as surplus property. The State of Minnesota made application for the tract with the intention of establishing and developing a state park. This tract, however, does not include the hexagonal tower, officers' quarters or commanding officer's home, all of which were part of the old fort.[22]

10. Fort Atkinson, Nebraska

Location. Washington County, 1 mile east of town of Fort Calhoun.

Ownership and Administration. The site of the post, including the cemetery, the fortified section and major scattered buildings, covers 140 acres. Of these, the fortified section and 90 percent of the outlying buildings are privately owned.

Significance. Fort Atkinson lay to the south and west of Fort Snelling, on the line of forts guarding the western frontier of the 1820's, and held this portion of the line from 1819 until its abandonment in 1827. Strategically located at Council Bluffs, and an important center of activity in the fur trade, the fort's primary function was to advance the interests of the fur trappers and traders in the upper Missouri country.

General Leavenworth had Fort Atkinson as his base for his 1823 expedition (described on pp. 6–7) against the Arikara Indians, who had attacked the trappers' brigade of the Rocky Mountain Fur Company under William H. Ashley. Two years later a second expedition had greater success, led by Colonel Henry Atkinson and Indian Agent Benjamin O'Fallon, who had established the Upper Missouri Indian Agency here in 1819. Fort Atkinson also played a significant part in the exploration of the West. In 1820 Major Stephen H. Long set out from nearby Engineer Cantonment to explore the Rocky Mountains. He marched up the Platte, south along the base of the Rockies, and returned down the Arkansas River. In 1824 Thomas Fitzpatrick, Jedediah Smith and other trappers of the Rocky Mountain Fur Company arrived at the fort after their dramatic rediscovery of South Pass and the North Platte route, which later became the Oregon Trail. Later in the same year William H. Ashley led an expedition from the fort to the Green River and discovered the canyon of the Upper Colorado River.

The Army abandoned Fort Atkinson in 1827 and, to afford better protection to the Santa Fe Trail, moved the garrison down the Missouri to establish Cantonment (later Fort) Leavenworth.

Present Appearance. The site of Fort Atkinson lies on a plateau crowning timbered bluffs that rise fifty-five feet from the flood plain on the west edge of the Missouri River Valley. In the 1820's the river ran at the foot of the bluffs. The old channel is still evident, but the modern channel is three miles to the east. The only visible remains at the site are low earth mounds on the east edge, the rest of the site having been leveled and placed in cultivation. Since 1956 the Nebraska State Historical Society has been conducting archaeological excavations, still incomplete at this writing, that have yielded many artifacts and exposed the building foundations.[23]

Parade ground and officers' row at Fort Robinson, Nebraska. National Park Service photograph.

11. Fort Robinson and Red Cloud Agency, Nebraska

Location. Dawes County. Fort Robinson is on U.S. Highway 20, 3 miles southwest of Crawford. Red Cloud Agency is 1½ miles by unimproved road east of Fort Robinson.

Ownership and Administration. Of the 21,404 acres in the Fort Robinson Reservation and Reserve, owned by the Federal Government and administered by the U.S. Department of Agriculture, there are 7 tracts comprising about 30 acres in all leased to the State Historical Society. Of these 30 acres, 19 are in the Red Cloud Agency site. The Nebraska Game, Forestation and Parks Commission has leased 45 to 50 acres; the University of Nebraska Museum 1½ acres; and both the Soil Conservation Service and the Fish and Wildlife Service hold, under lease, small portions.

Significance. Events that occurred at Red Cloud Agency and nearby Fort Robinson during the 1870's guided the course of Indian-white relations on the northern Plains during the final crucial years of Sioux and Cheyenne resistance. At these sites the United States attempted to force the Indians of the Powder River country into the mold of the reservation system.

Following the conclusion of the Treaty of 1868, which ended the conflict over the Bozeman Trail, part of the Sioux, including Red Cloud himself, elected to settle at a government agency. The remainder insisted upon a free life in the unceded Powder River country. Red Cloud Agency was established in 1871 on the Platte River to take care of the former. In 1873 it was moved farther north, away from the overland route, to a site on White River in northwestern Nebraska. The first years were hectic, with dishonest or inexperienced agents nominally in charge. The actual rulers, however, were the Sioux themselves, and the agent and his staff existed under virtual siege in constant terror for their lives. The situation was aggravated by the Powder River Sioux, who formed the custom of wintering at the agency, where food might be had from the Great Father, and then returning in the spring to the unceded territory. The situation grew so serious that in 1874 troops were sent from Fort Laramie to protect the agency employees and property. Fort Robinson was established near the agency, and the soldiers succeeded in stabilizing conditions among the Sioux.

In 1874 Red Cloud Agency was the scene of an investigation that assumed nationwide importance. A Yale professor, O. C. Marsh, had come west on a fossil-hunting expedition. Red Cloud convinced him that the agent was profiting from traffic in Indian supplies and that the Indians were being issued inferior food and annuity goods. Marsh stirred up a public controversy that led to an investigation. The testimony made it clear that contractors, freighters and government employees were profiting enormously, but no legally admissible evidence could be assembled.

Fort Robinson took on added importance with the discovery of gold in paying quantities in the Black Hills. (See pp. 49–51.) Troops from the post for a time tried to stem the flow of miners into the area, which had been guaranteed to the Indians by the Treaty of 1868. After the Government gave up this attempt, Fort

Robinson became a way station on the Sidney–Black Hills Trail, which linked the Union Pacific with the gold fields and was used by numerous prospectors.

Fort Robinson played a key role in the campaign of 1876 against the Powder River Sioux, who united under the leadership of Sitting Bull to contest the invasion of the Black Hills and the construction of the Northern Pacific Railroad. General Crook returned to Fort Robinson following the operations that included the Custer disaster and the Battles of the Rosebud and Slim Buttes. After disarming and dismounting Red Cloud's people at the agency, Crook sent Colonel Ranald S. Mackenzie and the 4th Cavalry against Dull Knife and the Cheyennes. On November 25 Mackenzie surprised these Indians on a branch of the Powder River and dealt them a severe blow, described on pp. 56–57. The survivors fled to Crazy Horse's camp farther north. During the winter Spotted Tail, an influential agency chief of the Brûlé Sioux, went north to talk to the hostiles. His persuasion, coupled with the

The White Cliffs, now Red Cloud Buttes, overlook the valley of upper White River and the site of Red Cloud Agency, Nebraska. National Park Service photograph.

aggressive campaigning of Colonel Nelson A. Miles, induced Crazy Horse with the Oglalas and Cheyennes to come to Red Cloud Agency and surrender to General Crook. A total of about 4500 Indians gave themselves up at the agency and Fort Robinson during late 1876 and 1877.

Indian politics and white suspicion led to the attempted arrest of Crazy Horse at Fort Robinson in September 1877. When he resisted, a soldier bayoneted him. He died shortly afterward. Dull Knife and his people had been moved to a reservation in Indian Territory, but in October 1878 they broke loose and made an epic fighting retreat north toward their old homes. They were finally captured in the sandhills near Fort Robinson and confined at the post. In January 1879 they made a concerted attempt to escape. Most of the band fell under the fire of Army rifles, and the rest were captured.

In 1878 new agencies were created in present South Dakota for the various tribes of Sioux. The Oglalas, Red Cloud's people, settled at Pine Ridge, about fifty miles north of their old agency. Fort Robinson continued as a military post. When the Ghost Dance troubles broke into open rebellion at Pine Ridge in 1890, 9th Cavalrymen from Fort Robinson were the first troops on the scene. A large force eventually reached Pine Ridge, and the trouble was brought under control. The Battle of Wounded Knee Creek, discussed on pp. 85 ff., marked the end of the outbreak and the end of the Indian wars. Fort Robinson, however, remained an Army installation until 1948.

Present Appearance. Having been an active military post until 1948, Fort Robinson is a mixture of historic and modern buildings. The principal historic buildings are six sets of adobe officers' quarters built in 1874 and 1875, and six more sets of brick officers' quarters built in 1887. Several miscellaneous structures—storehouses, shops, offices—date from the period between 1886 and 1910, and the rest were erected after 1910. The Nebraska State Historical Society maintains a museum in the frame headquarters building, constructed in 1905, and another exhibit in the saddlery shop. The other buildings are used by Federal and state agencies.

At the site of Red Cloud Agency, to the east, no remains of the building are visible. The site is marked by a monument, however, and the historic scene survives entirely unimpaired by modern intrusions. During the summer months the State Historical Society conducts tours from the museum at Fort Robinson to the agency site.[24]

12. Fort Union, North Dakota

Location. Williams County, 11.6 miles by gravel road southwest of Trenton, on the north bank of the Missouri above its confluence with the Yellowstone.

Ownership and Administration. The site of the main fort complex, eight acres, is owned by the State of North Dakota and administered by the State Historical Society. Another twelve acres, including the sites of related structures, are privately owned.

Significance. Fort Union was started in 1828 by the American Fur Company. It soon achieved a monopoly of the rich fur trade with the Plains and Mountain tribes that roamed the region now encompassing Montana, North Dakota and part of Wyoming.

The dominant historical values of Fort Union derive from its significance in the fur trade but, like Bent's Old Fort, Colorado, it was also an important center of cultural transmission. As a small projection of the white man's civilization, Fort Union afforded the tribes of the northern Plains—Crow, Blackfoot, Piegan, Blood, Cree and others—their first sustained view of the alien culture moving into their midst. At Fort Union and its subposts these Indians became acquainted with the trade goods that, in a matter of decades, transformed their material culture and made them dependent upon the white man for supply.

Fort Union also illustrates the evil effects of the white man's vices, which reached the Indian through the fur-trading posts. H. M. Chittenden, historian of the fur trade, wrote of liquor and disease: "That they corrupted the life of the people, enervated their physical force, poisoned their ambitions, rendered them an easy prey to the hard environment of their lives, and in the aggregate reduced the native population at an alarming rate, the testimony of contemporary observers conclusively proves."[25] Disease took a terrible toll and liquor proved demoralizing to whole bands and tribes as well as to individuals. But no matter how much some traders and companies lamented its use, it came to be an

Fort Union, North Dakota, and the distribution of goods to the Assiniboin Indians, probably 1853. From a tinted lithograph. John Mix Stanley, the artist, was with the U.S. Pacific Railroad Explorations and Surveys, 47–49th Parallels. Collections of the Library of Congress.

indispensable weapon of competition. If one firm employed it, all had to follow the example or retire from the field. The Government's attempts to enforce the prohibition laws were almost uniformly ineffective. Following the passage of the stringent prohibition law of 1832, Kenneth McKenzie, *bourgeois* of the American Fur Company at Fort Union, installed a distillery to manufacture corn whiskey. The experiment stirred a storm of denunciation from competitors and almost cost the company its license. Thereafter the old smuggling methods had to be employed.

The most spectacular and destructive disease to reach the tribes through Fort Union was smallpox, which came up the river on the company's annual supply boat in 1837. The Indians could not be prevented from coming to the fort to trade, and the epidemic swept with devastating effect through the Blackfeet, Crows, Assiniboines, Mandans, Minitaris and Arikaras. About fifteen thousand people died. "The destroying angel," wrote Prince Maximilian, who was there, "has visited the unfortunate sons of the wilderness with terrors never before known, and has converted the extensive hunting grounds, as well as the peaceful settlements of these tribes, into desolate and boundless cemeteries."

Fort Union was a conventional stockaded post. The log palisade, 240 by 200 feet, rose 20 feet from the bank of the Missouri and supported two-story bastions at opposite corners. Lining the inside of the palisade were cottonwood barracks, storehouses, workshops, stone powder room, and reception room for Indians. Opposite the massive wooden gate stood the *bourgeois'* house, a roomy two-story structure with glass windows and fireplaces—luxuries on the frontier. A tall flagstaff, flanked by two cannon, rose from the center of the quadrangle.

The fur trade began to decline in the 1840's, but Fort Union continued to be an active trading center. In 1864–65 it served briefly as a base of supply for General Alfred Sully in his campaign against the Sioux. (See p. 19.) Finally, after passing to the North West Company, then to Durfee and Peck, Fort Union in 1867 was abandoned and dismantled, and its material used in building Fort Buford, a military post three miles eastward.

Present Appearance. Although there are no remains of the stockade and buildings of Fort Union, such surface evidences as earth mounds and depressions suggest a rich field for archaeological excavations. The integrity of the natural scene has not survived altogether intact. Gravel operations have destroyed the site of the southwest bastion, while cultivated fields on three sides and the nearby main line of the Great Northern Railroad intrude somewhat less seriously. The Missouri River flows by the south side; until recently it threatened to cut into the bank and destroy the site, but this threat has now receded. A flagpole stands in the center of the site.[26]

13. Cherokee National Capitol, Oklahoma

Location. Tahlequah, Cherokee County.
Ownership and Administration. Cherokee County.
Significance. The Cherokee Indians were forced by the United States in 1838–39 to move west of the Mississippi and take up land in what is today eastern Oklahoma. One of the "Five Civilized Tribes," they had well-educated leaders and highly developed political institutions. The tribe produced outstanding statesmen, literary figures, soldiers and, above all, the inventor of the Cherokee alphabet, Sequoyah. Their "nation" once occupied virtually the entire region of the southern Appalachian Mountains.

In the years after their arrival in Oklahoma they broke into two hostile factions, one that had opposed the treaty of removal and the other that had favored it. The antagonisms thus created were compounded further by the Civil War, during which one group sided with the North and the other with the South. After the war, differences were smoothed over and a measure of harmony prevailed. The tribe lived under its own government until 1906, when land allotments were made and the remaining area thrown open to settlement.

Tahlequah was designated the permanent Cherokee capital when the eastern and western Cherokees signed an Act of Union on July 12, 1839. For four years the capital consisted only of council grounds where delegates camped while attending conferences. In 1843, however, the present town of Tahlequah was platted and three log cabins, housing council, senate and treasury, were constructed. In June of that year the Cherokees and Creeks held a grand council with representatives of sixteen other western

Cherokee National Capitol, Tahlequah, Oklahoma. Tahlequah Chamber of Commerce.

tribes to discuss mutual problems. Chief John Ross presided, and General Zachary Taylor and Governor Pierce M. Butler, Cherokee agent, were present. At the conclusion of the four-week meeting the tribal delegates signed a treaty of friendship. By this compact the tribes pledged not to cede any of their territory to the United States without the consent of all other parties. They also provided for extradition of criminals and restoration of property taken by a member of one tribe from a member of another.

On the square of the new town the Cherokees in 1845 erected a brick building to house their Supreme Court. Although fire razed it in 1874, it was rebuilt, utilizing the surviving walls of the old building. This Capitol, completed in 1869, stood in the center of the square and housed executive offices and legislative halls of the national government.

The Cherokee National Capitol represents the culmination of the tribe's successful period of adjustment that began in the colonial period. The Cherokees appear to have recognized at an early date that their survival lay not in war with the whites but in adjusting their culture to the changing circumstances of life thrust upon them by the development of the white colonies. They also recognized early (1765) the need for schools to educate their youth. Building on the aboriginal tradition of an agricultural economy and life in orderly towns with an informal type of representative government, they had progressed materially in what we term civilization by the time of their removal to the West. Their progress is typified most spectacularly, perhaps, by Sequoyah's contribution of the Cherokee syllabary.

The Cherokee constitution and representative government antedate similar achievements by the Creeks, and the example probably provided a stimulus to Creek governmental development. The Cherokees adopted their republican form of government in 1820, and in 1821 issued the first volume of laws ever published by people under comparable circumstances.

The Cherokee National Capitol is thus a landmark to the way one important aboriginal group solved the problem of survival when faced with invasion by a numerically superior and technologically dominant group.

Present Appearance. The Cherokee Capitol is a conventional two-story brick structure, now the county courthouse of Cherokee County and in appearance not unlike most other Oklahoma county courthouses. Although the interior has been altered for modern purposes, the exterior is little changed from the 1869 design. The Capitol is in generally good condition. The building that once housed the Cherokee Supreme Court is located on the southeast corner of the square, across from the Capitol. Reconstructed after the fire of 1874, the outer walls, which survived the fire, are original. It is also in good condition.[27]

Creek National Capitol, Okmulgee, Oklahoma. Kent Spring photo, courtesy Creek Indian Memorial Association.

14. Creek National Capitol, Oklahoma

Location. Okmulgee County, city of Okmulgee.

Ownership and Administration. Creek Indian Memorial Association.

Significance. The Creek National Capitol symbolizes the successful acculturation of a group of Indians whose way of life and very existence were threatened by overwhelming white pressure. As a "nation" in the southeastern United States they suffered greatly at the hands of white neighbors. They made early strides in the direction of attainments in our civilization, many of them being educated and well-to-do or even wealthy.

In the form of their old Confederacy, the Creeks had a representative government while they still lived in the Southeast. The government of the Confederacy consisted of a general council composed of representatives from the various villages. The Creeks were divided into two districts, Upper and Lower. Both attended this general council, but were otherwise independent. The Confederacy had a "head chief" elected by the general council.

Following the march over the "Trail of Tears," 1836–40, the Creeks settled in eastern Oklahoma. In 1859 they held an election in which a principal chief and a second chief were chosen. This democratic election was a successful venture into a governmental form approaching that of the whites. In 1860 the general council adopted a constitution and both the Upper and Lower Creeks were incorporated in one single "Muscogee Nation." The constitution provided for a supreme court, district judges and a police force. The constitution was changed in 1867, after the Civil War, to provide for a government of three branches modeled after that of the United States. The two legislative houses were called the "House of Kings" (comparable to the U.S. Senate) and the "House of Warriors" (comparable to the U.S. House of Representatives). Although the form of this constitutional government was patterned after that of the United States and the Cherokee Nation, the basic laws and structure can be considered a development from the old Creek Confederacy.

The Confederacy tradition was still strong. As a result, the Creeks were active in the promotion of an intertribal council. Composed of delegates from most of the tribes in Indian Territory, it also met periodically in the capital. The council passed out of existence after 1875, however, for the United States made it known that it would continue to exercise supreme authority in the territory.

Present Appearance. The original Creek capital was established at Okmulgee in 1868, and a two-story log Capitol constructed. The present Capitol, of modified Victorian architectural style, was built of native brown sandstone in 1878. This building served as the Capitol until 1907, when Oklahoma became a state. Thereafter, the building served as Okmulgee County Courthouse until 1916. The Creek Indian Memorial Association now maintains a museum of Creek history on the first floor, and the building is well preserved and in good condition. Other structures now surround the square in which the Capitol stands.[28]

15. Fort Gibson, Oklahoma

Location. Muskogee County, north edge of town of Fort
Gibson.

Ownership and Administration. Owned by the State of Oklahoma, administered by the Planning and Resources Board
through the Division of State Parks; the park contains fifty-five
acres.

Significance. Of the line of forts separating settlements of the
Mississippi Valley from the Indian Country—Snelling, Leavenworth, Gibson, Towson and Jesup—Fort Gibson was the most
important, for it was thrust into the Indian Country and was actively concerned with immediate Indian problems. Established
by Colonel Matthew Arbuckle in 1824, on the Grand (Verdigris)
River near its confluence with the Arkansas, Fort Gibson was intended to prevent Osage attacks on Cherokees who were already
filtering into Indian Territory. During the period of Indian Removal, 1825–40, the garrison helped to receive, care for and locate immigrant Cherokees, Creeks and Seminoles. It also enforced
peace among the newly arrived tribes and attempted to protect
them from the Plains Indians. For a time the fort housed the
Cherokee Agency. Troops from Fort Gibson provided escorts for
surveyors marking the boundaries of Indian lands, established
subposts such as Forts Coffee, Wayne, Holmes, Arbuckle and
Washita to police other parts of Indian Territory, laid out a network of roads, patrolled to prevent the flow of liquor into Indian
Territory, and on occasion furnished escorts for traffic on the
Santa Fe Trail. Peace commissions met at Fort Gibson to conclude treaties with both native and immigrant tribes. Scores of
new graduates of West Point gained their first military experience
at Fort Gibson, and newly activated units such as the Rangers
and the Dragoon Regiment were tested here.

Fort Gibson was base of operations for three important expeditions to the Plains, all aimed at persuading the untamed
tribes to conclude peace treaties with the United States. Those of
1832 and 1833 failed. The third, the Dragoon Expedition, set out
in 1834 under command of Brigadier General Henry Leaven-

worth, who died of fever; but his successor, Colonel Henry Dodge, met with Kiowas, Comanches and Wichitas. He persuaded them to send delegates to Fort Gibson for negotiations. Dodge's effort led to the conclusion in 1835 of the first treaties with the "wild" tribes. (See pp. 4–5, 214–15.) The Plains Indians promised not to molest travelers on the Santa Fe Trail and to quit warring on the immigrant tribes.

Not only was Fort Gibson the hub of military activity on the frontier, but it also became a center of trade and travel. Keelboats and later river steamers came up the Arkansas and unloaded passengers, military stores, and merchandise for the Indian trade at the fort. Return cargoes were obtained from Indian traders. The Texas Road, which linked the growing American settlements in Texas with the Mississippi Valley, ran by Fort Gibson, which became a way station for immigrants, freighters and traders.

Originally a four-company post, Fort Gibson was expanded in 1831 to accommodate a regiment. It became the headquarters of the 7th Infantry. The post consisted of a collection of closely packed log buildings surrounded by a log palisade. Blockhouses guarded two of the four corners and commanded all four sides. Log quarters and barracks also stood outside the stockade, together with the sutler's store, two hospitals and a variety of other structures. Troops who served here unanimously condemned the dilapidated log structures as wholly inadequate, and in 1846 new construction was begun on the hill overlooking the stockade. But by 1857 only one stone building had been finished. In that year Cherokee sentiment led the Army to abandon the fort.

During the Civil War it was reoccupied by Union troops in 1863 and played a vital part in strengthening the loyal element of the Cherokees. The Union Army was based here that in July defeated the Confederates at Honey Springs in an engagement that won Indian Territory for the Union. Regular troops replaced the volunteers in 1866 and garrisoned the post until its abandonment in 1889. During this period the post on the hill was completed; it consisted of seven large stone buildings and ten frame buildings.

Present Appearance. Although the original fort has long since disappeared, the State of Oklahoma, under a WPA grant in 1936, reconstructed the log stockade and a number of outlying buildings almost on the original site. With a few minor exceptions, the reconstruction is a faithful reproduction of the original. The principal departure from authentic construction lies in the use, for durability, of pine timber and lime chinking. Interpretive markers, well written and attractively designed, give much of the history of the fort.

On a ridge overlooking the reconstructed stockade is the site of the second Fort Gibson, built largely after the Civil War. It was a conventional post made up of a group of buildings arranged for utility rather than defense. Several stone buildings still survive in various stages of repair, together with some ruins. The buildings are privately owned and/or used. A two-story stone barracks, with porches running the length of the building on two levels, is the most imposing relic of this group, and is in good condition. This building is owned by the State Historical Society but is privately used.[29]

16. Fort Sill, Oklahoma

Location. Comanche County, north edge of Lawton.

Ownership and Administration. U.S. Government, Department of Defense, Department of the Army.

Significance. The need for Fort Sill evolved from the problem of controlling the Indians in the area near the Wichita Mountains as demonstrated in the winter campaign by Major General Philip H. Sheridan in 1868–69 against the southern Plains tribes, discussed on pp. 37–39, 210, 212, 216. This campaign brought peace to the southern Plains, but Sheridan feared that it would be only temporary. Acting under his general direction, Colonel B. H. Grierson selected the site, a pleasant spot on Medicine Bluff Creek, and Sheridan named the post after his West Point classmate, General Joshua Sill. Lieutenant Richard H. Pratt, who later founded the Carlisle Indian School, supervised construction of the first buildings. While they were being erected, Custer returned from the field with the 7th U.S. Cavalry and the 19th Kansas Cavalry, and camped on the site.

As the Kiowa-Comanche Agency from 1870 to 1878, Fort Sill became a testing ground for President Grant's Peace Policy.

Quaker agents promptly discovered that the philosophy of conquest through kindness, basis for the Peace Policy, failed to tame the Kiowas and Comanches. These Indians continued to raid the Texas frontier and return to their "city of refuge" at Fort Sill, where the Army was forbidden to follow. By 1874 the failure of the Peace Policy to protect the Texas settlements prompted a

Indian School, Fort Sill, Oklahoma. Undated Signal Corps photograph, National Archives.

return to sterner measures, and Fort Sill became a base of operations in the Red River War. The Kiowas and Comanches fled to the west, and military columns converged from four directions on the Staked Plains. By the end of 1875 the last of the Indians had been conquered, rounded up and confined to reservations. These operations ended warfare on the southern Plains.

Fort Sill continued to be an active frontier military post throughout the 1880's and 1890's, however. After his imprisonment in Florida, Geronimo and the Chiricahua Apaches were settled on the Fort Sill Reservation, where Geronimo died and was buried in 1909. In 1911 the post became the home of the Field Artillery School and today, as the Artillery and Missile Center, it remains one of the most important U.S. Army installations.

Present Appearance. Virtually all of the original Fort Sill, built in the early 1870's, is still standing. Only the cavalry stables have been torn down to make room for newer construction. Approximately twenty-five buildings dating from 1870 and 1871 are still used by the Army. These structures, built of native limestone, include residences for officers and noncommissioned officers on two adjacent sides of the parade ground, the commanding officer's quarters (Sherman House, where in 1871 an Indian attempted to murder General William T. Sherman), three barracks (in the basement of one of which three Kiowa chiefs were imprisoned in 1871), the quartermaster storehouse, the commissary, guardhouse and stone corral. In addition, about ten stone buildings erected during the 1880's are still standing. The quartermaster storehouse, commissary, and guardhouse now contain the Artillery and Missile Center Museum, which houses many displays portraying the history of the Army, with emphasis on the artillery arm and on Fort Sill. Outdoor displays in the corral portray frontier military and commercial modes of transportation, and the guardhouse contains a collection of frontier and Indian artifacts.[30]

17. Carlisle Indian School, Pennsylvania

Location. Cumberland County, east edge of Carlisle on U.S. Highway 11.

Ownership and Administration. U.S. Government, Department of Defense, Department of the Army.

Significance. In its thirty-nine-year existence, 1879 to 1918, the Carlisle Indian School gave to thousands of young Indians an elementary education and practical instruction in mechanical arts, agriculture and home economics. The experiment represented a sincere effort to better the lot of the Indians, and its success led to the founding of similar institutions across the country. Despite attempts to discredit them, Carlisle and the institutions that followed it played a conspicuous role in the education of Indian youth.

The school at Carlisle Barracks was the brainchild of Captain Richard H. Pratt, Civil War officer and, later, a cavalry commander in Indian Territory and Texas. In 1875 he escorted a group of young Indian prisoners, taken during the Red River campaigns, to Fort Marion (Castillo de San Marcos), St. Augustine, Florida, and remained as one of their caretakers. Close association with his prisoners gave Pratt a knowledge and admiration of the Indians shared by few of his fellow officers or, indeed, by other white Americans.

When the prisoners were released in 1878, seventeen young men were sent to the Negro school at Hampton, Virginia, at the urging of Pratt, and more young western Indians were recruited for the educational experiment. The pioneer effort at Hampton was successful and next year, again thanks to Pratt's persuasion, the former cavalry post at Carlisle Barracks was approved as the site of an Indian school. Beginning with 136 boys and girls, the school grew quickly. Although there is a popular misconception that it had the status of a university—thanks to its athletic achievements in collegiate competition—it actually offered only a limited elementary education combined with practical instruction in mechanical arts, agriculture and home economics. The length of term was first three and later five years, and an interesting feature of instruction was the "outing" system by which selected students, both boys and girls, were allowed to live with nearby white families and gain practical experience in farming and domestic arts. They were not servants, Pratt was careful to point out. While at the school students from various tribes, frequently traditional enemies, lived and worked together with less friction than did white students at other schools.

Although the "outing" system did much to familiarize each race with the other, the most spectacular advertisement of the Indian school was its famed athletic program, notably the powerhouse football teams turned out by "Pop" Warner. First among a number of top Carlisle athletes was Jim Thorpe, the Sac-Fox Indian who walked off with the decathlon and pentathlon of the 1912 Olympics and was named the all-around amateur athletic champion of the United States. Thorpe attended the school from 1909 to 1912.

Pratt retired from the Army as a brigadier general in 1904, and the Indian school was terminated in 1918. As the first of the off-reservation boarding schools and the model after which more than a score of others were patterned, Carlisle stands as a landmark to the attempts of reformers to find a humane and enduring solution to the perennial "Indian problem."

Present Appearance. A number of buildings of the Indian school era still survive. One of the most important is the commandant's quarters, occupied by Pratt when he served as first superintendent of the school. The house was in existence as early as 1821 and was the only building on the post not fired in the raid by General J. E. B. Stuart's Confederate cavalry during the Gettysburg campaign of 1863. The house today is the home of the commandant of the Army War College, which now occupies the post. Thorpe Hall, built with funds raised by pupils of the Indian School and from private donations, was the school gymnasium—a role it fulfills at the War College. The Coren Apartments, built immediately after the destruction of Carlisle Barracks in 1863, was a girls' dormitory during the time of the school and serves as officers' quarters today. Armstrong Hall, now containing offices of post headquarters, was the Indian school laundry. Quarters No. 2, now home of the deputy commandant of the college, was built in 1887 as the residence of the assistant superintendent of the Indian school. Washington Hall, another survivor of the school, is a guest house. All these buildings are grouped in close proximity near the western limits of the present military reservation.[31]

18. Fort Belknap, Texas

Location. Young County, northwest of Graham, 1 mile south of junction of State Highways 24 and 251.

Ownership and Administration. Owned by Young County and administered by the Young County Commissioners Court in cooperation with the Fort Belknap Society. The park contains about five acres.

Significance. Following the annexation of Texas and the Mexican War, the demands of settlers on the frontier of Texas for protection against Kiowa and Comanche raids from the north and west grew so insistent that the Government laid out a chain of forts. Before they had been completed, however, the frontier of settlement had advanced farther west and north. Lieutenant

Colonel William G. Belknap was therefore sent to survey the frontier and select sites for another system of forts. These were Forts Belknap (1851), Phantom Hill (1851), Chadbourne (1852), McKavett (1852) and Clark (1852). There were thus inner and outer rings of forts enclosing the frontier of settlement during the 1850's. On the outer ring, Fort Belknap was the key link in the chain, thrust northward toward the Kiowa-Comanche country.

Throughout the 1850's the Texas frontier was the object of destructive raids by Kiowas and Comanches. One-third of the U.S. Army, often bolstered by Texas Rangers and state troops, attempted to defend the Texas frontier. Judging from the catalogue of atrocities, Fort Belknap and vicinity was the most dangerous segment of the frontier. The infantry garrisons of this and other posts proved all but helpless in Indian warfare. In 1855, however, the newly organized 2nd Cavalry Regiment was assigned to Texas. It arrived at Fort Belknap under Colonel Albert Sidney Johnston on December 29 and was distributed among the forts of the outer chain. In 1858 Federal and state troops took the offensive. Captain Earl Van Dorn led a squadron of the 2nd Cavalry north from Fort Belknap and, at Rush Springs in Indian Territory, decisively defeated a large village of Comanches. The following spring he won another victory at the Battle of Nescutunga, in southwestern Kansas. (See pp. 12–14.) In 1860 a regiment of state troops organized at Fort Belknap also took the offensive and pushed north as far as Kansas without bringing on a fight.

The United States in 1855 turned to the reservation system as a complement to military operations. Supervising Agent Robert S. Neighbors and Captain Randolph B. Marcy established two reservations near Fort Belknap, one for the numerous small, docile tribes and the other for the southern Comanches. The experiment failed because some of the Comanches could not be restrained and because the frontier whites were violently hostile to all Indians. In 1859 the reservations were abolished and the Indians escorted to new land in Indian Territory by a squadron of cavalry under Major George H. Thomas.

In 1852 Fort Belknap served as base for the exploration of the upper Red River country conducted by Captain Marcy and Lieutenant George B. McClellan. During the decade a small settlement, also named Belknap, grew up near the fort. Between 1858 and 1861 it was an important station on the Butterfield Overland Mail.

Fort Belknap and the other Texas forts were evacuated by U.S. troops at the outbreak of the Civil War. It continued, however, to play a vital role in frontier defense. Troops of the Texas Frontier Regiment used it throughout the war as a base for operations against Kiowas and Comanches and for the protection of surrounding settlements. After the Civil War U.S. troops reoccupied the Texas forts. Fort Belknap was discontinued as a permanent post in 1867, because of the unreliable water supply, although small detachments were stationed there from time to time for protection of the mail road during periods of particularly intense Indian raiding activity. Fort Richardson, to the east, and Fort Griffin, to the southwest, took over Belknap's role in frontier defense.

A small body of soldiers garrisoned Fort Belknap in 1871 when General William T. Sherman visited it on an inspection of the Texas frontier. The next day, between Belknap and Richardson, he narrowly escaped death at the hands of a Kiowa raiding party that massacred the personnel of a wagon train following Sherman's party. This episode, the "Jacksboro Incident," led to the arrest of Satanta and Big Tree and their trial and conviction by a Texas state court. (See pp. 41–42, 226–27.) After the subjugation of the Kiowas and Comanches in 1874–75, Fort Belknap fell into disuse and, ultimately, ruins.

Present Appearance. Young County in cooperation with the Fort Belknap Society administers part of the fort site as a county park. The remainder of the site has been lost in surrounding farmland. The park was developed in 1936 by the State of Texas with Federal funds made available for observance of the Texas Centennial. The stone walls were repaired and stabilized and a new roof added. The only original structure on the site is the arsenal, built in 1852. The old well has also survived. The stone walls were repaired and stabilized and a new roof added. The corn house, largely a restoration, includes some of the original stone walls that were still standing in 1936. The rest of the structures, all of stone construction with shingled roofs, are reconstructions built by the state on the original foundations. These replicas include two barracks, a kitchen and the commissary. The last houses a museum collection of artifacts pertaining to the history of the region. Each barracks originally had a separate kitchen building. Available funds in 1936 were not sufficient to build a kitchen for each of the restored barracks, as planned. The problem was resolved by reconstructing one kitchen, not on original foundations but between the two barracks. Otherwise, the reconstruction appears to be as authentic as extant historical records and the memory of old settlers would permit.[32]

19. Fort Concho, Texas

Location. Tom Green County, south edge of San Angelo.

Ownership and Administration. City of San Angelo and various private owners; city-owned portions administered by the Fort Concho Museum Board. The complex of buildings covers about fifteen acres.

Significance. After the Civil War the Army reconstituted the antebellum Texas frontier defense system. Most of the posts guarding the El Paso Road—Stockton, Davis, Quitman and Bliss— were reoccupied. But the old inner-and-outer-ring device for shielding the eight-hundred-mile frontier of settlement was discarded. A new line of forts—Richardson, Griffin, Concho, McKavett and Clark—stood between the Indian Country and the interior settlements. Fort Concho occupied the center of the line. Here, because of geography to the north and south, the trans-Texas immigrant trails converged. And here Indian raiders were wont to slip through the defenses and strike the settlements to the east. Because of its strategic location, Fort Concho was the most important bastion of the postwar Texas defense system.

Erected at the forks of the Concho River in November 1867, Fort Concho served as headquarters in the next twenty years for such noted Indian fighters as Ranald S. Mackenzie, William R. Shafter, Wesley Merritt, Anson Mills and Benjamin H. Grierson. Troops from the fort performed constant patrols during the early 1870's in an effort to stem the raids of Kiowa and Comanche war

Fort Concho, Texas. The old headquarters building now houses a museum.
Fort Concho Museum Board photograph.

parties based on the Fort Sill sanctuary. Later, after Fort Sill
ceased to provide a haven, Mackenzie led his men into the almost
unknown expanse of the Staked Plains. Men from Concho were
with him at the Battle of Palo Duro Canyon on September 27,
1874, when he dealt one of the decisive blows of the last war
against the southern Plains tribes. (See pp. 47–48, 234–35.) Mackenzie's expedition against Kickapoo and Lipan raiders based in
Mexico in 1873 included troops stationed at Concho. The pursuit
led across the Rio Grande and, although it violated Mexican soil,
ended in a decisive defeat of the troublesome warriors. The last
major field service of the Fort Concho garrison took place in
1879 and 1880 when, led by Colonel B. H. Grierson, the men participated in campaigns against Victorio and the Warm Springs
Apaches. These operations covered the deserts of western Texas,
and ended only after the death of Victorio at the hands of Mexi-

Watching over the San Antonio–El Paso Road, Fort Davis nestled in a box canyon in the Davis Mountains of western Texas. This photograph was taken about 1885. Courtesy National Archives.

can soldiers in Chihuahua. (See pp. 69–71.) The Indians conquered and its necessity therefore gone, Fort Concho was abandoned in 1889.

Present Appearance. Beginning in 1930 and continuing to the present, a program has been pursued locally to acquire all the buildings and land of the original Fort Concho for historic site purposes. Designated the Fort Concho Museum, that portion of the site in public ownership is maintained and administered by the Fort Concho Museum Board, whose members are appointed by the City Commission of San Angelo.

Surviving buildings include nine sets of officers' quarters, two in public ownership, seven in private ownership and used as residences; the chapel; the administration building, now housing an extensive museum collection of artifacts relating to all phases of

Texas history; the powerhouse, moved stone by stone from its original site near the river and rebuilt; and two restored barracks, now housing large museum pieces such as pioneer vehicles. All the structures are of stone construction.[33]

20. Fort Davis, Texas

Location. Jeff Davis County, north edge of town of Fort Davis.

Ownership and Administration. Fort Davis was authorized by Congress in 1961 for addition to the National Park System contingent upon acquisition of necessary land. At this writing it is on the verge of formal announcement as a unit of the National Park Service, as Fort Davis National Historic Site.

Significance. The mounting tide of westward travel in the 1850's brought into service several transcontinental trails. An important link in the southern trail was the San Antonio–El Paso Road, which carried a large volume of immigrant and freight traffic between these two towns as well as "argonauts" bound for

The ruins of Fort Davis are the most extensive of any fort in the Southwest. This is officers' row. National Park Service photo.

the California gold fields. In 1854 stage service was inaugurated over this trail from San Antonio to Santa Fe by way of El Paso. In 1857 the Birch Company began service between San Antonio and San Diego, and the following year the Butterfield Overland Mail, St. Louis to San Francisco, used the western part of the San Antonio–El Paso Road. The relatively heavy traffic and rich opportunities for plunder attracted Kiowa, Comanche, and Mescalero Apache raiding parties that made travel dangerous and often disastrous. As the roads moved west from the settlements, therefore, a finger of military outposts likewise projected west. Forts Hudson, Lancaster, Stockton, Davis, Quitman and Bliss, together with numerous temporary subposts, extended military protection from the outer ring of Texas defense forts to El Paso.

Of these posts, Fort Davis was the largest and most important. Named for Secretary of War Jefferson Davis, it was established in 1854 by Lieutenant Colonel Washington Sewell in the Davis Mountains north of the Big Bend. It was strategically located to command the trans-Pecos segment of the El Paso Road, the southern stem of the Great Comanche War Trail, the major routes of Mescalero Apache war parties destined for Mexico, and the main crossings of the Rio Grande used by the Indians in their forays against Mexican settlements beyond the river. From 1854 to 1861 Colonel Sewell and his troops patrolled constantly and fought numerous skirmishes with the Kiowas, Comanches and Apaches.

At the outbreak of the Civil War in 1861, U.S. troops evacuated Fort Davis and Confederates moved in. In August a detachment of fourteen soldiers under Lieutenant Reuben E. Mays, pursuing an Apache raiding party, rode into an ambush that destroyed the entire command, proving at least that the Apaches were impartial in the Civil War. Only the Mexican guide escaped. After the Confederates failed in their attempt to conquer New Mexico, Fort Davis and the other forts in western Texas were abandoned.

Federal troops returned to Fort Davis in 1867 to find that the old establishment, primarily of log construction, had been all but wrecked by Indians. They built a new post, using substantial rock and adobe materials. It again became an important link in the frontier defenses of western Texas and a base for operations

Fort Phil Kearny, Wyoming, from a sketch drawn by Bugler Antonio Nicoli, 2nd Cavalry, in 1867. Indians patrol the hilltops; sentries stand beyond the line of trees, along the Big Piney River. Signal Corps reproduction. National Archives.

against Kiowas, Comanches and Apaches. In 1879–80 it played a major role in the campaign against Victorio and the Warm Springs Apaches. (See pp. 69–71, 225, 226, 227.) At the same time, the fort continued to serve as a way station on the roads to Mexico and California, and as the mother post of many scattered subposts. Cattlemen entered the area in the 1880's and established ranches after the Indian barrier was destroyed. The fort had outlived its usefulness and was abandoned in 1891.

Present Appearance. Today Fort Davis remains in a fairly good state of preservation. The walls of nine sets of adobe officers' quarters are still standing, several with roofs intact. Seven other sets of officers' quarters, of slab limestone construction, are in good condition, complete with roofs. Three of these, however, have been rehabilitated and are now used as guest cottages. On the opposite side of the parade ground stand the roofless walls

Scene of the Fetterman Disaster, near Fort Phil Kearny, Wyoming. Fighting occurred along the ridge to the right of the monument (upper left), where the last of Fetterman's men were killed. National Park Service photograph.

The Fetterman Massacre marker.

ON THIS FIELD ON THE 21 ST DAY OF
DECEMBER, 1866,
THREE COMMISSIONED OFFICERS AND
SEVENTY SIX PRIVATES
OF THE 18TH U.S. INFANTRY, AND OF THE
2ND U.S. CAVALRY, AND FOUR CIVILIANS,
UNDER THE COMMAND OF CAPTAIN BREVET-
LIEUTENANT COLONEL WILLIAM J. FETTERMAN
WERE KILLED BY AN OVERWHELMING
FORCE OF SIOUX UNDER THE COMMAND OF
RED CLOUD.
THERE WERE NO SURVIVORS.

of two adobe barracks, as well as a restored barracks. The adobe commissary and the barracks-like shop, together with the ruins of numerous utility buildings and other miscellaneous structures, complete the physical layout. It is picturesquely located at the mouth of a box canyon in the heart of the Davis Mountains near the Davis Mountains State Park. The Fort Davis Historical Society maintains a small museum in the restored barracks.[34]

21. Fort Phil Kearny and Related Sites, Wyoming

Location. Fort Phil Kearny and the sites of the Fetterman Massacre and Wagon Box Fight lie within a few miles of one another near U.S. Highway 87 in Johnson and Sheridan Counties, about 20 miles southeast of the city of Sheridan. Fort Phil Kearny may be reached by driving .6 mile northwest on the paved road to Story from its south junction with U.S. 87, then driving .4 mile west on a dirt road to the fort site. The monument on the site of the Fetterman Massacre lies adjacent to U.S. 87 on the east, 5.9 miles northwest of the south junction with the Story road, while the battlefield extends north and east a mile or more on a spur ridge from the monument. The Wagon Box Fight area is located 1.5 miles by gravel road southwest of the business section of Story.

Ownership and Administration. Three acres, containing the site of Fort Phil Kearny itself, are in state ownership. The remainder, estimated at 25 acres of grounds with related structures, is in private ownership. Of the estimated 40 acres in the site of the Wagon Box Fight, the state owns one acre. Of the estimated 60 acres in the site of the Fetterman Fight, the Federal Government owns a fraction of an acre, on which the monument is located. The rest is privately owned.

Significance. Some of the most significant and dramatic chapters in the history of the Indian wars occurred in and around Fort Phil Kearny as the Sioux fought to prevent invasion of their hunting grounds by prospectors bound over the Bozeman Trail for the Montana gold fields. Their efforts marked one of the few instances in which the Army bowed to hostile resistance and surrendered an occupied region. This is described in some detail on pp. 31–35, 234, 235.

Fort Phil Kearny was the largest and most important of the new forts in this area, constructed in 1866 and abandoned at Chief Red Cloud's demand before the peace commission at Fort Laramie in 1868, under the treaty of that occasion which designated the Powder River country as unceded Indian territory. The Sioux swarmed in to raze the forts as soon as they were evacuated by the soldiers, and thus they celebrated the zenith of their power on the northern Plains.

Present Appearance. Despite surrounding ranch operations, the sites of Fort Phil Kearny and the Fetterman and Wagon Box Fights have suffered little encroachment. Picturesquely located at the foot of the Bighorn Mountains, they preserve a natural setting that permits the historic scene to be visualized readily. There are no surface remains of the fort, but the site has been marked conspicuously. A Boy Scout clubhouse and miniature stockade have been erected on the site but have been permitted to deteriorate badly. Five miles north of the fort is the ridge where the Fetterman disaster occurred. Fighting began at one end of the ridge and progressed along it to where the monument now stands. Here the last remnant of Fetterman's command was wiped out. The natural setting of this ridge remains unimpaired, except for the highway that crosses its point at the monument site. The monument was erected by the War Department on a small tract of Federal land adjacent to the highway. Another monument marks the site of the Wagon Box Fight, which lies in an upland prairie 1½ miles southwest of Story. The natural setting at this site has also remained intact.[35]

C. Other Sites Considered

In the process of selecting the comparatively few historic sites of such outstanding character as to merit recognition as Registered National Historic Landmarks, a great many sites were studied, evaluated and found not to meet the criteria. The sites described below were deemed to possess noteworthy historical values, but not to possess "exceptional value" within the meaning of the criteria, within the segment of history discussed here. Such sites may satisfy the criteria as applied to other phases of history, however.

ARIZONA

1. Big Dry Wash Battlefield

Location: Navajo County, Coconino National Forest, 7 miles north of Mogollon Rim Road at General Springs

This is the site of the battle that took place on July 17, 1882, between Apaches who had left Fort Apache Reservation and a force led by Captain Adna R. Chaffee, as described on pp. 72–75. An unimproved Forest Service road, difficult to negotiate with a conventional automobile, leads northward from the Mogollon Rim Road along Chaffee's approach route. It terminates at the canyon brink where the fighting began. A large stone monument stands on the south edge of the canyon with a plaque on one side describing the action, on the other side a plaque bearing the names of the white participants. Remains of the old trail into the canyon are visible. The heavy pine forests and rugged canyon are unchanged from 1882. Another plaque describing the battle stands on the Mogollon Rim Road at General Springs.

2. Camp Verde

Location: Yavapai County, town of Camp Verde

Established to protect settlers in the Verde Valley of central Arizona, Camp Verde (1864–91) was the focal point of General Crook's campaign of 1872–73 in the Tonto Basin. Here the hostile Yavapai, or Apache-Mojave, surrendered unconditionally in April 1873. Three sets of officers' quarters are still standing, remodeled and used as private residences, together with the administration building which houses a small museum maintained by the Camp Verde Improvement Association.

3. Cibecue Creek Battlefield

Location: Navajo County, Cibecue Creek, 2.5 miles south of village of Cibecue

At this place the engagement took place between followers of Nakaidoklini, a White Mountain Apache medicine man who had begun practicing a new religion, and a cavalry force under Colonel E. A. Carr, on August 30, 1881. This is described on pp. 72–73. The valley of Cibecue Creek at the battle site is wide and open, in contrast to the broken, wooded terrain on either side. The creek meanders back and forth across it. Aside from an occasional Indian cornfield and scattered Apache dwellings, which are not out of character, the natural scene is unimpaired.

4. Fort Apache (Camp Apache)

Location: Navajo County, town of Fort Apache

Fort Apache (1869–1924) was strategically located on the northern edge of the San Carlos Reservation and was the key post in the Apache wars of 1872–73 and 1881–86. After removal of the Chiricahua Apaches to San Carlos in 1876, these most intractable Indians were settled near the fort, which was known officially as Camp Apache, 1871–79. Several times during the next decade renegade bands under leaders such as Geronimo, Natchez, Chato and Chihuahua escaped from the reservation and were pursued, generally without success, by soldiers from Fort Apache. During the Cibecue affair in 1881 (see opposite page) Apaches attacked the fort but failed to capture it. Fort Apache ceased to play a significant role in frontier defense after the surrender of Geronimo and the removal of the reservation Chiricahuas in 1886, but continued as an operating agency.

Officers' row, barracks, adjutant's office, commissary, guardhouse, quartermaster warehouse and cavalry stables are still standing. A log building at the west end of officers' row, one of the earliest buildings of the fort, is reputed to have been occupied by General Crook during the Apache wars. The fort is now used by the Bureau of Indian Affairs as headquarters of the Fort Apache Indian Reservation.

5. Fort Breckinridge (Old Camp Grant)

> *Location: Pinal County, 50 yards southeast of junction of State Highway 77 with road to Aravaipa Canyon*

Fort Breckinridge (1860–73) was built and garrisoned by troops from Fort Buchanan, and was the second military post in the Gadsden Purchase. Dragoons from the fort went to the relief of Lieutenant George N. Bascom in February 1861, when he provoked the fight with Cochise that led to twelve years of warfare with the Chiricahua Apaches, as described beginning on p. 25. The fort was abandoned at the outbreak of the Civil War but reoccupied in 1866 and named Camp Grant. The controversial Camp Grant Massacre took place here in April 1871. (See pp. 66–67.) Because of its unhealthy location Camp Grant was moved to a new site, on the south slope of Graham Mountain, in 1873. (See Fort Grant, p. 169.)

A few mounds of earth and melted adobe outlining the building foundations are all that remain. One or two walls are still standing several feet high, but are disappearing rapidly. The site is heavily matted with mesquite and cholla cactus.

Navajo dance, Fort Defiance Indian Agency, Arizona, 1873. Photographed by Timothy H. O'Sullivan of the U.S. Army Geographical and Geological Explorations and Surveys, under Lt. George M. Wheeler. Collections of the Library of Congress.

6. Fort Buchanan (Fort Crittenden)

Location: Santa Cruz County, State Highway 82, 3 miles west of Sonoita

Fort Buchanan (1857–61) and Fort Breckinridge were the first two military posts in the Gadsden Purchase. The garrisons guarded the Butterfield Overland Mail and operated against hostile Apaches. Shortly after the outbreak of the Civil War, both forts were evacuated and destroyed. Troops returned to Fort Buchanan after the war and, on a hill just east of the ruined fort, built Fort Crittenden (1867–73). The garrison helped to protect settlers of the Babocomari, Sonoita and Santa Cruz Valleys from marauding Apaches.

Mounds of earth outlining building foundations are all that remain of Fort Buchanan. Adobe ruins and mounds of earth mark the site of Fort Crittenden.

7. Fort Defiance

Location: Apache County, town of Fort Defiance

Fort Defiance (1852–60), the first military post in present Arizona, was founded by Colonel E. V. Sumner as a base for campaigns against the Navajos. Nine years of intermittent skirmishing culminated in April 1860, when a large body of Navajos attacked the fort itself. Although the issue was for a time in doubt, the defenders succeeded in beating off the assault. Troops were withdrawn in 1861, and in subsequent years, before the establishment of Window Rock, Fort Defiance served as the Navajo agency.

The site of the fort is now occupied by a Navajo tribal school and hospital, around which the village of Fort Defiance has grown up. A three-story stone building on the school site survives from the agency period.

8. Fort Grant

Location: Graham County, town of Fort Grant, 25 miles north of Willcox

Fort Grant (1873–1905) was the successor to Old Camp Grant (see above, p. 167), which was abandoned in 1873 in favor of a more healthful location on the southwestern slope of Graham Mountain. It was located convenient to the route usually taken by Apache renegades who periodically fled the San Carlos Reservation to raid in Mexico. The garrison saw much field service in attempting to intercept these bands and pursuing raiding parties of Apaches from Mexico. With the surrender of Geronimo in 1886, the post lost its importance. The garrison was withdrawn in 1898 and the fort abandoned officially in 1905.

Barracks at Fort Grant, Arizona, in the 1890's. Quartermaster's Photo Album. National Archives.

In 1911 Fort Grant was turned over to the State of Arizona for use as a reform school, and it is still the State Industrial School. Several buildings dating from the military era are still in use, but an extensive construction program has destroyed much of the historic setting.

9. Fort Huachuca

Location: Cochise County, Fort Huachuca

Fort Huachuca (1877–present) played a prominent role in the campaigns against Geronimo between 1877 and the final surrender in 1886. It was part of the system of forts guarding the border against raids by Apache renegades based in the Sierra Madre of Mexico. At Fort Huachuca Captain Henry W. Lawton and Assistant Surgeon Leonard Wood organized the striking column that, throughout the summer of 1886, pursued Geronimo and his band through the Sierra Madre. Lawton's operations proved instrumental in leading to the surrender of the Chiricahua renegades.

Fort Huachuca today houses the Army Electronic Proving Ground. The large adobe houses on officers' row, built in the 1880's, have been remodeled and are still used as officers' quarters. Several other residences that date from the 1880's have also been remodeled and are used as offices. Three large frame barracks today house classrooms and other administrative offices. A row of eight adobe huts, one-half mile north of the parade ground, were built about 1900 to house the Apache scouts, who had been living in wickiups. Modern construction has encroached surprisingly little on the historic setting.

10. Fort Lowell

Location: Pima County, east edge of Tucson

Fort Lowell (1862–91) served more as a supply depot and administrative center than as an active outpost in the Apache wars. Its extensive adobe ruins, however, form an outstanding specimen, very easily accessible, of the typical southwestern fort of the nineteenth century.

Non-Commissioned Staff Quarters, occupied by Commissary and Ordnance sergeants and their families, Fort Huachuca, Arizona, in the 1890's. Quartermaster's Photo Album. National Archives.

11. Salt River Canyon (Skeleton Cave) Battlefield

Location: Maricopa County, Salt River Canyon, 7 miles (by boat only) above Mormon Flat Dam

A group of more than a hundred Yavapai, or Apache-Mojave, Indians took refuge in Skeleton Cave, where they were attacked by a force under Captain W. H. Brown on December 28, 1872. Most were killed (see pp. 68–69). The Army victory here had an important influence in bringing Colonel (soon General) George Crook's Tonto Basin campaign to a successful close.

The cave lies on the north wall of the canyon in the angle of a sharp turn to the south. It is an elliptical undercut about 65 by 25 feet, situated at the base of a cliff 170 feet high and at the top of a steep slope falling away some 1200 feet to the water below. The ceiling is smoke-blackened from Indian fires and scarred by the bullets of Brown's carbines. The setting is unimpaired.

12. San Carlos Agency (lost site)

Location: Gila County, beneath waters of San Carlos Lake

The San Carlos Agency was established in the Gila River Valley in 1871. Here, following Crook's successful campaign of 1872–73, the Indian Bureau attempted to concentrate most of the Apache peoples of Arizona and New Mexico. Although many bands were moved to San Carlos, and between 1875 and 1878 remained reasonably content under the energetic administration of Agent John Clum, the Apaches were never gathered all together and the attempt failed in the end. (See pp. 69 ff.) Corrupt and inefficient agents, friction between military and civil authorities, the attempt to make farmers out of wild Indians, and encroachment of white settlers kept the reservation in constant turmoil. Renegade bands periodically left San Carlos and, taking refuge in Mexico, raided settlements in Arizona and New Mexico and skirmished with U.S. troops. After the final surrender of Geronimo in 1886, the chief troublemakers were imprisoned in Florida, and most of the remaining Apaches continued to live either on the

San Carlos Reservation or the Fort Apache Reservation, to the north.

After the completion of Coolidge Dam in 1928, the site of old San Carlos was inundated by San Carlos Lake and the agency moved to a new site up the San Carlos River.

13. Skeleton Canyon

> *Location: Cochise County, adjacent to Sloan's Ranch, 8 miles southeast of hamlet of Apache*

Here, on September 3 and 4, 1886, Geronimo, worst of the renegade Apaches, and Natchez, son of Cochise and hereditary chief of the Chiricahuas, surrendered for the last time. With them imprisoned in Florida, lasting peace came to the southwestern frontier. Geronimo had been induced to give up because of the relentless pursuit of his people through the Sierra Madre of Mexico by troops operating under Brigadier General Nelson A. Miles, and by the persuasion of Lieutenant Charles B. Gatewood. (See pp. 78–80.)

A cairn of rocks about six feet high, overgrown with mesquite, marks the site of Geronimo's surrender. It stands on a bench just south of the creek that flows out of Skeleton Canyon, about one hundred yards east of the Sloan Ranch house and barn, and immediately above a stock pond and corral. The ranch facilities constitute a minor intrusion, but the desert character of the terrain remains unimpaired. A large stone monument on U.S. Highway 80 at Apache commemorates the surrender.

CALIFORNIA

14. Fort Bidwell

Location: Modoc County, town of Fort Bidwell

Fort Bidwell (1865–93) was established to protect the settlers of Surprise Valley from Indian depredations. It served as a base for troops operating against Bannocks, Paiutes, Snakes and Modocs between 1865 and 1873. Abandoned by the Army in 1893, it was

View of the Presidio, San Francisco, California, in the 1890's, looking toward
Fort Point (Fort Winfield Scott) and the Golden Gate. Quartermaster's Photo
Album. National Archives.

taken over by the Bureau of Indian Affairs and still functions as
the headquarters of an Indian reservation. The stable, a school
and the parade ground are all that survive from the military
period. The site is marked by a bronze plaque as California Registered Historical Landmark No. 430.

15. Fort Point (Fort Winfield Scott)

Location: San Francisco, south end of Golden Gate Bridge

A harbor defense fortification, Fort Point was active during the
period of the Indian wars but not directly associated with them.
It occupies historic ground on which the Spanish built Castillo de
San Joaquin in 1793 to protect San Francisco Bay. Of brick construction, mounting 146 guns, the fort was completed in 1861 and
is the largest fortification of its kind on the Pacific Coast. Its setting is also notable. The Golden Gate Bridge passes directly
above the fort.

16. Fort Tejon

Location: Kern County, U.S. Highway 99, 36 miles south of Bakersfield

Situated in scenic Grapevine Canyon near Tejon Pass, Fort Tejon (1854–64) was established to keep peace between white settlers and the inhabitants of the Sebastian Indian Reservation in Tulare Valley, twenty miles to the north. In 1858–59 it was a stop on the Butterfield Overland Mail, and from 1857 to 1861 the camels brought overland from Texas were stationed here. Inactivated in 1861, the fort was reoccupied in 1863 by California volunteers during local Indian troubles. After its final abandonment in 1864 Fort Tejon became part of the Rancho Tejon of E. F. Beale, who used the buildings as residences and stables.

Established as a California State Historical Monument in 1939, Fort Tejon now offers as visitor attractions three restored adobe buildings—a barracks and two officers' quarters—and a visitor center.

17. Fort Yuma

Location: Imperial County, U.S. Highway 80, across Colorado River from Yuma, Arizona

Fort Yuma (1850–85) was built to protect from Yuma and Mojave Indians the Yuma Crossing of the Colorado River, one of the most strategic locations on the southern transcontinental trail. Associated with the Yuma Quartermaster Depot, across the river, it was not only a way station for California-bound immigrants, but also a processing point for supplies and personnel destined for service at the Arizona forts. Steamboat transportation linked Yuma, by way of the Colorado River and Gulf of California, with San Francisco and Los Angeles.

Fort Yuma stands on a bluff at the west end of the highway bridge and is now headquarters of the Yuma Indian Reservation. About a dozen buildings, greatly altered and in poor condition, date from the late military period. Several buildings of the quartermaster depot are still standing on the east bank of the river.

Colorado River ferry, 1880, showing Fort Yuma, California, on the opposite hilltop. Signal Corps photograph. National Archives.

COLORADO

18. Beecher's Island Battlefield (lost site)

Location: Yuma County, 17 miles southeast of town of Wray, north edge of village of Beecher Island

The Battle of Beecher's Island was one of the dramatic conflicts of the Indian wars. Here in September 1868, about fifty veteran frontiersmen under Major George A. Forsyth held off a large war party of Sioux and Cheyennes estimated at more than a thousand until help arrived from Fort Wallace, Kansas. (See pp. 35–37, 187.)

The island on which Forsyth and his men were besieged, in the Arikara Fork of the Republican River, has long since disappeared. The battle is commemorated by a large monument that stands near the post office of Beecher Island.

19. Fort Garland

> *Location: Costilla County, south edge of town of Fort Garland.*

Fort Garland (1858–83) was built in the San Luis Valley of southern Colorado following the abandonment of Fort Massachusetts. Its function was to keep watch on nearby Ute and Navajo Indians. Colonel Christopher "Kit" Carson commanded the fort

Main entrance to Fort Garland, Colorado, 1874. The ropes which brace the flagpole show more distinctly than the pole itself. Photographer probably Timothy H. O'Sullivan. Collections of the Library of Congress.

from 1866 until his death two years later. He and Lieutenant General William T. Sherman held a council here in 1866 with the Ute Chief, Ouray, to discuss white invasion of Ute lands. In 1881 troops from Fort Garland escorted the Utes to new homes in Utah, and the post was abandoned shortly thereafter.

Army officer, wife and children at Fort Garland, 1874. Photographer probably Timothy H. O'Sullivan. Collections of the Library of Congress.

Seven of the original adobe buildings of Fort Garland have been restored by the State of Colorado and an eighth, the post trader's store, not owned by the state, is currently in use as a private residence. A large museum, divided among the various buildings, interprets the history of the fort and the San Luis Valley. The site is a state monument administered by the State Historical Society of Colorado.

20. Julesburg and Fort Sedgwick

Location: Sedgwick County. The site of Fort Sedgwick is 1.3 miles south and .3 mile east of the village of Ovid and U.S. Highway 138. The site of old Julesburg is 1.1 miles east of the site of Fort Sedgwick.

Fort Sedgwick (1864–71) was established by volunteer troops to protect the overland route to Denver during the outbreak of the Plains tribes in 1864. It was first called Camp Rankin and then renamed Fort Sedgwick in September 1865.

The town of Julesburg, an important way station on the stage-coach and freight lines to Denver, stood just east of the camp. Early in 1865 the camp and town were attacked several times by parties of Sioux, Cheyennes and Arapahoes, aroused by Chivington's Sand Creek Massacre. The town was sacked and burned to the ground. Thereafter the focus of hostility shifted north of the Platte. A second town sprang up three miles east of old Julesburg in 1867. The present Julesburg, still farther east, was founded in 1881 when the Union Pacific built up the South Platte to Denver. (See pp. 20–22, 180.)

The site of Fort Sedgwick lies in a pasture on the south side of the South Platte. The outlines of the adobe buildings may be traced. A stone monument stands in another pasture to the east, where old Julesburg was located, but there are no surface remains of the town.

21. Meeker Massacre Site

Location: Rio Blanco County, 4.5 miles west of Meeker

This is the site of the former White River Agency for the Ute Indians, which was established in 1873. Agent N. C. Meeker was killed here along with several of his employees in September 1879 by disgruntled Indians, in an episode described on pp. 63, 65, 180.

The Ute Agency site is located in an irrigated hay meadow on the north side of White River near present Meeker. A few traces of the building foundations and a flagpole standing on the site where Meeker was killed are all that remain to mark the location of the White River Agency.

22. Milk Creek Battlefield

Location: Moffat County, 20 miles by graded road north-east of Meeker, near Thornburg

Following their uprising against Agent N. C. Meeker at the White River Agency (see pp. 63, 65, and Meeker Massacre Site, above), the Utes set up an ambush of the relief column marching from Fort Fred Steele, Wyoming, at Milk Creek. Forming a corral with their wagons, the soldiers fought off the Utes from September 29 to October 5, 1879, when reinforcements arrived to lift the siege.

The battlefield remains much as it appeared in 1879, located in a brushy canyon. A monument bearing the names of the soldiers killed in the engagement stands in the center of the field.

23. Sand Creek Battlefield

Location: Kiowa County; drive from village of Chivington on graded road .7 mile east, 7.2 miles north and 1.5 miles east.

The event that gives this site historic value is often referred to as the Sand Creek or Chivington Massacre. Black Kettle and his band of Southern Cheyennes were camped here on November 29, 1864, when they were attacked without warning by Colonel J. M. Chivington and a regiment of Colorado volunteer soldiers. The Indians considered themselves to be at peace and under the protection of nearby Fort Lyon. About three hundred were slain, including over two hundred women and children. (See pp. 20–22.)

The valley of Sand Creek, used today as range land, has changed very little since 1864. A small marker stands on the ridge overlooking the bottomland where Black Kettle's village lay.

24. Summit Springs Battlefield

Location: Logan-Washington County line; 8.3 miles south from Atwood on State Highway 63, 4.8 miles east by un-improved road

The Battle of Summit Springs was one of the most shattering defeats suffered by the Plains Indians. It occurred on July 11,

1869, when Major E. A. Carr surprised Tall Bull and his Cheyenne "Dog Soldiers," killed fifty and captured more than a hundred with the loss of only one cavalryman. (See pp. 36–39.)

The battlefield is an open cattle pasture. A stone marker stands near the springs from which the battle took its name.

IDAHO

25. Fort Boise

Location: Ada County, Boise

Fort Boise (1863–1913) was established for the purpose of protecting Oregon Trail travelers and Idaho miners from Indian attacks. The garrison participated in the major Indian outbreaks of the Northwest between 1863 and 1879. During the Bannock War of 1878 the post was temporary headquarters for the field forces. Fort Boise was turned over to the Public Health Service in 1919, and to the Veterans Administration in 1938. Several stone buildings surviving from the military period may be seen on the present Veterans Hospital grounds, part of which is maintained as a city park.

26. Fort Hall

Location: Bingham County, Snake River Valley, 11 miles by dirt road west of U.S. Highway 91–191 at Evans' Trading Post

Although it was significant chiefly in the history of the fur trade and overland migrations, Fort Hall also merits attention in the story of Indian affairs. It was built in 1834 in the midst of the Snake Indian range, and served as a trading post operated by Nathaniel Wyeth until 1837 and by the Hudson's Bay Company thereafter. It performed among the intermountain tribes much the same acculturative role as did the other prominent fur posts of Fort Union (North Dakota) and Bent's Fort among the Plains tribes. After the collapse of the fur empire, Fort Hall was used occasionally during the 1850's and 1860's as a military post by regular and volunteer troops. The War Department made Fort Hall a formal establishment in 1870 and abandoned it in 1883.

Virtually all traces of the bastioned adobe fortress have been carried away by flood waters. The only remains consist of a group of low earth mounds forming a rough enclosure about 125 feet in diameter. A small monument marks the site. (Fort Hall is classified "exceptionally valuable" in the study dealing with overland migrations.)

27. Lolo Trail

Location: Clearwater and Lolo National Forests, between Lolo, Montana, and Pierce, Idaho

The Lolo Trail is important mainly as the route used by Lewis and Clark to cross the Bitterroot Mountains. It was also traversed by the Nez Percé Indians in their annual trek to the buffalo range. Chief Joseph conducted his people over the trail in 1877 in the masterly fighting retreat from General Howard's pursuing column. (See pp. 59–61.) A newly paved road across the Bitterroots from Lolo, Montana, to Pierce, Idaho, partially duplicates the old Lolo Trail of Indian times. Howard's Camp is now a packer's camp on a camp site used by General Howard in 1877. (The Lolo Trail is classified "exceptionally valuable" in the study dealing with the Lewis and Clark Expedition.)

28. Spalding Mission

Location: Nez Percé County, junction of U.S. Highway 95 and State Highway 9

The Spalding or Lapwai Mission was established by the Reverend and Mrs. Henry H. Spalding among the Nez Percé Indians in 1836, a sister station to the Waiilatpu Mission (see Whitman Mission National Historic Site). The missionaries made some progress in converting their charges to Christianity and in persuading them to settle down as farmers. The Whitman Massacre of 1847 wrecked the missionary effort in the Pacific Northwest, however, and the Spaldings closed the mission and withdrew. Spalding Memorial Park of the Idaho State Park Service, chiefly a recre-

White Bird Battle marker, Idaho. Signal Corps photograph. National Archives.

ational and picnic area, covers the site of the mission and includes traces of foundations of the buildings.

29. White Bird Battlefield

Location: Lewis County, U.S. Highway 95, 15 miles south of Grangeville

The first engagement of the Nez Percé War was fought in White Bird Canyon on June 17, 1877. It was a decisive and humiliating defeat for the Army, and served notice that in Chief Joseph the West Point officers had found a tactical skill that matched if not surpassed their own. (See p. 59.)

The site, in White Bird Canyon, lies just north of the town of White Bird. A state highway marker is on White Bird Summit, along U.S. Highway 95, where the battle site may be viewed among the deep gorges of the mountainous terrain. A granite shaft marks the place where the body of one of the soldier dead was found in 1919.

KANSAS

30. Fort Harker

Location: Ellsworth County, town of Kanopolis

First named Fort Ellsworth, Fort Harker (1864–73) served as an important operating and distributing post for the line of forts guarding the Smoky Hill Trail to Denver and later the Kansas Pacific Railroad. The town of Kanopolis has grown up around the site of the fort, and several of the original buildings are still standing as part of the town.

31. Fort Hays

Location: Ellis County, U.S. Highway 40, 2 miles west of Hays

Fort Hays (1865–69) was a key part of the defense system which helped to protect travelers on the Smoky Hill Trail to Denver and construction workers on the Kansas Pacific Railroad. From temporary headquarters at Fort Hays, Major General Philip H. Sheridan in 1868–69 directed the operations of columns in the winter campaign against the southern Plains tribes. (See pp. 37–39.) From 1867 to 1870 Fort Hays was also the headquarters of Lieutenant Colonel George A. Custer and the 7th Cavalry.

Only two buildings, the stone guardhouse and stone blockhouse, have survived. The site itself has been leveled and is used as a golf course.

32. Fort Riley

Location: Geary County, U.S. Highway 40, east of Junction City

Fort Riley (1855–present) was established at the junction of the Smoky Hill and Republican forks of the Kansas River, close to the area of Indian troubles. It served as base for several expeditions against the hostile tribes during the 1850's and 1860's. Lieutenant Colonel George A. Custer organized the newly authorized 7th Cavalry Regiment here in 1866. In 1891 the fort became headquarters of the School of Application for Cavalry and Light Artillery, which in 1908 became the Mounted Service School and in 1919 the Cavalry School. Fort Riley is still an Army installation, now as the home of the Army General School.

Fort Hays, Kansas, 1873. Barracks, mess halls, kitchens and wash houses. Signal Corps photograph. National Archives.

A number of buildings erected in the early years are still standing, including officers' quarters (1855) once occupied by Custer and the post chapel (1855), which has undergone some alteration.

33. Fort Scott

Location: Bourbon County, town of Fort Scott

Fort Scott (1842–53, 1863–65, 1870–73) represented an extension of the "Permanent Indian Frontier" of the 1820's and 1830's. Troops from Fort Scott helped to protect traffic on the Santa Fe Trail and participated in exploring expeditions to the northern Plains and Rocky Mountains. Abandoned in 1853, it was reactivated during the Civil War as a Union headquarters and supply depot. Abandoned again after the war, it was reoccupied for three years in 1870–73 to police the Fort Scott and Gulf Railroad,

Fort Riley, Kansas, about 1878. From a pen drawing by L. Leduc, 16th Infantry Band. Signal Corps reproduction. National Archives.

which was threatened by troubles resulting from illegal white settlement of Cherokee lands in Indian Territory.

The parade ground, one-and-a-half officers' quarters, Headquarters House (1842) and several outbuildings are still standing. Near the parade ground is a blockhouse, Fort Blair, built during the Civil War some miles distant from the fort and subsequently moved. The site is largely though not entirely owned by the city of Fort Scott, within which it is located.

34. Fort Wallace

Location: Wallace County, 1.5 miles southeast of town of Wallace

Fort Wallace (1865–82), the westernmost of the Smoky Hill forts, bore the brunt of Indian hostility during the wars of the 1860's and 1870's. A party of two or three hundred Cheyennes under Roman Nose attacked Fort Wallace itself in June 1867, but were driven off by the garrison after losing several men. Here in 1868 Major George A. Forsyth set forth on the expedition that culminated at the Battle of Beecher's Island. The siege of Forsyth was lifted by a relief column from Fort Wallace. (See pp. 35–37, 176.)

Although buildings of the fort disappeared long ago, some traces of the building outlines are still visible, and the site itself is comparatively unspoiled.

35. Highland Indian Mission

Location: Doniphan County, U.S. Highway 36, 2 miles east of Highland

Highland Mission was built about 1846 among Iowa, Sac and Fox Indians who had recently moved to Kansas from the East. Until 1863 Indian children here received elementary schooling and instruction in domestic arts, manual trades and agriculture. The mission was a large, three-story building with thirty-two rooms. Part of it, subsequently destroyed, has been restored by the state. It is now owned and administered by the Northeast Kansas Historical Society.

36. Medicine Lodge Treaty Site

Location: Barber County, 1½ miles south of town of Medicine Lodge, at junction of Elm and Medicine Lodge Creeks; inaccessible by automobile

The two treaties concluded by the Peace Commission of 1867–68 were landmarks in the evolution of Indian policy and constituted important parts of the foundation on which President Grant in 1869 erected the famous Peace Policy. The treaty with the tribes of the northern Plains was signed at Fort Laramie in April 1868, that with the tribes of the southern Plains at Medicine Lodge, Kansas, in October 1867. Neither treaty solved the Indian problem. Instead of peace, there followed the Sioux War of 1876–81 in the north, and the Washita campaign of 1868–69 and the Red River War of 1874–75 in the south.

The Medicine Lodge Treaty was signed in a large natural amphitheater at the junction of Elm and Medicine Lodge Creeks. The integrity of the site has been largely destroyed by a drainage ditch that cuts through the area and by cultivation of surrounding fields. The spot is not marked and can be reached only by walking half a mile across a plowed field.

37. Shawnee Indian Mission

Location: Wyandotte County, Fairway

The Shawnee Methodist Mission (1839–62) was a center for the education and religious instruction of Indian children moved from eastern homes to Indian Territory. At the height of its activity, the mission comprised two thousand acres, sixteen buildings, and two hundred students. On the antebellum frontier, the mission was an outpost of civilization and a social center. Among its visitors during these years were John C. Frémont, Marcus Whitman, Francis Parkman and John W. Gunnison. Of the original sixteen buildings, three two-story brick structures survive. Located in a suburb of Kansas City, Kansas, they are owned by the state and administered by the State Historical Society.

MINNESOTA

38. Birch Coulee Battlefield

Location: Renville County, U.S. Highway 71, 1½ miles north of Morton

The Battle of Birch Coulee, on September 2–3, 1862, marked the high tide of the Sioux in their revolt against the settlers who were populating the valley of the Minnesota River. Hundreds of settlers were killed in the area (see pp. 15 ff.), and at Birch Coulee the Sioux surrounded a force of 170 volunteer soldiers under Major Joseph R. Brown. The whites lost thirteen killed and forty-seven severely wounded; the Sioux reportedly had two killed and five or six wounded, in two days of fighting. The Indians withdrew when reinforcements arrived about 11 A.M. on September 3 under Colonel Henry Hastings Sibley.

The rolling, tree-studded battlefield has not changed much. A state memorial park preserves the scene of the fighting.

39. Fort Ridgely

Location: Brown County, State Highway 4, 5 miles south of Fairfax

Fort Ridgely (1853–67) was located on the south bank of the Minnesota River fifteen miles below the Lower Sioux Agency, where the Sioux under Little Crow began their revolt in August 1862. (See pp. 15 ff.) Refugees poured into the fort, which was attacked on August 20 by about four hundred Sioux warriors, and two days later by eight hundred. The defenders, about 180 civilians and volunteer soldiers, beat off repeated charges until the Indians withdrew in discouragement.

Surrounded by unimpaired prairie and woodlands, the site of Fort Ridgely is now a state park. Archaeological excavations in the 1930's revealed the building foundations, some of which were stabilized and left exposed. The reconstructed commissary building houses a small museum.

40. New Ulm (lost site)

Location: Brown County, town of New Ulm

New Ulm was a town of about nine hundred population, located below Fort Ridgely in the Minnesota River Valley, when the Sioux revolt of 1862 began. (See pp. 15 ff. and Fort Ridgely, above.) A body of about one hundred Sioux attacked the town while the larger force invested Fort Ridgely until, on August 23, the attack on Ridgely having failed, the Indians turned their full fury on New Ulm. Thirty-four whites were killed and sixty wounded before the attack was called off. Fire consumed 190 of the community's buildings.

The scene of the fighting in the western outskirts of New Ulm has been completely changed by urban expansion and development of the modern New Ulm, a city of ten thousand population.

41. Wood Lake Battlefield

Location: Yellow Medicine County, Minnesota Highway 274, 7 miles south of Granite Falls

The Battle of Wood Lake was the first decisive defeat of the Sioux in the outbreak of 1862. Colonel Henry H. Sibley had assembled about fourteen hundred volunteer troops and occupied Fort Ridgely near the end of August. (See above, Fort Ridgely, and pp. 17–19.) He moved on against the Indians on September 18 and effectively frustrated the effort of Little Crow to ambush his command near Wood Lake. Little Crow was decisively defeated on September 23, with a loss of perhaps thirty Indians killed and many wounded. Sibley was commissioned a brigadier general six days later. This ended the Minnesota uprising, although many of the Sioux fled into Dakota Territory.

The State of Minnesota preserves an acre of the Wood Lake Battlefield. The terrain is gently rolling prairie with occasional cultivated fields. Lone Tree Lake, where the battle actually took place, has disappeared since 1862. Sibley's guide mistook it for Wood Lake, several miles to the west, hence the misnomer. A monument has been erected on the site.

MONTANA

42. Bear Paw Mountain Battlefield

Location: Blaine County, 16 miles by graded road south of Chinook.

At this spot ended the epic flight of the Nez Percé Indians under Chief Joseph from the threatened confinement of a reservation in Idaho to hoped-for freedom in Canada. (See pp. 59–61, 192.) Colonel Nelson A. Miles led a column from Fort Keogh which overtook the weary Indians and surrounded them on September 30, 1877. Three days of savage fighting ensued before Joseph concluded that further resistance was hopeless and surrendered. His people were forced into a reservation in Indian Territory but later were permitted to return to Idaho.

The Bear Paw State Monument preserves 160 acres of slightly rolling grasslands where the fighting took place. Two monuments stand in the park. The historic scene has changed little.

43. Fort C. F. Smith and Hayfield Battlefield

Location: Bighorn County, south of Hardin, 2 miles below the site of Yellowtail Dam on the south bank of the Bighorn River

Fort C. F. Smith, a companion post of Fort Phil Kearny, guarded the northern segment of the Bozeman Trail from 1866 to 1868. Like Forts Phil Kearny and Reno, it lay under almost constant siege by Red Cloud's Sioux for two years. On August 1, 1867, the Hayfield Fight took place nearby. (See p. 34.) Fort C. F. Smith was abandoned in August 1868 and burned by the Sioux, together with the other Bozeman Trail posts.

Mounds of earth tracing the foundations of the log and adobe buildings are all that remain of Fort C. F. Smith. A monument marks the site of the Hayfield Fight. This is a scenic locale on the bank of the Bighorn River at the mouth of Bighorn Canyon, which cuts through the northern tip of the Bighorn Mountains.

44. Fort Ellis

*Location: Gallatin County, U. S. Highway 10, 3.4 miles
east of Bozeman*

Fort Ellis (1867–86) was built as part of the program of protecting Montana miners from hostile Indians in the Gallatin Valley of western Montana, to guard nearby Bozeman and the Bridger and Flathead Passes. Troops from Fort Ellis participated in the Sioux wars of 1876–81. It was the base for Colonel John Gibbon in the ill-fated campaign of 1876 which ended in the Custer disaster. (See pp. 53 ff.) After the collapse of the Sioux, Fort Ellis no longer served a useful purpose and was abandoned.

There are few remains of the old fort, and the site is now occupied by modern buildings of the Fort Ellis Experiment Station, part of Montana State University. A commemorative monument stands on U.S. Highway 10 nearby.

45. Fort Keogh

*Location: Custer County, U.S. Highway 10, 2 miles west
of Miles City*

Colonel Nelson A. Miles established his command in a temporary cantonment on the south bank of the Yellowstone River at the mouth of Tongue River in September 1876. From this base, which later became a permanent installation about a mile away named Fort Keogh, in memory of one of Custer's officers killed at the Little Bighorn, Miles campaigned against the allied Sioux and Cheyennes. Through a brilliant combination of war and diplomacy, he played an instrumental role in compelling the hostiles to surrender. Most had gone to their agencies by the spring of 1877, but Sitting Bull and his immediate following took refuge in Canada. Miles patrolled the international boundary so closely that Sitting Bull and his people, prevented from following the buffalo into the United States, surrendered in 1881. From Fort Keogh, too, Miles marched against Chief Joseph and the Nez Percés in September 1877, and met them in the Battle of Bear Paw Mountain. (See pp. 59–61, 191.) An eleven-company post, Fort Keogh was continuously garrisoned until 1908.

Fort Keogh is now the site of a Range and Livestock Experiment Station of the U.S. Department of Agriculture. Although several residences on officers' row are still standing and used by employees, most of the buildings associated with the military period have given way to modern construction, which obscures the historic scene.

46. Lame Deer Battlefield

Location: Rosebud County, 1.3 miles southwest of Lame Deer

Lame Deer Battlefield is on Lame Deer Creek, a tributary of the Rosebud River, and is the site of the defeat of Lame Deer's band of Miniconjou Sioux, one of the last remnants of the Indian coalition that had previously overwhelmed Custer at the Little Bighorn. Colonel Nelson A. Miles was the victor here when he surprised and surrounded Lame Deer on May 7, 1877. Fourteen Indians including the chief and his son, as well as four soldiers, were killed. The surviving Indians were returned to their reservation. (See p. 58.)

The battlefield is located near the present Northern Cheyenne Agency, surrounded by rugged hills dotted with scrub pine. A gravel road runs up the valley from Lame Deer but the site has suffered no important modern intrusions.

47. Powder River Battlefield

Location: Powder River County, 4 miles by graded road northeast of Moorhead, on the west bank of Powder River

Opening battle of the campaign of 1876 against the Sioux and Cheyennes, the battle of Powder River was a victory for the Indians. (See pp. 51–53.)

The Indian village was situated on the west side of Powder River. In 1923 the river overflowed here, and the bottomland was covered with about a foot of silt. The mesa and bluffs from which the Indians counterattacked are unchanged.

48. Rosebud Battlefield

Location: Bighorn County, 8.5 miles by gravel road south of Kirby and 2 miles west, on Elmer Kobolt Ranch

Brigadier General George Crook, after his retreat from Montana in March 1876 (see Powder River Battlefield), advanced north again from Fort Fetterman in June, in concert now with columns under Brigadier General Alfred H. Terry and Colonel John Gibbon. As Crook moved down Rosebud Creek, Crazy Horse led a large force of warriors to meet him from the vast camp of Sioux and Cheyennes on the Little Bighorn River. The ensuing Battle of the Rosebud was very fiercely contested. The Indians were driven from the field, but Crook suffered such heavy losses that he withdrew and was unable to join Terry. It was one week later that Terry's subordinate, George A. Custer, attacked the village on the Little Bighorn and met disaster at the hands of the triumphant Sioux and Cheyenne warriors. (See pp. 53 ff.)

The Rosebud Battlefield is located on terrain that is in places rugged, in places rolling. Occasional grain fields dot the rolling part. Most of the battlefield, however, is stock range that has changed little since 1876. A monument stands near a gravel road east of the scene of the fight.

49. St. Ignatius Mission

Location: Lake County, St. Ignatius

St. Ignatius was established in 1855 as part of Father DeSmet's mission program. (See also Cataldo Mission, Idaho.) Here the Jesuit missionaries taught their charges farming, carpentry and milling. The century-old mission, several buildings of the girls' boarding school and the church (built in 1891) are still standing. The complex is owned and used by the Society of Jesus.

50. Wolf Mountain (Tongue River) Battlefield

Location: Rosebud County, 15 miles by gravel road southwest of Birney, at a crossing of Tongue River

Colonel Nelson A. Miles in the winter of 1876–77 led a force in pursuit of the fugitive Sioux under Crazy Horse who had annihilated Custer the previous summer on the Little Bighorn. Crazy Horse attacked his camp beside Tongue River, on the southern flank of the Wolf Mountains, on the morning of January 8. The Indians' surprise was counterbalanced by an Army surprise: howitzers in the guise of supply wagons. The attackers withdrew. (See pp. 57–58.)

The battlefield is on the east side of Tongue River beneath a landmark now known as Pyramid Butte, a spur of the Wolf Mountains. An unnumbered gravel road bridges the river from the west, crosses the valley where Miles camped, ascends the bluffs just south of Pyramid Butte where the Indians fortified to fight the troops, and continues toward the town of Birney. Except for this minor intrusion, the battlefield has not changed since 1877.

NEBRASKA

51. Bluewater (Ash Hollow) Battlefield

Location: Garden County, U.S. Highway 26, 2 miles west of Lewellen. The battle area extends north from the highway bridge across Blue Creek for a distance of about 8 miles up the valley.

The Battle of Bluewater, September 3, 1855, was the first major clash between U.S. soldiers and Sioux Indians. Because of the Grattan Massacre near Fort Laramie in 1854 and other disturbances, the Army determined to punish the Sioux. Colonel William S. Harney was placed at the head of an expedition of twelve hundred men in 1855 and sent across the northern Plains. He discovered and attacked the Brûlé Sioux village of Little Thunder, exacting severe losses upon the Indians. (See pp. 11–12.)

The terrain near the mouth of Blue Creek is rugged, but farther upstream where the village was located the valley becomes more level, with broken hills on each side in which the Indians took refuge from Harney's dragoons. Except for a few patches of cultivation along the stream itself, Bluewater Valley is largely stock range and therefore comparatively free from intrusions.

52. Fort Hartsuff

Location: Valley County, State Highway 11, 10 miles northwest of Ord

Fort Hartsuff (1874–81) was established to protect settlers and resident Pawnee Indians from the warlike Sioux farther north and west. This necessity disappeared with the conquest of the Sioux, and the post was abandoned in 1881. There remain the stable, commissary storehouse, guardhouse, library-schoolhouse, officers' quarters, hospital, and a combination barracks, kitchen and dining room.

53. Fort Kearny

Location: Kearney County, 3.8 miles south on State Highway 44 from city of Kearney and 4.4 miles east on State Highway 10

Forts Kearny and Laramie were the first two posts garrisoned to protect the Oregon Trail. Fort Kearny was first established on the Missouri River near present Nebraska City in 1846, but was relocated in January 1849 at the permanent site on the south bank of the Platte River. For Oregon and California immigrants, it marked the completion of the first leg of the journey, and they usually paused a day or more at the fort to repair wagons and prepare for the next leg, which would take them to the halfway point at Fort Laramie. The first buildings, of log and adobe, were replaced by ones of frame construction. The post was abandoned in 1871, after the Pacific railroad had been completed.

Fort Kearny State Park, primarily a recreational area, contains most of the site of the fort. Traces can be found of the location of some buildings, and a monument stands in the park. Archaeological excavations were in progress at this writing.

54. Warbonnet (Hat) Creek Battlefield

Location: Sioux County, north edge of Montrose

Here, on July 17, 1876, the 5th Cavalry under Colonel Wesley Merritt intercepted and defeated a band of Cheyenne warriors from the Spotted Tail and Red Cloud Agencies, driving them back to their reservations. The Cheyennes had been en route to join the victorious Sioux after their great victory over Custer on the Little Bighorn. (See p. 56.) Merritt had been ordered to reinforce General Crook, but delayed his movement in order to head off the Cheyennes.

The rolling grassland where the battle was fought has changed little since 1876. Two stone monuments stand on the battlefield.

NEVADA

55. Camp Ruby

Location: White Pine County, 8 miles south of Cave Creek, at headquarters of Fort Ruby Ranch

Camp Ruby (1862–67) was established at the southern end of the Ruby Valley to protect the overland stage and telegraph lines from Indian depredations. During 1862–63 the Goshute and Paiute Indians focused their attacks mainly on the stations of the Overland Mail. The garrison of Camp Ruby, two companies of California volunteers, fought several skirmishes before the trouble subsided. Nevada volunteers relieved the Californians in 1864 and held the post until its abandonment three years later.

The site of Camp Ruby is located on the Fort Ruby Ranch. Two one-story log structures, the old post office and a residence, stand adjacent to the modern ranch buildings.

56. Camp Schellbourne

Location: White Pine County, State Highway 2, at western approach to Schellbourne Pass

Schell Creek was a station on the Pony Express and Overland Stage Route from 1859 to 1869. The first building was destroyed by Indians in 1860, and in 1862 troops were stationed at Schell Creek to patrol Schellbourne Pass and Egan Canyon. The post was abandoned in 1869 when the completion of the Pacific railroad ended transcontinental stagecoaching. (See pp. 27 ff.)

Stone ruins reputed to be remains of the stage station and military post are standing at Schell Creek, although there is a possibility that they were associated instead with the gold-mining operations of 1872.

57. Fort Churchill

Location: Lyon County, U.S. Highway 95-A, 8 miles south of junction with U.S. Highway 50

Fort Churchill (1860–70) was established in the Carson Valley as a result of the Paiute outbreak in the spring of 1860 (see Pyramid Lake Battlefield). The post's function was to impress the Paiutes and to protect the Central Overland Mail route, the Pony Express and the projected transcontinental telegraph. This purpose was achieved, and there was no further trouble with the Paiutes until 1869. (See pp. 27–29.)

Sold at auction after abandonment in 1870, Fort Churchill was stripped for building materials, and over the years the adobe walls disintegrated. A number of buildings were reconstructed on the original foundations in 1935 as a CCC project, but these reconstructions have now fallen into ruin also. Some fifteen such ruins form a rough quadrangle about 300 by 500 feet. The site is a state park.

58. Fort Halleck

Location: Elko County, 7 miles northeast of State Highway 11 at Secret Canyon

When Camp Ruby was abandoned in 1867 the garrison moved northward to a new site, close to the route of the projected Central Pacific Railroad, and established Fort Halleck, which remained an active post until 1886. The troops did no Indian fighting, but by their presence settlement of the surrounding valleys was encouraged. The buildings have now disappeared but the site is identified by a historical marker.

59. Pyramid Lake Battlefield

Location: Washoe County, State Highway 34, about 2½ miles south of the southern tip of Pyramid Lake, immmediately south of Nixon, on the banks of the Truckee River

Paiute Indians fought here twice in 1860 against the encroachment into their territory of miners and associated settlers in the

Carson Valley. On May 12 they killed in ambush here almost half of a 105-man expedition of Nevada volunteers which was attempting to subdue them. With reinforcements including some regular soldiers, from California, a force of about eight hundred whites returned to the place and defeated the Paiutes, killing twenty-five and dispersing the remainder. (See pp. 27–29.)

The site of the two battles is virtually unchanged from its appearance in 1860. Black-topped Nevada Highway 34 and a railroad run along the western rim of the Truckee River Gorge, but the lowlands and eastern bank, where the fighting occurred, are undisturbed. A marker, located across the street from the Nixon Post Office, commemorates the action.

NEW MEXICO

60. Fort Craig

> *Location: Socorro County, 5 miles by gravel road east of the Fort Craig marker on U.S. Highway 85, 37 miles south of Socorro*

Fort Craig was established in April 1854 on the west bank of the Rio Grande at the northern entrance to the Jornada del Muerto. A two-company post, its purpose was to protect westbound miners from Navajo and Apache Indians and to guard the road between Santa Fe and El Paso. The first major battle of the Civil War in the Southwest, Valverde, was fought across the river from Fort Craig in February 1862. The fort figured in the Navajo and Apache conflicts of the 1850's and in the Apache wars of the 1860's and 1870's. It was abandoned in 1885.

At Fort Craig, the walls of eighteen adobe buildings are still visible in varying stages of disintegration, together with earth mounds representing fortifications erected at the outbreak of the Civil War. The site is located on the banks of the Rio Grande, with the San Mateo and Magdalena Mountains visible on two sides and a large volcanic mesa lying to the north. A New Mexico historical marker on U.S. 85, five miles to the west, gives a brief sketch of the fort's history.

61. Fort Cummings

Location: Doña Ana County, 6 miles northwest of Florida

Fort Cummings was established by command of Brigadier General James H. Carleton on October 2, 1863. Located at the mouth of Cooke's Canyon, it was placed to guard strategic Cooke's Spring and to control the Apaches who roamed in the vicinity. From 1858 to 1861 a Butterfield stage station was located here. Fort Cummings was a one-company post entirely surrounded by an adobe wall. It was abandoned in 1880. Ruins of adobe walls, together with mounds of earth tracing foundation outlines, today mark the site of Fort Cummings. A tablet commemorating the Butterfield Overland Mail marks the site of the stage station.

62. Fort Selden

Location: Doña Ana County, east side of U.S. Highway 85, 16 miles north of Las Cruces

Fort Selden was located on a slight elevation overlooking the Rio Grande at the southern end of the Jornada del Muerto, in 1865. Its purpose was to afford protection to settlers in the Mesilla

A portion of the ruins of Fort Craig, New Mexico. Courtesy New Mexico State Travel Bureau.

F. W. Klopfer, Troop H, 4th Cavalry, and a group of Mescalero Apache scouts at Fort Stanton, New Mexico, 1885. Signal Corps photograph. National Archives.

Valley and to travelers on the post road between El Paso and Santa Fe. Troops from Fort Selden participated in the early Apache wars, but when the railroad came down the Rio Grande in 1879 it was abandoned. In 1881, during the Geronimo war, the fort was reactivated to serve as a base for patrolling the Mexican border, but it was permanently abandoned in 1892.

At Fort Selden eroding adobe walls of twenty-five or more buildings are still standing as high as ten feet. A New Mexico historical marker on U.S. Highway 85 gives a brief sketch of the fort, which may be seen from the highway.

63. Fort Stanton

Location: Lincoln County, U.S. Highway 380, 4 miles west of Capitan, 3 miles south on State Highway 214

Fort Stanton was established in 1855 to control the Mescalero and White Mountain Apaches who had been subjugated in an energetic campaign conducted by Captain R. S. Ewell and Lieutenant S. D. Sturgis. The post consisted of a blockhouse surrounded by an adobe wall, on a level hilltop. From 1855 until

1861 it was the agency for the Mescaleros. U.S. troops abandoned the fort when the Confederates invaded New Mexico, and moved to Albuquerque. The Mescaleros began to commit depredations throughout central New Mexico, however, and General Carleton ordered Stanton reoccupied in 1862. Colonel Kit Carson was sent to deal with these Indians, using the fort as a base. He rounded them up in a short campaign and moved them to the Bosque Redondo Reservation at Fort Sumner. He then conducted a vigorous campaign that crowded the Gila Apaches out of the Territory. After the flight of the Mescaleros from Bosque Redondo in 1865, they were rounded up and, in 1871, re-established on the Fort Stanton Reservation, where they were joined in 1883 by Jicarilla Apaches. The fort had been rebuilt of stone and brick in 1868, and for almost thirty years was garrisoned to keep watch on these Apaches. (See pp. 24, 26–27, 69.)

Fort Stanton was abandoned by the Army in 1896, and became a U.S. Public Health Service hospital for the Merchant Marine three years later. It is now a tuberculosis sanitarium operated by the New Mexico Department of Public Welfare. Many of the stone buildings erected in 1868, though remodeled, are still in use as residences, wards and administrative offices. They are grouped around a seeded parade ground shaded by large trees.

64. Fort Sumner

Location: DeBaca County, 3 miles east of town of Fort Sumner on U.S. Highway 60, 4 miles south on New Mexico Highway 212

Fort Sumner (1862–68) was established at Bosque Redondo (Round Grove of Trees) in eastern New Mexico to guard the reservation on which General James H. Carleton colonized the Navajos and Mescalero Apaches conquered by Colonel Kit Carson. By 1865 more than eight hundred Navajos and four hundred Mescaleros had been settled there. Flood, drought, lack of skill, and the raids of Kiowas and Comanches doomed all attempts at agriculture. The Mescaleros, who detested the Navajos, fled the reservation in 1865. Three years later, in 1868, a peace commission signed a treaty with the Navajos permitting them to return to the west to their homes; the fort was abandoned. (See pp. 26–27.)

The site of Fort Sumner is identifiable, in a pasture on the east bank of the Pecos River, but the ruins were washed away by a flood in 1941. A small cemetery adjacent to a curio shop on New

Fort Sumner, New Mexico, about 1865. Company quarters being constructed by Indian labor. Signal Corps photograph. National Archives.

Mexico Highway 212 a mile east of the site contains the grave of Billy the Kid, who was shot and killed at Fort Sumner in 1881, after it had become headquarters of Lucien Maxwell's ranch.

65. Fort Wingate

Location: McKinley County, town of Fort Wingate

Fort Wingate has occupied two sites and borne three names. It was located first at Ojo del Oso in April 1860 and named Fort Fauntleroy, then renamed Fort Lyon in 1861 after Colonel Fauntleroy's defection to the Confederacy. Fort Lyon was abandoned late in 1861 when Federal troops were concentrated on the

Rio Grande to meet the Confederate invasion of New Mexico. In September 1862 Fort Wingate was established on a new site sixty miles southeast of Fort Lyon. It served actively in Colonel Kit Carson's campaign against the Navajos in 1863–64. When the Navajos returned to their homeland from Bosque Redondo in 1868, Fort Wingate was moved back to the site of Fort Fauntleroy—Lyon at Ojo del Oso, where it remained a large and active installation until troops were withdrawn in 1910. In 1918 it was reactivated and designated the Wingate Ordnance Depot.

The ordnance depot, still in use, was moved to a new site nearer the railroad. The buildings of the old fort were taken over by a Navajo Indian school in 1925. Until 1960 Fort Wingate was one of the best-preserved frontier forts in the Southwest, complete with eight sets of adobe officers' quarters and stone and adobe barracks. In that year, however, many of the old buildings were razed to make way for modern school facilities. The other site of Fort Wingate lies on the southern edge of the village of San Rafael. There are no remains.

NORTH DAKOTA

66. Big Mound Battlefield

Location: Kidder County, about ten miles north-northwest of Tappen

This place was the scene of a disaster for the rebellious Sioux of Minnesota. (See pp. 17–18.) Brigadier General Henry Hastings Sibley pursued Little Crow and Inkpaduta, the principal leaders, with their followers, into Dakota in June 1863. On July 24, he surprised a group of about three thousand Sioux under Inkpaduta. The Indians, along with some Sissetons, were hunting buffalo. At a parley one of the Sioux shot and killed an army surgeon, Dr. Joseph Weiser, whereupon a running fight developed immediately. Defeated here and at Buffalo Lake and Stony Lake soon after, Sibley pursued the refugees as far as the Missouri River before returning to Minnesota.

The site of Big Mound Battlefield is gently rolling terrain

covered with prairie grass and dotted with small lakes. A marker stands on the spot where Dr. Weiser was killed and the battle began.

67. Fort Abercrombie

> *Location: Richland County, U.S. Highway 81, 32 miles south of Fargo*

Fort Abercrombie (1857–59, 1860–78) was established at the head of navigation on the Red River of the North to protect settlers on the Minnesota frontier. During the Sioux outbreak of 1862, described on pp. 16–17, many settlers sought refuge at the fort, which was itself attacked and besieged for almost two months. General H. H. Sibley returned to Abercrombie following his expedition of 1863 against the Sioux in Dakota. During the 1860's the post was also the point of departure for several expeditions that pioneered a northern route to the Montana gold fields, including that of James L. Fiske.

Fort Abercrombie occupied two successive locations. During the 1860's it was on the Minnesota side of the river. This site is now in private ownership. The later Fort Abercrombie, on the west side of the river, is now a North Dakota State Park. The reported original guardhouse is on the site and the state has reconstructed three blockhouses and two sides of the stockade.

68. Fort Abraham Lincoln

> *Location: Morton County, State Highway 6, 5 miles south of Mandan*

Fort Abraham Lincoln (1872–91) was established on the west side of the Missouri River below Bismarck to protect surveyors and construction workers on the Northern Pacific Railroad. First named Fort McKeen, it became Fort Abraham Lincoln in 1872. From 1873 to 1876 Lieutenant Colonel George A. Custer was post commander, and it was from here that he set forth in 1876 on the ill-fated campaign that ended at the Little Bighorn. (See pp. 53–56.) In the fall of 1876 Brigadier General Alfred H. Terry returned with the Fort Lincoln column and marched down the river to the Standing Rock and Cheyenne River Agencies to disarm and dismount the agency Sioux. After completion of the Northern Pacific in 1883, the fort was no longer useful, but it was not abandoned until 1891.

Now a North Dakota State Park, the site of Fort Lincoln retains much of its integrity. The foundations of the buildings have been exposed and identified with markers. A museum, open in the summer months only, tells the story of Fort Lincoln. Several restored Mandan earth lodges and the restored blockhouses of Fort McKeen, on the bluffs above, complete the visitor attractions.

69. Fort Buford

Location: McKenzie County, southeast edge of Buford

Fort Buford (1866–95) was established near the confluence of the Missouri and Yellowstone Rivers to guard routes of travel to the Montana gold fields. It served as a base of operations and supply depot during the campaign against the Sioux in 1876 and participated actively in the Nez Percé War of 1877 and the operations against Sitting Bull, 1877–81. (See pp. 31 ff., 50 ff. and 58 f.) Sitting Bull and a small following fled to Canada following the Custer battle, but in 1881 finally recrossed the border and surrendered to the post commander at Fort Buford.

The site of Fort Buford now comprises about twenty acres owned by the state and administered by the State Historical Society. Surviving remains include frame officers' quarters, walls of the powder magazine, the morgue and buildings that have been converted for modern use. A mile west of the site are two buildings that have been moved from their original locations at the fort. An irrigation ditch runs through a corner of the site.

70. Killdeer Mountain Battlefield

Location: Dunn County, 10.6 miles northwest of Killdeer, on the Diamond C Ranch

Inkpaduta, a Sioux chief who had figured prominently in the Minnesota uprising of 1862 and in ensuing campaigns (see pp. 15–19), was defeated again on the battlefield at Killdeer Mountain, July 28, 1864. On this occasion he had about sixteen hundred

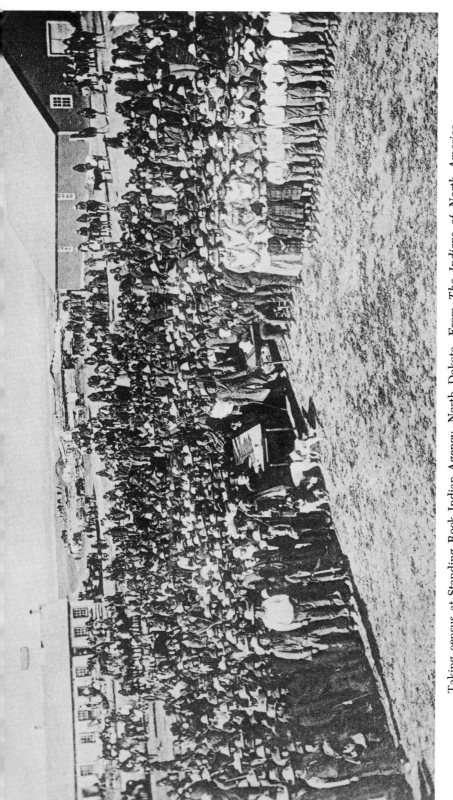

Taking census at Standing Rock Indian Agency, North Dakota. From *The Indians of North America; Life Pictures in Photo-Gravure*, by A. Wittemann, New York, 1895. Collections of the Library of Congress.

warriors, both Santee and Teton Sioux, and decided to engage Brigadier General Alfred Sully and his volunteers in open battle.

The site is at the south base of Killdeer Mountain. Except for a few patches of cultivation and an artificial lake, the plain in this area is cattle range. Ranch buildings and corrals occupy the site of the Sioux camp. Two markers and a large interpretive sign identify the site and explain the action.

71. Standing Rock Agency and Fort Yates

Location: Sioux County, town of Fort Yates

Established in 1868 or 1869 near the mouth of Grand River, Standing Rock Agency was moved, in July 1873, to a location near the sacred "standing rock" of the Sioux, farther up the Missouri River. Fort Yates was built and garrisoned adjacent to the agency to keep watch on the Hunkpapa, Yanktonai and Blackfeet Sioux whose affairs the agency managed. Together with the Cheyenne River, Red Cloud and Spotted Tail Agencies, Standing Rock was a center of unrest during the Sioux troubles of the 1870's, and in the war of 1876 renegades and supplies taken from here added to the strength of Sitting Bull's hostiles. In September 1876, following the Custer disaster, Brigadier General A. H. Terry marched down from Fort Lincoln to disarm and dismount the agency Indians at Standing Rock, and as the hostile Sioux began to surrender, the Hunkpapas among them were sent to Standing Rock. In 1883, after two years of confinement at Fort Randall, Sitting Bull himself returned to live on Grand River near his birthplace. Throughout the 1880's he exerted his influence against the efforts of the Indian Bureau to make farmers of his people. A leading spirit in the Ghost Dance troubles of 1890, he was shot and killed at his home on December 15, 1890, while resisting arrest by Indian policemen.

Neither Standing Rock Agency nor Fort Yates exhibits historic structures. Although Standing Rock is still a Sioux agency, the old frame buildings have given way to more modern buildings. Fort Yates was abandoned by the Army in 1903 and the town of Fort Yates has grown up on the site.

72. Whitestone Hill Battlefield

Location: Dickey County, 27.6 miles northwest of Ellendale and 5.5 miles southwest of Merricourt

Brigadier General Alfred Sully had intended to unite with Brigadier General H. H. Sibley in the summer of 1863 in a campaign against the Sioux, especially those like Chief Inkpaduta who had fled from the disorders they had created in Wisconsin. Sully was delayed by low water, however, while Sibley fought at Big

Water tank and Bath House at Fort Yates, North Dakota, in the 1890's. Quartermaster's Photo Album. National Archives.

Mound, Buffalo Lake and Stony Lake in July. He had his opportunity on September 3, however, and won a hard-fought battle near Whitestone Hill, in present southeast North Dakota. (See pp. 17–19.)

The State Historical Society administers approximately sixty-six acres of the battlefield. The terrain consists mainly of small hills covered with prairie grass. On Whitestone Hill is a monument surrounded by twenty-two markers bearing the names of the soldiers killed in the battle. Nearby is a small combination exhibit room and picnic shelter.

OKLAHOMA

73. Anadarko Agency

Location: Caddo County, north edge of Anadarko

The Wichita Indian Agency was established in 1871 beside the Washita River on the north edge of the present city of Anadarko. The first battle of the Red River War was fought here in 1874, when Kiowas and Comanches raided in the area and stirred up the peaceful Wichitas. (See p. 47.) Troops from Fort Sill joined with the infantry guard in defending the agency. Six civilians were killed and four soldiers wounded. In 1878 the Kiowa-Comanche Agency at Fort Sill was eliminated by consolidation with the Wichita Agency at Anadarko. The Kiowas, Comanches and Kiowa-Apaches at Fort Sill were moved to Anadarko in the fall of 1879 and located with the Wichitas, Wacos, Tawakones, Keechis, Caddoes and Delawares. Thus nine tribes were administered from the new Kiowa-Comanche Agency.

Nothing remains today of the Wichita Agency, just north of the river, or of the first Kiowa-Comanche Agency south of the river. Nearly all the buildings of the second Kiowa-Comanche Agency, erected in the 1890's adjacent to the first, are still standing. These include about fifteen frame houses that served as residences for agency employees, the old brick agency headquarters, a two-story office building, the stone jail, a brick blacksmith shop and two frame warehouses. These buildings were abandoned in 1957 and declared surplus by the Bureau of Indian Affairs.

74. Armstrong Academy

Location: Bryan County, 3 miles northeast of Bokchito

Founded in 1844 as a unit of the Choctaw Indian school system, Armstrong Academy provided both adult and child education under supervision of Baptist missionaries. The school operated until the Civil War forced its closing. From 1863 to 1883 it served as capital of the Choctaw Nation. Presbyterians reopened the school in 1882 and operated it until it was destroyed by fire in 1921. The ruins may still be seen.

75. Chilocco Indian School

Location: Kay County, U.S. Highway 77 at Kansas line

Chilocco Indian School was established in 1883 by the Federal Government, based on the Carlisle pattern. The original structure that housed the school still stands on the campus, a four-story brick building constructed in 1884 which now contains dormitories and is designated Home Number Two.

76. Darlington Agency

Location: Canadian County, 4 miles north, 2 miles west of El Reno

Headquarters of the Cheyenne-Arapaho Reservation—4.3 million acres carved from land ceded by the Five Civilized Tribes—Darlington Agency was founded in 1869 and served during the early 1870's as a major testing ground for President Grant's Peace Policy. Although the reservation was thrown open to white settlement in 1892, the agency continued to manage the affairs of the Cheyennes and Arapahoes. In 1909 it was moved several miles to the north and today the original site, its historical setting largely obscured, is occupied by the Oklahoma State Game Farm.

77. Fort Cobb

Location: Caddo County, south edge of village of Fort Cobb

Fort Cobb (1859–69) was established on the Washita River to protect the small tribes administered by the nearby Wichita Agency from the Kiowas and Comanches, and to restrain the latter from raiding on the Texas frontier. Confederates garrisoned the post after the outbreak of the Civil War. In October 1862 a large party of Indians from various tribes in Kansas joined the local Caddoes in a massacre of the Tonkawas, who were accused of cannibalism. They also drove out the Confederates and burned the fort. Reoccupied by Federal troops after the war, Fort Cobb served significantly in General Sheridan's winter campaign of 1868–69 against the southern Plains tribes. After the establishment of Fort Sill in 1869, Fort Cobb was abandoned. (See pp. 37–39.)

There are now no surface remains of Fort Cobb but the site, situated in a cottonwood grove beside the Washita River, has remained comparatively undisturbed.

78. Fort Reno

Location: Canadian County, U.S. Highway 66, 3 miles west of El Reno

Fort Reno (1874–1949) was built across the North Canadian River from Darlington Agency to keep watch on the Cheyennes and Arapahoes. Troops from Fort Reno pursued Dull Knife's Cheyennes, who escaped from the agency in 1879 and made a spectacular fighting retreat toward their homes in the north, only to be captured near Fort Robinson, Nebraska.

Fort Reno is now owned by the U.S. Government and operated as an Experiment Station by the Department of Agriculture. Sixteen buildings erected between 1876 and 1890 are still standing and are used by the staff of the Experiment Station. A log cabin, reputed to have been built in 1874 and occupied for a short time by General Sheridan, has been moved from Fort Reno to a site on U.S. 66 on the west edge of El Reno.

79. Fort Towson

Location: Choctaw County, U.S. Highway 70, .6 mile east of town of Fort Towson, then .5 mile north

Fort Towson (1824–54) was built as a sister post of Fort Gibson to protect the interests of Indians immigrating from the East to Indian Territory. During the 1830's it was an important link in the line of forts that formed the military frontier. When the frontier moved farther west the post was abandoned. It was used briefly by both Confederate and Union forces during the Civil War. Ruins of several stone buildings, overgrown by vegetation, still survive. (See pp. 4 ff.)

80. Fort Washita

Location: Bryan County, State Highway 199, 3.5 miles west of junction with State Highway 78

Fort Washita (1842–61), established by General Zachary Taylor at the mouth of the Washita River, represented an advance of the frontier from the Forts Gibson-Towson line. It was founded specifically to protect immigrant Choctaws and Chickasaws from

General view, northern half of Fort Reno, Oklahoma, in the 1890's. Large building on the left is the Quartermaster and Commissary Storehouse. Quartermaster's Photo Album. National Archives.

the Plains Indians. After the Mexican War it became a way station on a heavily traveled road to Texas and on the Marcy Trail followed by gold-seekers to California. Abandoned at the outbreak of the Civil War, the fort was reoccupied and held by Confederate troops throughout the war. Ruins of two stone buildings, one used as a cowbarn, stand on a farm south of the village of Nida. Preservation and restoration activities are being carried forward by the Oklahoma Historical Society, which recently acquired the property.

81. New Hope Seminary

Location: LeFlore County, 7 miles northeast of Spiro

New Hope was the leading educational institution for Choctaw Indian girls. Founded in 1844 at Skullyville, the educational, political and social center of the Choctaw Nation, the school operated until the Civil War and from 1870 to 1897, when it was destroyed by fire. Only the foundations of the building remain to mark the site.

82. Park Hill Mission and Cherokee Female Seminary

Location: Cherokee County, 4 miles south of Tahlequah

Park Hill Mission, founded by Presbyterians in 1836, became the religious and educational center of the Cherokee Nation and retained this status until it was destroyed during the Civil War. The Cherokee National Council in 1846 established a female seminary immediately to the south, which served as an educational center for Cherokee girls until destroyed by fire in 1887. There are no remains at the site of Park Hill Mission, but extensive ruins of the seminary may still be seen.

83. Peace-on-the-Plains Site and Soldier Spring Battlefield

Location: Greer County, 5 miles southeast of junction of U.S. Highway 283 and State Highway 44

At the Wichita villages of western Indian Territory, Colonel Henry Dodge, commander of the Dragoon Expedition of 1834, met with representatives of the Wichitas, Kiowas and Comanches in conferences that led to the conclusion, in 1835, of the first treaties with the southern Plains tribes. (See pp. 4–5.) Here, thirty-four years later, on Christmas Day, 1868, Major A. W. Evans and troops of the 3rd Cavalry attacked a Comanche village and won a decisive victory at the Battle of Soldier Spring. (See p. 37.) The site of the Wichita villages is at the mouth of Devil's Canyon where it joins the north fork of Red River. Quartz Mountain State Park overlooks the canyon. The Battle of Soldier Spring occurred along the north bank of the river for a distance of two miles below the mouth of the canyon.

84. Rush Springs Battlefield

Location: Grady County, 5 miles south of Rush Springs, east of U.S. Highway 81

Rush Springs was the site of a battle—tragic because it came about due to a misunderstanding—between U.S. troops under Captain Earl Van Dorn and Comanche Indians who had come north from Texas in order to discuss peace, on October 1, 1858. This is described on p. 14.

The site of the battle is on a private farm and is partly used as pasture and partly for cultivation.

85. Sequoyah's Home

Location: Sequoyah County, 7 miles northeast of Sallisaw

Sequoyah was one of the leading statesmen of the Cherokee Nation, and perhaps even more notable as an educator and the compiler of the Cherokee syllabary. As a result of this invention the Cherokees were quickly transformed into a literate people. Half of Sequoyah's cabin, built in 1829, is preserved by the state in a public park. A small one-room log cabin with stone fireplace and chimney, it is housed in a stone building where also are displayed a few relics and documents associated with Sequoyah's life.

86. Union Mission

Location: Mayes County, 2 miles south of Chouteau

Union Mission was an educational and religious center established in 1819 by a Presbyterian missionary, Epaphras Chapman, serving primarily the Osage Indians until 1833. The first printing press in Oklahoma was installed here in 1835 by another Presbyterian minister and was used to print textbooks and religious tracts in the Creek language. Only the cemetery and a few foundation stones remain to mark the site.

87. Washita Battlefield

Location: Roger Mills County, northwest edge of Cheyenne

Lieutenant Colonel George A. Custer and the 7th Cavalry, based on Camp Supply, seventy miles to the north, surprised and defeated Black Kettle's Cheyennes at this site on November 7, 1868. General Philip Sheridan's winter campaign of 1868–69 owed much of its success to the outcome of this initial engagement. (See pp. 37–38.)

The site has been marked by the State of Oklahoma, but is largely under cultivation.

OREGON

88. Fort Dalles

Location: Wasco County, The Dalles

Fort Dalles (1850–67) occupied a strategic location where a series of falls and rapids interrupted navigation of the Columbia River. A temporary stockade erected during the Cayuse War of 1847 gave way in 1850 to a permanent military post. Because of its location Fort Dalles was a key post during the Indian wars of the 1850's, and its garrison participated in a number of engagements. The value of Fort Dalles declined during the 1860's and it was abandoned in 1867.

The town of The Dalles now occupies the site of the fort. One building, the surgeon's quarters, is still standing at 15th and Garrison Streets. Owned by the Oregon Historical Society and operated by the Wasco County–Dalles City Museum Commission, it displays a variety of historical artifacts.

89. Fort Klamath

Location: Klamath County, State Highway 62, just outside town of Fort Klamath and 10 miles south of Crater Lake National Park

Fort Klamath (1863–90) was established to provide protection to settlers in the Klamath Basin from Modoc, Klamath and Shasta Indians. It was chiefly important for its role in the Modoc War of 1872–73 (see pp. 43–45). Efforts to place the Modocs on a reservation led to a series of incidents and, in November 1872, Captain James Jackson rode out of Fort Klamath with a detach-

Methodist Mission at The Dalles, on the Columbia River, Oregon, in 1849. Fort Dalles was later constructed about one mile from this site. Signal Corps reproduction. National Archives.

ment of cavalry to arrest Captain Jack and other Modoc leaders. The result was the first battle of the Modoc War. During the war Fort Klamath was the principal supply and replacement depot and medical receiving station for casualties. After the surrender, the Modoc prisoners-of-war were assembled at Fort Klamath in a specially constructed stockade. The trial of Captain Jack was held

Post hospital, Fort Klamath, Oregon, May 1876. Signal Corps photograph. National Archives.

at the fort, and here he and three of his followers were hanged in October 1873.

All traces of Fort Klamath have disappeared. The site, now part of a ranch, is marked by a stone monument.

90. Willamette (Lee) Mission

Location: Clackamas County, one-half mile south of east landing of Wheatland Ferry across the Willamette River, 10 miles north of Salem

Jason and Daniel Lee, acting as agents of the Methodist Missionary Society, founded the Willamette Mission in October 1834 on the east bank of the Willamette River, near French Prairie, with the objective of converting the Indians of Oregon to Christianity. In 1838 the two brothers established a branch mission at The Dalles and in 1841 another at Fort Nisqually. The missionary program made little headway, and the Lees turned their efforts increasingly to promoting the colonization of Oregon and attending to the spiritual wants of the colonists. The mission was moved to a new site ten miles to the south in 1840. The "Great Reinforcement" of American immigrants settled there in 1840 and founded the town of Salem. In 1844 the Lees dissolved the mission and sold the property to settlers.

The site of the first Lee Mission is now in the center of a cultivated field. There are no surface remains, but the general location is marked by a bronze plaque mounted on a large boulder at the edge of the field. The City of Salem has encroached upon the site of the second mission. Two original structures, built in 1840–41, are still standing. These are the parsonage, located on 13th Street, an architecturally intact building, and the Jason Lee Home at 960 Broadway, which has been considerably altered over the years.

SOUTH DAKOTA

91. Arikara Villages

> *Location: Corson County, west side of Missouri River 14 miles north of Mobridge*

The Arikaras were one of the most powerful tribes of the Upper Missouri River in the early nineteenth century. William H. Ashley's fur brigade was attacked treacherously at their villages in 1823 and forced to withdraw. General Henry Leavenworth thereupon marched up from Fort Atkinson on a punitive expedition and attacked the villages, with unsatisfactory results, as described on pp. 133 f.

Remains of the Arikara earth lodges may be seen along the Missouri River, but most will be submerged by the filling up of Oahe Reservoir.

Ration day at Cheyenne River Agency, South Dakota, December 22, 1890. Signal Corps photograph. National Archives.

92. Cheyenne River Agency and Fort Bennett (lost site)

Location: Stanley County, mouth of Cheyenne River. The site lies under the waters of Oahe Reservoir.

Cheyenne River Agency was established in 1868, following conclusion of the Fort Laramie Treaty, as agency for the Two Kettle, Sans Arc and Miniconjou Sioux. Fort Bennett was built next to the agency in 1870 to afford military protection. Some of the Cheyenne River Indians fought in the Sioux War of 1876 and, after the surrender, were returned to the agency. It was also a focal point of trouble during the Ghost Dance uprising of 1890. In 1891, the Great Sioux Reservation having been reduced and divided, the fort was abandoned and the Cheyenne River Agency was moved fifty-six miles up the Missouri, where until recently it administered the affairs of these Indians. As a result of the construction of Oahe Dam, the agency has moved to a new site.

93. Pine Ridge Agency

Location: Shannon County, U.S. Highway 18, Pine Ridge

When the Nebraska–South Dakota boundary was surveyed, the Red Cloud and Spotted Tail Agencies were found to lie on the Nebraska side of the line. Nebraskans demanded their removal to within the Great Sioux Reservation. In 1878 Red Cloud Agency was relocated on White Clay Creek, within the reservation, and renamed Pine Ridge. Throughout the 1880's the history of Pine Ridge was largely the story of a clash of wills between Agent V. T. McGillycuddy and Chief Red Cloud, the former attempting to impose the farming education program on the Oglalas, and the latter resisting changes that spelled doom to the old way of life, including the paramount position of the chiefs in tribal life. Pine Ridge was the center of the Ghost Dance difficulty of 1890 and the large-scale military operations to suppress it. (See pp. 84–89.)

Pine Ridge is a town of about nine hundred inhabitants, still

Government school for Indians, Pine Ridge, South Dakota, in 1891. Photograph by Grabill, of Deadwood, South Dakota. Collections of the Library of Congress.

the agency for the Oglalas. Although a few of the buildings date from the turn of the century, most are of recent origin.

94. Rosebud Agency

Location: Todd County, town of Rosebud

In 1878, when Red Cloud Agency was moved and became Pine Ridge, Spotted Tail Agency was also moved and renamed Rosebud. The new location of this Brûlé Sioux Agency was on the south fork of White River, east of Pine Ridge Agency. The Rosebud agents were usually weaker than McGillycuddy at Pine Ridge, so Rosebud experienced little of the strife that characterized the program of civilization at Pine Ridge. Chief Spotted Tail was killed by another Indian in 1881, and thereafter the Brûlés had no single strong leader. The Brûlés were the most zealous and intractable of the Sioux Ghost Dancers in 1890, but their activities occurred chiefly on the Pine Ridge Reservation.

Rosebud is still the Brûlé agency. A village of about 700 people, its buildings are nearly all of twentieth-century origin.

Rosebud Agency, South Dakota. Military Camp included two troops 9th Cavalry, four companies 8th Infantry and six companies 21st Infantry. Signal Corps photograph. National Archives.

95. Slim Buttes Battlefield

Location: Harding County, State Highway 8, 2.1 miles west of Reva

At Slim Buttes, north of the Black Hills, the village of American Horse was attacked and captured by Captain Anson Mills' advance guard of General George Crook's army, on September 8, 1876. Losses were not great on either side, and Crook was able to continue on to the Black Hills, ending his summer campaign with a victory, one of the first over the Sioux since the Custer disaster on the Little Bighorn. (See p. 56.)

Slim Buttes Battlefield is unbroken prairie surrounded by pine-dotted hills. A monument and several markers stand on a small hill near the highway.

96. Whetstone Agency (lost site)

Location: Gregory County, mouth of Whetstone Creek. The site lies beneath the waters of Fort Randall Reservoir.

After the conclusion of the Treaty of 1868 with the Sioux, the Government, in an attempt to clear these Indians from the overland route, established agencies along the Missouri River in Dakota Territory. As the home of Spotted Tail's Brûlé Sioux, Whetstone (1868–73) was one of the more important. In 1870 about 4500 Indians drew rations at Whetstone. Most of the Indians despised the Missouri River location and persuaded the Government to move the agency farther west, to the headwaters of White River in Nebraska, where it was later named Spotted Tail Agency.

97. Wounded Knee Battlefield

Location: Shannon County, village of Wounded Knee

The Indians of the West looked to a new religion, which the whites called the Ghost Dance religion, for restoration of their old way of life. Among the Sioux the religion took on militant characteristics, and troops were called to Pine Ridge Agency in

November 1890. At Wounded Knee Creek, east of the agency, on December 29, Colonel James W. Forsyth and the 7th Cavalry attempted to disarm Big Foot's band of Miniconjou Sioux, who had fled from Cheyenne River Reservation. A fight broke out, as described on pp. 85, 88. The Battle of Wounded Knee was the last important armed encounter in nearly four hundred years of conflict between Indians and whites in the United States. It represented the final subjugation of the American Indian by the advancing frontier. Now there was acquiescence, albeit reluctant, in the new scheme of life devised for him by his conquerors.

The natural scene along Wounded Knee Creek at the battle site has changed little since 1890. On the hill where the artillery was posted, the Indian dead were buried in a mass grave which has been marked appropriately by a monument erected by the Sioux. A small white frame mission church stands in front of the cemetery. Below, where the village lay and the main fighting took place, the State Historical Society has placed markers at key sites to denote the positions of troops and Indians, and has erected a large sign which tells briefly the story of the battle.

TEXAS

98. Adobe Walls Battlefield

Location: Hutchinson County, State Highway 281, 5 miles east from junction with State Highway 15, then 5 miles south and east on farm road

The name "Adobe Walls" was used in later times for an adobe trading post built on the Canadian River by William Bent in 1845, which was soon abandoned because of Indian hostility. Twice, in 1864 and 1874, it was the site of battles with Kiowas and Comanches, first against Colonel Kit Carson and his New Mexico Volunteers (see pp. 22–23) and second against a group of white buffalo hunters (see pp. 46–47).

The Adobe Walls site is owned by the Panhandle-Plains Historical Society of Canyon, which has erected a marker. The remains of the buildings, however, have largely disappeared.

99. Fort Clark

Location: Kinney County, south edge of Brackettville

Fort Clark (1852–1949), southern anchor of the Texas defense line in the 1850's, guarded the San Antonio–El Paso Road and policed the Mexican border. After an interlude of Confederate control, U.S. troops resumed their frontier duties after the Civil War. Fort Clark was headquarters of Colonel Ranald S. Mackenzie in 1873 when he conducted a daring expedition to punish Kickapoo and Lipan raiders using Mexico as a sanctuary. His command crossed into Mexico and defeated the fugitives, creating thus an international incident. From 1876 to 1880 Fort Clark figured prominently in the war against Victorio's Apaches.

About twenty-five or thirty buildings dating from the 1850's and 1880's are still in use at Fort Clark, although the setting has been somewhat impaired by twentieth-century military construction. Abandoned by the Army in 1949, the fort is now a privately owned guest ranch.

100. Fort Griffin

Location: Shackelford County, U.S. Highway 283, 20 miles north of Albany

A unit of the post-Civil War Texas defense system, Fort Griffin (1867–81) furnished escorts for mail riders, surveyors and cattle drivers, and patrols to follow up and punish depredating Kiowas, Comanches and Apaches. The nearby town of Fort Griffin was a typical wild frontier settlement, and in the 1870's an important supply and shipping center for buffalo hide hunters.

The site of the military post lies on a flat hilltop overlooking the valley of the Clear Fork of the Brazos River. The stone walls and chimney of one set of officers' quarters, ruins of the bakery, hospital, arsenal, and the chimney of the sutler's store are all that have survived. A granite shaft erected by the Texas Centennial Commission in 1936 stands in the center of the parade ground. The site is part of a Texas State Park.

101. Fort Lancaster

Location: Crockett County, U.S. Highway 290, one-half mile east of bridge across Live Oak Creek

Fort Lancaster was established on August 20, 1855, one-half mile above the confluence of Live Oak Creek with the Pecos River. It guarded the Pecos crossing of the San Antonio–El Paso Road and was one of the important posts in the frontier defense system of western Texas. Federal troops abandoned the fort on March 19, 1861, following the secession of Texas from the Union. At the height of the Kiowa-Comanche depredations on the Texas frontier in 1871, it was reactivated and for a short time served as a subpost to facilitate troop movements.

The stone ruins of Fort Lancaster are visible from the highway, where the Texas Centennial Commission placed a marker. One chimney, partial walls of several buildings, and rubble piles are all that remain of the post.

102. Fort McKavett

Location: Menard County, village of Fort McKavett

Fort McKavett (1852–83) furnished troops for the Red River War of 1874–75 and for the Victorio campaign of 1878–80. Extensive stone ruins and some repaired buildings are still standing. The village of Fort McKavett has grown up amid the ruins, and the whole presents a quaint and picturesque appearance.

103. Fort Richardson

Location: Jack County, U.S. Highway 281, south edge of Jacksboro

Fort Richardson in 1867 took the place of prewar Fort Belknap in the Texas defense scheme. It was the key bastion of the Texas frontier against Kiowa and Comanche raids, based on the Fort Sill "sanctuary." Near the fort in 1871 the Indians ambushed the Warren wagon train and narrowly missed according similar treatment to a party that included General Sherman. This "Jacksboro Affair" led to a hardening of the Peace Policy and the trial of

Satanta and Big Tree in a Texas state court at Jacksboro. Troops from Richardson participated in the Red River War of 1874–75 and in the Battle of Palo Duro Canyon, September 27, 1874. (Refer to pp. 41, 46–48, 155–57 and below.)

Urban and industrial development have encroached on Fort Richardson, but the main part of the post has survived relatively intact. It is in public ownership, administered by the Jacksboro Historical Society. The hospital building, built of native stone and housing a museum and community center, is the central feature. Other structures, also of stone, include the deadhouse, guard-house, bakery and powder magazine. One frame officers' quarters has been preserved. The parade ground remains free of intrusions.

104. Fort Stockton

Location: Pecos County, town of Fort Stockton

Part of the frontier defenses of western Texas, Fort Stockton (1859–86) was built at Comanche Springs, a strategic watering place on the Comanche War Trail to Mexico. The purpose of the fort was to protect a segment of the San Antonio–El Paso Road, which also went by way of Comanche Springs. U.S. soldiers evacuated the post at the beginning of the Civil War and it was deserted until their return in 1867. Troops from Stockton took part in the campaigns against Victorio and the Warm Springs Apaches, 1878–80.

The site of Fort Stockton is located in the town of the same name bordering James Rooney Park, created around Comanche Springs, from which the fort drew its water. Still standing are the guardhouse and three sets of officers' quarters, constructed of slabs of hewn limestone. The guardhouse is unused but the offi-cers' quarters have been remodeled and are occupied as resi-dences. The Chamber of Commerce has marked these buildings as well as other historical structures in the town.

105. Palo Duro Canyon Battlefield

Location: Armstrong County, 20 miles southeast of Canyon

At the Battle of Palo Duro Canyon, September 27, 1874, Colonel Ranald S. Mackenzie and the 4th Cavalry dealt a severe blow to

Comanche power and hastened the end of the Red River War. The Comanches scattered in the difficult terrain but the capture of their pony herd, which Mackenzie destroyed, hurt enemy mobility, wealth and morale, and contributed significantly to ultimate surrender. (See pp. 46–48.)

Part of Palo Duro Canyon, which is formed by the Prairie Dog Town fork of Red River, is now a state park. The battle site, however, is down the canyon from the park. It is inaccessible by wheeled vehicle but may be viewed from the south rim of the canyon at a point about ten miles northwest of the village of Wayside. At this overlook a trail, the only one on the south rim for miles and the one used by Mackenzie, leads into the canyon.

UTAH

106. Fort Douglas

Location: Salt Lake County, east edge of Salt Lake City

Camp Douglas, later to be called Fort Douglas, was established in 1862 by Colonel Patrick E. Connor and his California Volunteers for the purpose of protecting the overland mail route from hostile Indians. During the Civil War years and afterward it served as a base for patrolling the routes of transportation that crossed Utah in all directions, for surveying parties that laid out new and improved old roads, and for a major Indian campaign. (See p. 29.) After the Civil War regular soldiers replaced the Californians and the post became and still remains a permanent installation.

Twelve sets of stone officers' quarters, three stone barracks buildings and the stone officers' club date from the approximate period of the 1880's. More recent construction mingles with the old, however, somewhat impairing the historic appearance. Still partially used by the Army, Fort Douglas is well maintained and retains much of the appearance of a nineteenth-century military post.

107. Gunnison Massacre Site

Location: Millard County, near west side of Deseret

The exploring party of Captain John W. Gunnison was assigned in 1853 the task of surveying the southern Rockies and Great Basin as part of the Pacific Railroad Surveys. On October 21, 1853, Gunnison and eleven men set out from camp at Cedar Springs to explore Sevier Lake. On the morning of the twenty-fifth they were attacked by a band of Pahvant Indians and slaughtered, every one. A search party found the bodies so badly mutilated that they were deemed impossible to move and were buried on the spot. Lieutenant E. G. Beckwith completed the survey to the Pacific. The site is relatively intact today, marked by a small monument.

WASHINGTON

108. Fort Simcoe

Location: Yakima County, State Highway 3B, 30 miles west of Toppenish

Fort Simcoe (1856–59) was established to preserve peace between settlers and Indians, and its garrison participated in the campaign of 1858 against the Yakimas. The following year the Army turned the post over to the Bureau of Indian Affairs for use as the Yakima agency. For more than twenty years the Fort Simcoe Agency was considered a model of Indian administration.

Acquired by the Washington State Park and Recreation Commission in 1953, Fort Simcoe is being restored to its appearance of 1856–59. Four officers' quarters have been restored and one, the commanding officer's house, has been refurnished. One of the original blockhouses and several structures dating from the agency period, in poor condition, are also included in the park. The setting, in the midst of a grove of live oaks, isolated from any habitation, is particularly attractive.

109. Fort Steilacoom

Location: Pierce County, 2 miles east of Steilacoom

Fort Steilacoom (1849–68), established on Puget Sound to protect settlers from the local Indians, played an instrumental part in the Indian wars of 1855–56. The Western State Hospital for the Insane now occupies the site. Four officers' quarters have survived and are used as residences by doctors assigned to the hospital.

Old Block House at Fort Simcoe, Washington. Rose Collection, undated. National Archives.

110. Fort Walla Walla

Location: Walla Walla County, city of Walla Walla

Founded by Lieutenant Colonel E. J. Steptoe as a result of the Indian troubles that disturbed the Pacific Northwest in the middle 1850's, Fort Walla Walla (1856–1910) was Colonel Steptoe's base in 1858 when he narrowly missed destruction at the hands of the Spokane Indians and their allies (see below). Colonel George Wright, placed in command of a large expedition assembled at Fort Walla Walla, took the field and broke Spokane resistance forever. In the fall of 1858 the Walla Walla Valley was opened to

Fort Walla Walla, Washington, about 1854. From a lithograph by John Mix Stanley, artist with the U.S. Pacific Railroad Explorations and Surveys, 47–49th Parallels. Collections of the Library of Congress.

white settlement, and thereafter the influx of settlers caused friction that kept the Walla Walla garrison constantly occupied. Troops stationed at the fort also participated in the Nez Percé War of 1877, suffering losses at White Bird Canyon, and in the Bannock War of 1878. (See pp. 59–63, 183–84.)

The site of Fort Walla Walla, within the city of Walla Walla,

Front view, Commanding Officer's residence, Fort Bridger, Wyoming. This building was constructed in 1858; picture taken in 1935, before a protective roof was placed over it. The area is a Wyoming State Park. National Park Service photograph.

is used as a Veterans Hospital. Several buildings dating from the late military period are still standing on the hospital grounds. The post cemetery is maintained by the city as a park.

111. Steptoe Battlefield

Location: Whitman County, U.S. Highway 195, 3 miles south of Rosalia

The Spokane and allied tribes of western Washington and Oregon concluded a treaty with the United States in 1855 ending the Rogue River War, but in the next few years grew increasingly restless and troublesome. In the spring of 1858 Lieutenant Colonel E. J. Steptoe, with three companies of dragoons and one of infantry, was ordered to march through the Indian country from Fort Walla Walla to Colville. On May 16 a force of about a thousand Indians—Spokanes, Pelouses, Coeur d'Alenes, Yakimas and others—fell upon his command. Severe fighting lasted all day, with both sides sustaining heavy casualties. During the night Steptoe broke contact and made a forced march of eighty-five miles to the Snake River, which the command crossed to find safety on the other side. A punitive expedition later sought out the Indians and on September 1, 1858, at the Battle of Four Lakes, won a decisive victory over the allied tribes.

The site of the Steptoe battle is now included in a five-acre state park, which features a twenty-six-foot memorial shaft of granite.

WYOMING

112. Dull Knife Battlefield

Location: Johnson County, 23 miles west of Kaycee, on the Red Fork of Powder River

Dull Knife's Cheyennes, who had participated in the fight with Custer on the Little Bighorn, were surprised in their winter camp at dawn of November 25, 1876. Colonel Ranald S. Mackenzie's command was entirely successful in destroying the bulk of the Indians' shelter, clothing and food. Most of the suffering survivors surrendered the following spring. (See pp. 56–57.)

The battlefield occupies a picturesque setting among rugged hills, and is marked by a monument. A ranch headquarters stands at the upper end of the canyon and a hay meadow is located lower downstream, but the natural scene has not been altered appreciably.

113. Fort Bridger

Location: Uinta County, U. S. Highway 30S, town of Fort Bridger

Fort Bridger as a military post (1858–78, 1880–90) was established initially by Colonel Albert Sidney Johnston as headquarters for operations against the Mormons in the "Utah War." It later furnished protection to the Overland Mail and stage lines and to construction crews building the Union Pacific Railroad. The fort's earlier history was as an Indian trading post established in 1842 or 1843 by the famous mountain man, Jim Bridger. In this capacity it served importantly in supplying goods and information to emigrants bound for Oregon and California in the 1840's and early 1850's, until it was abandoned and the primitive buildings burned in 1853 or 1854.

The site is administered now by the State Historical Society, and the remains of the military post are well preserved. There are the quarters of the commanding officer (1858), guardhouse (1884), sentry box, ruins of the commissary and old guardhouse (1858), and soldiers' barracks (1884) reconstructed to house a museum.

114. Fort Fetterman

Location: Converse County, 6.8 miles by paved road north of U.S. Highway 26 at a point 2.7 miles west of Douglas

Fort Fetterman (1867–82) was placed on the south side of the North Platte River and served as the southern anchor among the forts protecting the Bozeman Trail. After the abandonment of the Bozeman Trail forts in 1868 it took on added importance as the forward base for military operations in the Powder River country. Thus it was the base for General Crook's column in the campaign of 1876 against the allied Sioux and Cheyennes and for Colonel Mackenzie in the campaign in November 1876 that ended in the Dull Knife battle. (See pp. 51 ff.)

An adobe post designed for three hundred men, Fort Fetterman has only two surviving buildings, an adobe barn covered with corrugated iron and a log duplex residence that once served as officers' quarters. The State of Wyoming recently acquired the property with the reported intention of preserving and interpreting it.

115. Fort Fred Steele

Location: Carbon County, U.S. Highway 30, 15 miles east of Rawlins

Fort Fred Steele (1868–86) was established by Colonel Richard I. Dodge to help protect workers on the Union Pacific Railroad. After completion of the road, the post continued to guard the stretch of track across central Wyoming during the period of the Sioux troubles. The fort was principally important as base for Major T. T. Thornburgh in the Ute campaign of 1879. (See pp. 63, 65, 180.)

Several barracks and officers' quarters are still standing at the site of Fort Fred Steele, although altered for modern use. The stone powder magazine remains intact and unchanged. Mounds of earth define the foundations of a number of other buildings.

116. Fort Reno

Location: Johnson County, 27 miles by paved road east and north of Kaycee

General P. E. Connor established Fort Connor as a temporary base for the Powder River campaign of 1865. In the spring of 1866 Colonel Henry B. Carrington, laying out the Bozeman Trail defense line, established Fort Reno in the same location, on the Powder River. A log stockade with blockhouses and bastion, it served as a link in the defense line and, together with Forts Phil Kearny and C. F. Smith, was abandoned following conclusion of the Fort Laramie Treaty of 1868. (See pp. 31–36, 163–64, 191.)

Mounds of earth trace the outlines of the stockade and blockhouses, and a small granite monument marks the site.

117. Platte Bridge Battlefield

Location: Natrona County, Casper

In the summer of 1865 an expedition of about three thousand warriors—Sioux, Cheyenne and Arapaho—descended from the Powder River country to cut the Oregon Trail again, as they had already done earlier in the year. Near the military post at Platte

Bridge, where the road crossed the North Platte River, they ambushed Lieutenant Caspar Collins and his troop of cavalry and a wagon train. Collins and twenty-four soldiers were slain, July 26. (See pp. 19–20.) The Platte Bridge post, originally occupied in 1858, was renamed Fort Caspar, and the city that later grew up there adopted the same name although with different spelling.

The site where Collins was killed is just west of a modern bridge across the North Platte, one mile above the U.S. Highway 20–26 bridge on the northwest edge of Casper. A cow pasture at 4000 Yellowstone Avenue is the place where the wagon train was wiped out. A replica of Fort Caspar stands on the original site of the fort on the southwestern edge of Casper.

D. Sites Also Noted

The historic sites listed in this group were noted in the course of the survey but were considered to be of less importance in this phase of history than those already given.

ARIZONA

Cochise Stronghold
Fort McDowell
Fort Mohave

Fort Thomas
Whipple Barracks
Pima Villages

CALIFORNIA

Fort Bragg
Fort Crook
Fort Humboldt

Fort Independence
Fort Jones
Pala Chapel

COLORADO

Poncha Pass Battlefield

IDAHO

Bennett's Creek Battlefield
Clearwater Battlefield
Clark's Fork Battlefield
Camus Meadows Battlefield

Camus Prairie Battlefield
Fort Lapwai
Fourth of July Canyon (Mullan Road)

KANSAS

Kickapoo Cemetery
Nescutunga Battlefield

Osage Catholic Mission

MONTANA

Fort Assiniboine
Fort Benton
Fort Custer
Fort Missoula

Fort Shaw
St. Paul's Mission
St. Xavier Mission
St. Labré Mission

NEBRASKA

Fort Niobrara
Fort Omaha
Plum Creek Battlefield

Santee Normal Training School
Spotted Tail Agency

NEVADA

Fort McDermitt

NEW MEXICO

Cantonment Burgwin
Fort Bascom
Fort Bayard
Fort Conrad

Fort Fillmore
Fort Thorn
Fort Webster
Rio Caliente Battlefield

NORTH DAKOTA

Fort Berthold Congregational
    Mission
Fort Rice

Fort Stevenson
Fort Totten
St. Michael's Mission

OKLAHOMA

Camp Mason
Camp Supply
Dwight Mission

Fort Arbuckle
Skullyville and Fort Coffee
Wheelock Mission

OREGON

Camp Smith
Camp Warner
Camp Watson
Dalles (Wascopham) Mission
Fort Harney

Fort Hoskins
Fort Lane
Fort Yamhill
Silver Creek Battlefield
Willow Springs Battlefield

SOUTH DAKOTA

Fort Meade
Fort Randall
Fort Rice
Fort Sisseton

Fort Sully
Holy Rosary Mission
Oahe Chapel
St. Elizabeth Indian Mission

TEXAS

Buffalo Wallow Battlefield
Fort Bliss
Fort Chadbourne
Fort Duncan
Fort Elliott

Fort Mason
Fort McIntosh
Fort Phantom Hill
Fort Quitman
McClellan Creek Battlefield

WASHINGTON

Cowlitz Mission
Fort Colville
St. Mary's Mission

Tshimakain Mission
Walla Walla Treaty Council Site

WYOMING

Fort D. A. Russell

Fort McKinney

SUGGESTED READING

No single work gives a satisfactory account of the interplay between the civil, military and cultural factors that explain the struggle between Indian and white. The following books illuminate many aspects of the subject, however. No attempt has been made to be comprehensive in the selection of these titles. Many extremely valuable older books and some splendid recent books have been omitted because of their limited availability. In pursuing the subject of Indian-white relations, and special aspects of the subject, reference may be made to the Notes, to other books written by authors listed below, and to the bibliographies included in many of these titles.

ATHEARN, ROBERT G. *William Tecumseh Sherman and the Settlement of the West.* Norman, Okla., 1956.

BANCROFT, HUBERT H. *History of the Pacific States of North America.* 34 vols. San Francisco, 1882–90. (Includes North Mexican States, Texas, Colorado, Wyoming, Montana and states west of these.)

————. *Native Races of the Pacific States of North America.* 5 vols. New York, 1874–76.

BILLINGTON, RAY A. *Westward Expansion, a History of the American Frontier.* New York, 1949; later edition, 1960.

BOURKE, JOHN G. *On the Border with Crook.* New York, 1891.

CARLEY, KENNETH. *The Sioux Uprising of 1862.* Publications of the Minnesota Historical Society, Russell W. Fridley, Director and Editor. St. Paul, 1961.

CATLIN, GEORGE. *Episodes from Life Among the Indians, and Last Rambles,* ed. by Marvin C. Ross. Norman, Okla., 1959.

CHITTENDEN, HIRAM M. *The American Fur Trade of the Far West.* 3 vols. New York, 1902; several reprintings.

CROOK, GEORGE. *General George Crook: His Autobiography,* ed. by Martin F. Schmitt. Norman, Okla., 1945.

DALE, EDWARD E. *Indians of the Southwest.* Norman, Okla., 1949.

DEBO, ANGIE. *The Road to Disappearance.* Norman, Okla., 1941.

DOWNEY, F. D. *Indian-Fighting Army.* New York, 1941.

DUNN, JACOB P., JR. *Massacres of the Mountains.* New York, 1886; reprinted recently.

Editors of *American Heritage. Book of Indians.* New York, 1961.

FEY, HAROLD E., and D'ARCY McNICKLE. *Indians and Other Americans: Two Ways of Life Meet.* New York, 1959.

FOREMAN, GRANT. *The Five Civilized Tribes.* Norman, Okla., 1934.

GLASSLEY, RAY H. *Pacific Northwest Indian Wars.* Portland, Ore., 1953.

GRINNELL, GEORGE B. *The Fighting Cheyennes.* New Haven, 1926; other editions 1915, 1956.

HAFEN, LeRoy R., and CARL C. RISTER. *Western America.* New York, 1941.

HAGAN, WILLIAM T. *American Indians.* Chicago, 1961.

HAINES, FRANCIS. *The Nez Percés: Tribesmen of the Columbia Plateau.* Norman, Okla., 1955.

HALEY, J. EVETTS. *Fort Concho and the Texas Frontier.* San Angelo, 1952.

HALLOWELL, A. IRVING. "The Backwash of the Frontier: The Impact of the Indian on American Culture." *Smithsonian Institution, Annual Report for 1958.* Washington, 1959.

HERR, JOHN K., and E. A. WALLACE. *The Story of the U.S. Cavalry.* Boston, 1953.

HYDE, GEORGE E. *Red Cloud's Folk: A History of the Oglala Sioux Indians.* Norman, Okla., 1937; 2nd ed., 1957.

LA FARGE, OLIVER. *A Pictorial History of the American Indian.* New York, 1956.

LAVENDER, DAVID. *Bent's Fort.* Garden City, 1954.

LINTON, RALPH, ed. *Acculturation in Seven North American Indian Tribes.* New York, 1940.

LOCKWOOD, FRANK C. *The Apache Indians.* New York, 1938.

LOWIE, ROBERT H. *Indians of the Plains.* New York, 1954.

McNICKLE, D'ARCY. *They Came Here First: The Epic of the American Indian.* Philadelphia, 1949.

MATTES, MERRILL J. *Indians, Infants, and Infantry; Andrew and Elizabeth Burt on the Frontier.* Denver, 1960.

NYE, W. S. *Carbine and Lance: The Story of Old Fort Sill.* Norman, Okla., 1937.

Potomac Corral of Westerners. *Great Western Indian Fights.* New York, 1960.

PRIEST, LORING B. *Uncle Sam's Stepchildren: The Reformation of United States Indian Policy, 1865–1887.* New Brunswick, N.J., 1942.

RADIN, PAUL. *The Story of the American Indian.* New York, 1934; enlarged ed., 1944.

RICHARDSON, RUPERT N. *The Comanche Barrier to South Plains Settlement.* Glendale, Cal., 1933.

RISTER, CARL C. *Border Command: General Phil Sheridan in the West.* Norman, Okla., 1944.

SANDOZ, MARI. *Crazy Horse, the Strange Man of the Oglalas, a Biography.* New York, 1942.

SCHMITT, MARTIN F., and DEE BROWN. *Fighting Indians of the West.* New York, 1948.

SEYMOUR, FLORA W. *Indian Agents of the Old Frontier.* New York, 1941.

STEWART, EDGAR I. *Custer's Luck.* Norman, Okla., 1956.

STIRLING, MATTHEW W., *et al. National Geographic on Indians of the Americas.* Washington, 1955.

UNDERHILL, RUTH. *The Navajos.* Norman, Okla., 1956.

———. *Red Man's America; a History of Indians in the United States.* Chicago, 1953.

WEBB, WALTER P. *The Great Plains.* Boston, 1931.

WELLMAN, PAUL I. *Death on Horseback: Seventy Years of War for the American West.* Philadelphia, 1947.

WINTHER, O. O. *The Great Northwest.* New York, 1947.

WISSLER, CLARK. *Indians of the United States: Four Centuries of Their History and Culture.* New York, 1940; reissued 1946.

———. *Indian Cavalcade: Life on the Old-Time Indian Reservation.* New York, 1938.

Works Projects Administration. Guides to all states, mostly published in the 1930's, many updated in 1950's and reissued.

NOTES

1. A separate study of the National Survey of Historic Sites and Buildings deals with the fur trade. The sites of a few fur trading posts that were especially important as agents of cultural transmission, however, have been included in this study also.

2. Indian-white conflict east of the Mississippi River is discussed in the study of the National Survey of Historic Sites and Buildings that deals with the advance of the frontier, 1763–1830.

3. Grace R. Hebard and E. A. Brininstool, *The Bozeman Trail* (2 vols., Cleveland, 1922), I, 271–72.

4. Paul I. Wellman, *Death on Horseback: Seventy Years of War for the American West* (Philadelphia, 1947), 50.

5. See Merrill J. Mattes, "Report on Historic Sites in the Fort Randall Reservoir Area, Missouri River, South Dakota," *South Dakota Historical Collections and Report*, XXIV (1949); Ray H. Mattison, "Report on Historical Aspects of the Oahe Reservoir Area, Missouri River, South and North Dakota," *ibid.*, XXVII (Pierre, 1954); Mattison, "Report on Historic Sites in the Garrison Reservoir Area, Missouri River," *North Dakota History*, XXII (1955); Mattison, "Report on Historic Sites Adjacent to the Missouri River Between the Big Sioux River and Fort Randall Dam, Including Those in the Gavins Point Reservoir Area," *South Dakota Historical Collections and Report*, XXVIII (1956).

6. Canyon de Chelly National Monument, Arizona: Ruth Underhill, *The Navajos* (Norman, 1956); Edwin L. Sabin, *Kit Carson Days, 1809–1869* (2 vols., New York, 1935), Vol. II; "Canyon de Chelly National Monument, Arizona," three-fold leaflet available at the Monument.

7. Lava Beds National Monument, California: Keith A. Murray, *The Modocs and Their War* (Norman, 1960); Cyrus T. Brady, *Northwestern Fights and Fighters, 1876–1890* (New York, 1904); Max L. Heyman, Jr., *Prudent Soldier: A Biography of Major General E. R. S. Canby, 1817–1873* (Glendale, 1959); "Lava Beds National Monument, California," three-fold leaflet available at the Monument.

8. Big Hole Battlefield National Monument, Montana: Cyrus T. Brady, *Northwestern Fights and Fighters, 1876–1890* (New York, 1904); Chester

A. Fee, *Chief Joseph* (New York, 1936); "Big Hole Battlefield National Monument, Montana," three-fold leaflet available at the Monument.

9. Custer Battlefield National Monument, Montana: W. A. Graham, *The Story of the Little Big Horn* (2nd ed., Harrisburg, 1945); E. I. Stewart, *Custer's Luck* (Norman, 1956); Edward S. and Evelyn S. Luce, *Custer Battlefield National Monument, Montana* (National Park Service, Historical Handbook Series, No. 1, Washington, 1949).

10. Fort Union National Monument, New Mexico: A. B. Bender, *The March of Empire: Frontier Defense in the Southwest, 1848–1860* (Lawrence, Kansas, 1952); Robert M. Utley, "Fort Union and the Santa Fe Trail" (Ms. Report, National Park Service, January 1960); "Fort Union National Monument, New Mexico," three-fold leaflet available at the Monument.

11. Fort Vancouver National Monument, Washington: H. H. Bancroft, *History of Washington, Idaho, and Montana* (San Francisco, 1890); R. Glassley, *Pacific Northwest Indian Wars* (Portland, Oregon, 1953); A. G. Brackett, *History of the United States Cavalry* (New York, 1865).

12. Whitman Mission National Historic Site, Washington: O. O. Winther, *The Great Northwest* (New York, 1947); Myron Ells, *Marcus Whitman, Pathfinder and Patriot* (New York, 1909); A. B. and D. P. Hulbert, *Marcus Whitman, Crusader* (2 vols., Denver, 1936); C. M. Drury, *Henry Harmon Spalding* (Caldwell, Idaho, 1936); "Whitman Mission National Historic Site, Washington," three-fold leaflet available at the Monument.

13. Fort Laramie National Historic Site, Wyoming: George E. Hyde, *Red Cloud's Folk: A History of the Oglala Sioux Indians* (Norman, 1937); LeRoy Hafen and Francis Marion Young, *Fort Laramie and the Pageant of the West, 1834–1890* (Glendale, 1938); David L. Hieb, *Fort Laramie National Monument, Wyoming* (National Park Service, Historical Handbook Series, No. 20, Washington, 1954). Fort Laramie's associations with the trapper's frontier and with overland migrations are treated at greater length in other studies of the National Survey of Historic Sites and Buildings.

14. Fort Bowie, Arizona: Richard Y. Murray, "The History of Fort Bowie" (Master's Thesis, University of Arizona, 1951); Frank C. Lockwood, *The Apache Indians* (New York, 1938); Robert M. Utley, "Historical Report on Fort Bowie, Arizona" (Ms. Report, National Park Service, January 1958); Utley, "Supplementary Report on Fort Bowie, Arizona: Site Identification Study" (Ms. Report, National Park Service, April 1959).

15. Hubbell Trading Post, Arizona: Harold S. Colton, "The Hubbell Trading Post at Ganado," *Plateau*, XX (1958); John Lorenzo Hubbell, "Forty Years an Indian Trader," *Touring Topics*, XII (1930); Frank C. Lockwood, "John Lorenzo Hubbell: Navajo Indian Trader," in *More Arizona Characters* (University of Arizona General Bulletin No. 8, Tucson, 1942); Ruth Underhill, *The Navajos* (Norman, 1956); Robert M. Utley,

"Special Report on Hubbell Trading Post, Ganado, Arizona" (Ms. Report, National Park Service, January 1959).

16. Fort Smith, Arkansas: Grant Foreman, *Indians and Pioneers: The Story of the American Southwest before 1830* (New Haven, 1930); Walter Lowrie *et al.* (eds.), *American State Papers: . . . Indian Affairs* (2 vols., Washington, 1832–34); David Y. Thomas, "Isaac Charles Parker," *Dictionary of American Biography*, XIV.

17. Formal establishment of Bent's Old Fort National Historic Site, a unit of the National Park System, including a total of 178 acres, was announced in March 1963.

17a. Bent's Old Fort, Colorado: David Lavender, *Bent's Fort* (Garden City, 1954); Nolie Mumey, *Bent's Old Fort and Bent's New Fort on the Arkansas* (Denver, 1956); Herbert W. Dick, "The Excavation of Fort Bent," *Colorado Magazine*, XXXIII (1956). Bent's Fort is also treated in studies of the National Survey of Historic Sites and Buildings dealing with the fur trade, the Santa Fe Trail and the Mexican War.

18. Cataldo Mission, Idaho: William N. Bischoff, *The Jesuits in Old Oregon* (Caldwell, 1945); E. R. Cody, *History of the Coeur d'Alene Mission of the Sacred Heart* (Caldwell, 1930); Donald R. Ruohy, "Horseshoes and Handstones: The Meeting of History and Prehistory at the Old Mission of the Sacred Heart," *Idaho Yesterdays* (Summer, 1958).

19. Fort Larned, Kansas: William E. Unrau, "The Story of Fort Larned," *Kansas Historical Quarterly*, XIII (1957); P. H. Sheridan, *Personal Memoirs* (2 vols., New York, 1888), II; C. C. Rister, *The Southwestern Frontier, 1865–1881* (Cleveland, 1928). Fort Larned is also evaluated as nationally important in the study of the Santa Fe Trail.

20. Fort Leavenworth, Kansas: Elvid Hunt, *History of Fort Leavenworth, 1827–1927* (Fort Leavenworth, 1926); *Fort Leavenworth and the Command and General Staff College* (Fort Leavenworth, n.d.); Otis E. Young, *The West of Philip St. George Cooke* (Glendale, 1955).

21. Haskell Institute, Kansas: Annual Reports of the Commissioner of Indian Affairs, 1884–1945; Haskell Institute Catalog (1956); Works Projects Administration, *Kansas: A Guide to the Sunflower State* (New York, 1939), 228–30.

22. Fort Snelling, Minnesota: Marcus L. Hansen, *Old Fort Snelling, 1819 to 1958* (Minneapolis, 1958); John M. Callender, *New Light on Old Fort Snelling: An Archeological Exploration, 1957 to 1958* (St. Paul, 1959); Russell W. Fridley, "Fort Snelling, from Military Post to Historic Site," *Minnesota History*, XXXV (1956); O. T. Hagen, "Special Report on Fort Snelling" (Ms. Report, National Park Service, June 3, 1946).

23. Fort Atkinson, Nebraska: Edgar B. Wesley, *Guarding the Frontier: A Study of Frontier Defense from 1815 to 1825* (Minneapolis, 1935); Wesley, "Life at Fort Atkinson," *Nebraska History*, XXX (1949); Sally A. Johnson, "Fort Atkinson, Council Bluffs," *ibid.*, XXXVIII (1957); Johnson,

"The Sixth's Elysian Fields—Fort Atkinson on Council Bluffs," *ibid.*, XL (1959); Marvin F. Kivett, "Excavations at Fort Atkinson, Nebraska, a Preliminary Report," *ibid.*; Chester L. Guthrie and Leo L. Gerald, "Upper Missouri Agency: An Account of Indian Administration on the Frontier," *Pacific Historical Review*, X (1941); O. T. Hagen, "Report on Fort Atkinson" (Ms. Report, National Park Service, April 7, 1949).

24. Fort Robinson and Red Cloud Agency, Nebraska: Robert T. Grange, Jr., "Fort Robinson, Outpost on the Plains," *Nebraska History*, XXXIX (1958); George E. Hyde, *Red Cloud's Folk* (2nd ed., Norman, 1957); George Crook, *General George Crook: His Autobiography*, ed. by Martin F. Schmitt (Norman, 1945).

25. H. M. Chittenden, *The American Fur Trade of the Far West* (3 vols., New York, 1902), II, 619.

26. Fort Union, North Dakota: *Ibid.*, I, 325–28, III, 958–60; *Maximilian's Travels in North America*, Early Western Travels Series, ed. R. G. Thwaites (Cleveland, 1904), 376–88; Maria R. Audubon (ed.), *Audubon and His Journals* (2 vols., New York, 1900), II, 180–88. Fort Union's principal significance was achieved in the history of the fur trade, and the site is dealt with at greater length in the study of that subject.

27. Cherokee National Capitol, Oklahoma: Grant Foreman, *Advancing the Frontier* (Norman, 1933); Foreman, *The Five Civilized Tribes* (Norman, 1934); Charles C. Royce, *The Cherokee Nation of Indians*, Bureau of Ethnology, *Fifth Annual Report, 1883–84* (Washington, 1887); Marion L. Starkey, *The Cherokee Nation* (New York, 1946); Morris L. Wardell, *A Political History of the Cherokee Nation, 1837–1907* (Norman, 1938); W. A. Gilbert and S. A. Langone, "The National Significance of the Cherokee Indians" (Ms. Report, Library of Congress, Legislative Reference Section, 1957).

28. Creek National Capitol, Oklahoma: Angie Debo, *The Road to Disappearance* (Norman, 1941); Grant Foreman, *Indian Removal: The Emigration of the Five Civilized Tribes of Indians* (Norman, 1932); Foreman, *The Five Civilized Tribes* (Norman, 1934); W. H. Gilbert and S. A. Langone, "The National Significance of the Creek Indians" (Ms. Report, Library of Congress, Legislative Reference Section, 1957).

29. Fort Gibson, Oklahoma: Grant Foreman, *Fort Gibson: A Brief History* (Norman, 1936); Foreman, *Advancing the Frontier* (Norman, 1933); Foreman, "The Centennial of Fort Gibson," *Chronicles of Oklahoma*, II (1924); W. B. Morrison, *Military Posts and Camps in Oklahoma* (Oklahoma City, 1936); William R. Hogan, "Special Report on Fort Gibson, Oklahoma" (Ms. Report, National Park Service, October 16, 1936).

30. Fort Sill, Oklahoma: W. S. Nye, *Carbine and Lance: The History of Old Fort Sill* (Norman, 1937); Rupert N. Richardson, *The Comanche Barrier to South Plains Settlement* (Glendale, 1933); C. C. Rister, *The Southwestern Frontier, 1865–1881* (Cleveland, 1928); W. B. Morrison, *Military Posts and Camps in Oklahoma* (Oklahoma City, 1945).

31. Carlisle Indian School, Pennsylvania: Elaine Goodale Eastman, *Pratt, the Red Man's Moses* (Norman, 1935); "Carlisle Barracks, Pennsylvania, Guide for Visitors," pamphlet issued at Carlisle Barracks; Letter from Major Robert H. West, Hq., Carlisle Barracks, to National Park Service, Region Five (Northeast Region), Philadelphia, April 28, 1960.

32. Fort Belknap, Texas: Ben G. Oneal, "The Beginnings of Fort Belknap," *Southwestern Historical Quarterly*, LXI (1958); C. C. Rister, *The Southwestern Frontier, 1865–1881* (Cleveland, 1928); Rupert N. Richardson, *The Comanche Barrier to South Plains Settlement* (Glendale, 1933); W. S. Nye, *Carbine and Lance: The History of Old Fort Sill* (Norman, 1937); W. C. Holden, "Frontier Defense, 1846–1860," West Texas Historical Association, *Yearbook*, VI (1930).

33. Fort Concho, Texas: J. Evetts Haley, *Fort Concho and the Texas Frontier* (San Angelo, 1952); J. N. Gregory, *Fort Concho: Its Why and Wherefore* (San Angelo, Texas, n.d.); C. C. Rister, *The Southwestern Frontier, 1865–1881* (Cleveland, 1928); M. L. Crimmins, "General Mackenzie and Fort Concho," West Texas Historical Association, *Yearbook*, Vol. X (1934).

34. Fort Davis, Texas: Barry Scobee, *The Story of Fort Davis* (Fort Davis, Texas, 1936); C. C. Rister, *The Southwestern Frontier, 1865–1881* (Cleveland, 1928); J. H. and J. R. Toulouse, *Pioneer Posts of Texas* (San Antonio, 1936); U.S. War Department, *A Report on the Hygiene of the U.S. Army, with Descriptions of Military Posts* (Circular No. 8, Washington, 1875); Robert M. Utley, "Special Report on Fort Davis, Texas" (Ms. Report, National Park Service, June 1960).

35. Fort Phil Kearny and Related Sites, Wyoming: Grace R. Hebard and E. A. Brininstool, *The Bozeman Trail* (2 vols., Cleveland, 1922); Cyrus T. Brady, *Indian Fights and Fighters* (New York, 1909); Paul I. Wellman, *Death on Horseback: Seventy Years of War for the American West* (New York, 1947); Charles J. Kappler, *Indian Affairs: Laws and Treaties* (2 vols., Washington, 1903); Roy E. Appleman, "Action on the Bozeman Trail," in Potomac Corral of Westerners, *Great Western Indian Fights* (New York, 1960).

CRITERIA FOR SELECTION
OF HISTORIC SITES OF
EXCEPTIONAL VALUE

1. Structures or sites at which occurred events that have made an outstanding contribution to, and are identified prominently with, or which best represent, the broad cultural, political, economic, military or social history of the nation and from which the visitor may grasp the larger patterns of our American heritage.

2. Structures or sites associated importantly with the lives of outstanding historic personages.

3. Structures or sites associated significantly with an important event that best represents some great idea or ideal of the American people.

4. Structures that embody the distinguishing characteristics of an architectural type specimen, exceptionally valuable for a study of a period style or method of construction; or a notable structure representing the work of a master builder, designer or architect.

5. Archaeological sites that have produced information of major scientific importance by revealing new cultures, or by shedding light upon periods of occupation over large areas of the United States. Such sites are those that have produced, or that may reasonably be expected to produce, data affecting theories, concepts and ideas to a major degree.

6. Every historic and archaeological site and structure should have integrity—that is, there should not be doubt as to whether it is the original site or structure and, in the case of a structure, that it represents original materials and workmanship. Intangible elements of feeling and association, although difficult to describe, may be factors in weighing the integrity of a site or structure.

7. Structures or sites that are primarily of significance in the field of religion or to religious bodies but are not of national importance in other fields of the history of the United States, such as political, military or architectural history, will not be eligible for consideration.

8. Structures or sites of recent historical importance, relating to events or persons within fifty years, will not as a rule be eligible for consideration.

COLLABORATORS FOR VOLUME XII

Editorial Collaborators

John Porter Bloom, Staff Historian, National Park Service, Washington, D.C.

Robert M. Utley, Southwest Region Historian, National Park Service, Santa Fe, New Mexico

M. S. Wyeth, Jr., Harper & Row, Publishers, Inc., New York, New York

National Park Service Contributing Historians (1958–59)

William C. Everhart, Western Region, San Francisco, California

Ray H. Mattison, Midwest Region, Omaha, Nebraska

Charles W. Snell, Western Region, San Francisco, California

Robert M. Utley, Southwest Region, Santa Fe, New Mexico—Coordinating Historian

Frank B. Sarles, Southeast Region, Richmond, Virginia

Charles E. Shedd, Jr., Northeast Region, Philadelphia, Pennsylvania

Contract Historian for Historical Background Narrative (1958–59)

Lessing H. Nohl, Jr., University of New Mexico, Albuquerque

National Park Service Reviewing Committee (1959–62)

Herbert E. Kahler, Chief, Division of History and Archaeology, Washington, D.C.

Charles W. Porter III, Acting Chief Historian

John O. Littleton, Chief, National Survey of Historic Sites and Buildings

Roy E. Appleman, Staff Historian

J. Walter Coleman, Staff Historian

Wilfred D. Logan, Staff Archaeologist

COLLABORATORS FOR VOLUME XII   [254

Harold L. Peterson, Staff Historian
Rogers W. Young, Staff Historian

Consulting Committee (1959)

Richard Howland, Smithsonian Institution (Chairman)
J. O. Brew, Peabody Museum of Archaeology and Ethnology
Eric Gugler, American Scenic and Historical Preservation Society
Frederick Johnson, Robert S. Peabody Foundation for Archaeology,
    Phillips Academy
Waldo Leland, American Council of Learned Societies
Earl H. Reed, American Institute of Architects
S. K. Stevens, Pennsylvania Historical and Museum Commission
Louis Wright, Folger Shakespeare Library

Advisory Board
on National Parks, Historic Sites, Buildings and Monuments (1959)

Frank E. Masland, Jr., Carlisle, Pennsylvania (Chairman)
Harold P. Fabian, Utah State Park and Recreation Commission (Vice-
    Chairman)
Edward B. Danson, Museum of Northern Arizona (Secretary)
E. Raymond Hall, University of Kansas
John A. Krout, Columbia University
John B. Oakes, New York City
Sigurd Olson, Ely, Minnesota
Earl H. Reed, American Institute of Architects
Fred Smith, Newark, New Jersey
Robert Sproul, Berkeley, California
Carl I. Wheat, Menlo Park, California

ACKNOWLEDGMENTS

The work of the National Survey of Historic Sites and Buildings profits from the experience and knowledge of many persons and organizations. Efforts are made to solicit the considered opinion of as many qualified people as possible in reaching final selection of the most significant sites. Assistance in the preparation of this volume from the following is acknowledged: John A. Hussey, Regional Historian, National Park Service, San Francisco, Calif.; Merrill J. Mattes, Regional Historian, National Park Service, Omaha, Neb.; Frank Barnes, Regional Historian, National Park Service, Philadelphia, Pa.; James W. Holland, Regional Historian, National Park Service, Richmond, Va.; Don Rickey, Jr., Historian, Jefferson National Expansion Memorial, St. Louis, Mo.; Maurice Frink, Executive Director, State Historical Society of Colorado, Denver; J. W. Vaughn, Windsor, Colo.; William J. Peterson, Superintendent, State Historical Society of Iowa, Iowa City; K. Ross Toole, former Director, Historical Society of Montana, Helena; Russell Reid, Superintendent, State Historical Society of North Dakota, Bismarck; Miss Lola Homsher, Executive Secretary, Wyoming State Historical Society, Cheyenne; Nyle H. Miller, Secretary, Kansas State Historical Society, Topeka; Russell W. Fridley, Director, Minnesota Historical Society, St. Paul; William D. Aeschbacher, Director, Nebraska State Historical Society, Lincoln; William G. Robinson, Secretary, South Dakota State Historical Society, Pierre; William Center, Chamber of Commerce, Fort Smith, Ark.; Miss Muriel H. Wright, Secretary, Oklahoma Historical Society, Oklahoma City; Gillett Griswold, Director, Artillery and Missile Center Museum, Fort Sill, Okla.; M. A. Hagerstrand, Chamber of Commerce, Tahlequah, Okla.; Creek Indian Memorial Association, Okmulgee, Okla.; C. Boone McClure, Director, Panhandle-Plains Historical Museum, Canyon, Tex.; Rupert N. Richardson, Professor of History, Hardin-Simmons University, Abilene, Tex.; H. Bailey Carroll, Editor of *Southwestern Historical Quarterly*, University of Texas, Austin; J. N. Gregory, Mrs. Eugene Bonham, and The Fort Concho Museum Board, San Angelo, Tex.; Frank D. Reeve, Editor of *New Mexico Historical Review*, University of New Mexico, Albuquerque; Mr. and Mrs. Ben G. Oneal, Fort Belknap Society, Fort Belknap, Tex.; Barry Scobee, President, Fort Davis Historical Society, Fort Davis, Tex.; L. C. Knape, Bowie, Ariz.; Mrs. R. J. Hubbell, Ganado, Ariz.;

Emil W. Haury and W. W. Wasley, Arizona State Museum, Tucson; Aubrey Neasham, State Historian, California Division of Beaches and Parks, Sacramento; Leo Crawford, Assistant District Superintendent, California Division of Beaches and Parks, Sacramento; Thomas Vaughan, Director, Oregon Historical Society, Portland; Albert Culverwell, State Historian, Washington State Park Commission, Olympia; H. J. Swinney, Director, Idaho Historical Society, Boise; Merle Wells, Historian, Idaho Historical Society, Boise; Thomas Miller, Chairman, Nevada State Parks Commission, Carson City; Mrs. Clara S. Beatty, Director, Nevada Historical Society, Reno.

LIST OF ILLUSTRATIONS

Index

Format by Sidney Feinberg
Set in Linotype Caledonia
Composed by American Book–Stratford Press, Inc.
Printed by Murray Printing Co.
Bound by American Book–Stratford Press, Inc.
HARPER & ROW, PUBLISHERS, INCORPORATED

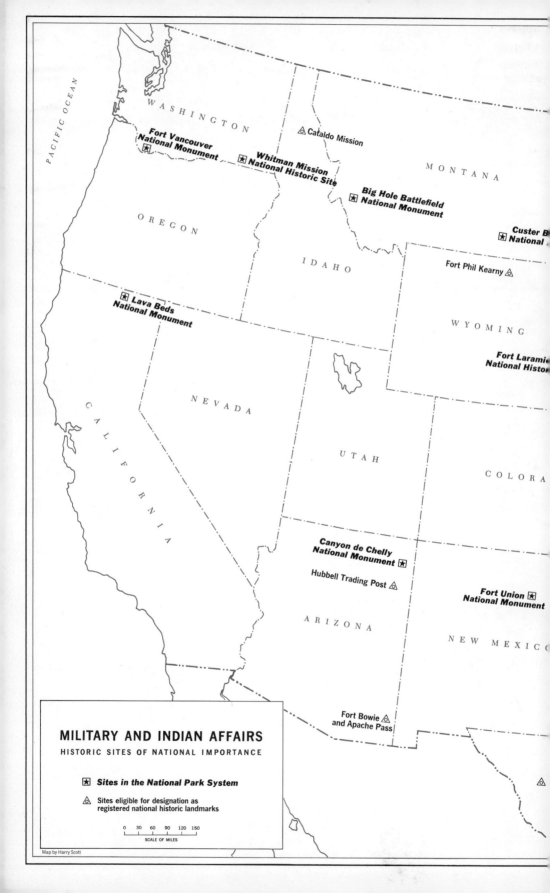

WASHINGTON

Cataldo Mission

MONTANA

Fort Vancouver
National Monument

Whitman Mission
National Historic Site

Big Hole Battlefield
National Monument

Custer B
National

OREGON

Fort Phil Kearny

IDAHO

WYOMING

Lava Beds
National Monument

Fort Larami
National Histor

NEVADA

CALIFORNIA

UTAH

COLORA

Canyon de Chelly
National Monument

Hubbell Trading Post

Fort Union
National Monument

ARIZONA

NEW MEXICO

PACIFIC OCEAN

Fort Bowie
and Apache Pass

MILITARY AND INDIAN AFFAIRS

HISTORIC SITES OF NATIONAL IMPORTANCE

⊠ **Sites in the National Park System**

⚠ Sites eligible for designation as
registered national historic landmarks

0   30   60   90   120   150
SCALE OF MILES

Map by Harry Scott